the **ART** *of*
ESCAPISM COOKING

the ART of
ESCAPISM COOKING

a survival story, with intensely good flavors

MANDY LEE

wm

WILLIAM MORROW

An Imprint of HarperCollins *Publishers*

to my future cynical self,
"THINGS HAPPEN FOR A REASON"
is not the dumbest delusion to work with

CONTENTS

Beijing, China–December 31, 2015

INTRODUCTION

One hazy Beijing afternoon, one no more particularly dreadful than the others, I stood behind my closed kitchen window, stone cold, as I dragged a serrated knife through the body of a sandwich. I felt the unforgiving blade lacerate the wobbly stack of steaming pastrami short ribs tucked under a runny egg fried in browned butter and mustard seeds, watching its blood-like fluid weep into a layer of charred and pickled shishito peppers on top of still-warm rye bread anointed with mustard. I exhaled, tilting my head, as a cold rush of solace eased through my veins. Through the window a neighboring building disappeared, swallowed in the thickening soot outside. I knew I was next.

Yet there was a sense of calm in watching the heap of meat wiggle, an unstable formation of rendered fat and loosened muscle; I felt delight in the dark pink coloring of its flesh, a successful result of its silent four-day immersion in a meticulously constructed brine. My head lowered along with my breaths as I listened to the soothing sound of my fingernails dragging across the crusty, goose-bumped skin of my homemade rye bread. With its body laid open and hollow, sacrificial, I counted the air bubbles in a cross section freckled with caraway seeds, an act that tenderly overran my urge to scream. For a second it felt strange, but nothing was out of the ordinary: neither the constant current of my bubbling discontent nor my surgical infatuation with a sandwich. It was just me making lunch, with each and every component composed from scratch, on a Tuesday.

This is not a moment of boasting.

Instead, this is the moment when I tell you that right then and there—that second, as if I were waking up from a deep neurotic trance— was when it hit me. Not how wonderfully the yolks lubricated the spice-encrusted sticky meat, nor how the sandwich sang in a savory, spicy, and smoky symphony. But how . . . *sick* this thing had become. When and how had I gone from a moderately motivated home cook who hovered in the aisles of frozen pizzas and dumplings over the edge into an obsessive kitchen extremist? When and how had I stopped making meals but, instead, begun making fantasies? When and how did I no longer cook, but escape? Why did I spend six years of my life buried in a little corner that most people would call a kitchen, but that for me was a sanctuary?

I stared impassively at the hellish cityscape of Beijing outside, then down at the nirvanic pink meat sparkling with fat as the mustard-stained yolk bled slowly onto my pristinely white kitchen counter. . . .

I knew the exact answer to that.

But let's make one thing clear. That's not why you've picked up this book, to talk about me, an angry food blogger. Well, at least not entirely. The story of how cooking, my once harmless hobby, mutated into a recreational addiction after I moved from New York City to Beijing; how I crawled out of my expat limbo by splashing my rage with pain-inflicting chile sauces and ducked my head into a bucket of butter frosting to cope; or even how I became what I call an *escapist cook*—that will all be clear by the end of the book.

But first things first—we're here to cook. Not for necessity, not as a chore or responsibility, not for convenience. This book is written for those who share the same perverse tendency to engage in cooking as a loner spends time with his Xbox or a teenager with porn—ultimately as a delicious evasion of unpalatable realities.

Escapism cooking.

It's not a passion; it's a drug. I'm not selling you a lifestyle; I'm telling you how I evaded one. If you need to know how to cook a chicken breast with one hand while you hold a baby in the other, sorry, I'm not about solving your problems. But I can show you how I cooked mine. This book is a memoir of recipes and stories that I documented during a desperately unpleasant time of my life, the delicious aftermath of how I cooked my way out of six miserable years in Beijing, my lemons and lemonade.

If you're still not sure that this book is right for you, then let me say this. Escapism cooking is about neither simplicity nor complication. I find equal rapture in nurturing a hunk of meat that is four days in the making as in cooking "Shit I Eat When I'm by Myself" (see page 301) in only minutes. When it comes to cooking, as far as I'm concerned, there's no hard or easy, new or old, real or fake. There is only good or bad. It's about orchestrating an idea, mapping the most sensible way to get there, chasing the high.

In fact, to me, cooking isn't even about love. As much as I would like to say that I cook to make other people happy, I don't. Truth is, I cook largely to make *myself* happy, as medication, as therapy. I cooked in Beijing because it was the one positive thing I could harvest from a place abundant with negativity. In life, I guess, we're all after some sort of abstraction of happiness. Cooking, whether by choice or not, just turned out to be my medium. If you ask me, the most important thing in learning how to cook is not the techniques but how to harness curiosity and fulfillment from the process, the puzzles and the answers, the failures and the triumphs, the hunt. It's a deeply personal, ever-evolving, solitary sport.

The food that comes as a result—which I'm told has made a lot of others happy, too—is the pleasant byproduct, the overspilled muffin top. So, if you're experiencing thoughts of suicide along with the midnight urge to butcher a chicken, this book may be right for you, my friends—those of you who find yourselves, likewise, cooking for one reason and one reason only.

Happiness.

FIRST, PANTRY

Hey, look, we're all scared of the unfamiliar. We all huddle inside our comfort zones, passive, waiting for someone else to break the mold first. In some aspects of life, this may even be considered smart, safe, a vital animal instinct for survival. Nobody wants to be that moron in the movie who goes, "There's a curiously dark tunnel behind this tombstone. Let's check it out." *He dies*.

But when it comes to unfamiliar ingredients in cooking, come on, what have we got to lose?

One of the hardest things about writing recipes that use possibly unfamiliar ingredients is convincing people that the future of their happiness—or even the world's—depends on their using them. Just think what kind of a joyless world it would be if the Japanese hadn't convinced us to gnaw on raw fish? Or if the Koreans didn't make a good case for keeping a bag of stinking cabbage in our fridge? Or what if a few hundred years ago, the good people

in what is now the Sichuan region of China hadn't embraced the chilies brought in by the Spanish conquistadors? Or if the Italians hadn't welcomed the tomatoes brought in by the Spanish conquistadors? Or if the Europeans had shied away from chocolate brought back . . . by the Spanish conquistadors. Okay, you get my point. Spanish conquistadors were the founding fathers of many things we eat today, and also, *you need to try new things*.

So here's a list of ingredients that if you aren't at least willing to be *friendly* with by now, there's no hope for the future. And you should start apologizing to your children.

Chile Flakes

Not all chilies are created equal, and such truth passes down to chile flakes as well. Generally speaking, look for the right balance between two components: fragrance and heat level. Based on that objective, my favorite chile is a common

Sichuan variety called *haijiao.* It has a medium heat level, is richly pigmented, and carries an intensely peppery aroma. If you can't find this specific type of chile flake, I would substitute the Korean chile called *gochugaru,* although it is much milder in heat level. It can easily be found online.

Dried Shrimp

Dried shrimp are sun-dried, salted baby shrimp. There are only two recipes in this book that call for them, but their application in Asian cooking is far-reaching. Both recipes have something to do with a Singaporean dish called *laksa.* If you've ever had the blessing of tasting a proper bowl of laksa, you know you need to keep a large bag of dried shrimp in your freezer. It's crucial, inarguable. Don't even think about substituting fresh shrimp.

Fish Sauce

I almost always season with fish sauce instead of salt whenever it makes sense. It is, simply put, just better tasting. If you smell the bottle of sauce itself, a suspicious funk will alarm your nose, but when added to food the sauce just melts into a deeply savory saltiness booming with naturally occurring MSG.

However, it's important to note that quality matters when it comes to fish sauce (and everything else). My go-to brand is Megachef from Thailand, and it's available worldwide and online.

Flours

Besides wheat flours, there are a few other types of flour used in this cookbook that may be confusing to some people.

First, **potato starch**, which is similar to cornstarch, but don't substitute it unless a recipe specifies that you can.

Then, **rice flour** and **sticky rice flour**, the difference being that rice flour is made from Asian short-grain rice, whereas sticky rice flour is made from sticky rice (sometimes called glutinous rice, but fyi it's gluten-free). They have entirely different applications and characteristics and *cannot,* under any circumstances, be substituted for each other.

Finally, **tapioca flour** (or, more accurately, tapioca starch). It's a crucial ingredient in many chewy elements in Asian foods, such as the black pearls in boba tea. Again, it *cannot* be substituted by any other type of starch.

All of these flours can be found easily online.

Lemongrass, Galangal, Makrut Lime Leaf

I'm grouping these three ingredients into one lot because (a) I consider them to be the holy trinity of Southeast Asian cooking and (b) where you can find one, chances are you can find the other two. Fresh produce can be harder to source online, so I suggest that whenever you see these in your local Asian supermarket, just buy them in bulk and keep them in the freezer. In fact, all three of the photos at top opposite show ingredients taken straight from the freezer.

Lemongrass

Galangal

Makrut Lime Leaves

Dried Shrimp

Chile Flakes

Sichuan Peppercons

Sichuan Broad Bean Chile Paste

Flours

Bonito Powder

Kombu Powder

Mushroom Powder

Dried Shiitake Mushrooms

There's really no substitute for galangal's unique and incredible floral quality, but if you must, you can use ginger in its place . . . okay, that was a bit painful to say, so please try not to.

Shrimp Paste

There are many different types of shrimp pastes in Asia. Generally speaking, Cantonese-style paste, called *xiajiang,* is typically used for stir-fries and is loose in consistency, extremely pungent, and funky in smell. Thai-style, called *kapi,* is used for making curry paste and comes in a thick paste. It's slightly milder and more rounded in taste and smell. Malaysian-style, called *belacan,* is a crucial ingredient for Southeast Asian curries and laksa. It's solid and brick-shaped and also milder and rounded in taste and smell.

I keep all three for different purposes, but that's a big commitment for people who aren't yet familiar with shrimp paste. So I'm going to go out on a limb and say that for the recipes in this book, you can substitute one with the other unless otherwise specified (although adjustments may be needed due to differing salt levels among them).

Sichuan Broad Bean Chile Paste (Doubanjiang)

Doubanjiang, Sichuan fermented broad bean chile paste, is the soul of Sichuan cooking. It's like tomatoes in Italy, corn in Mexico, or gochujang in Korea. *Irreplaceable. Undebatable. Necessary.* It provides an intensely aromatic chile flavor, a fermented savoriness, and an intermediate heat level to iconic Sichuan dishes like mapo tofu—and just about anything else. You can't do without it.

Doubanjiang comes in pure paste form or in a paste with oil. All the recipes in this book call for *pure paste form.* Depending on which brand you buy (my standard brand is Juan Cheng Pixian Douban, which is available online), doubanjiang can be very chunky at times. I like to use an immersion blender to process it to a smooth consistency, then I store it in an airtight glass jar (it will stain plastic).

Sichuan Peppercorns

Mala is a notorious characteristic of Sichuan dishes that translates to "numbing and spicy." The numbing comes first, for a reason. Many misunderstand Sichuan cuisine as heat-centric, but more accurately, it's that tingling, the numbing, and the addictive fragrance, more floral than peppery, that separate the heat of Sichuan cuisine from all other burns. It comes from the Sichuan peppercorn, which is in fact not a peppercorn at all but the husks and seeds of a few types of shrubs commonly referred to as prickly ash. The red variety is more common, and more pronounced in its floral quality than numbing. The green variety can be harder to source in North America (but can be found online) and is known for its hyper-numbing boost in specific dishes. All the recipes in this book use the red variety, which can be found easily in Asian grocery stores and online.

Powders

I'm a bit obsessed with powderizing everything. From a flavor point of view, it allows more surface area from which the flavors can release, and from an economic point of view, I get to use less product for greater effect. I highly recommend a spice grinder with a large removable bowl for easy and thorough cleaning.

GROUND SPICES

On any given day you'll find twenty to thirty different spices in my pantry. Whenever possible, I buy them whole and grind them myself, including black and white peppers. But if you ask me for a list of must-haves, I would say cumin, coriander, star anise, cinnamon, allspice, cloves, paprika, and nutmeg.

KOMBU AND BONITO POWDERS

Kombu is Japanese dried kelp. It is one of the ingredients out there with a very high concentration of natural MSG. Bonito is a type of fish that is often dried, then shaved thinly and used as a seasoning in Japanese cooking. Together, they make up a unique flavor profile that is the essence of an overwhelming majority of Japanese dishes. Like, I'm talking about 70 percent of all Japanese cooking. Kombu and bonito can sometimes be relatively expensive, so I grind them finely to maximize their flavors. Their sole use in this book is to make the ramen seasoning that is part of all the ramen recipes—and that's reason enough to buy them. They're widely available online.

MUSHROOM POWDER

This is basically ground dried shiitake mushrooms, another ingredient with a high concentration of natural MSG. It's everywhere in any Chinatown or Asian grocery store, whether Chinese, Korean, or Japanese. After you buy dried shiitake mushrooms, keep them frozen in an unzipped bag, which will make them extra dry and brittle, resulting in a much finer grind.

ROASTED BARLEY TEA POWDER

Roasted barley is either a stand-alone or an added ingredient in tea beverages in Japan and Korea. It has a dark, almost coffee-like aroma. I like to grind it and add it to bread doughs to give them a boost of subtle malty and wheaty flavor. Find it online.

TOOLS

In my experience, what often determines whether you walk away from a recipe basking in glory and high self-esteem or collapsing in defeat and thumb-sucking hopelessness is simply *if you used the right tool*. I can't stress this enough; I learned it the hard way. As far as I'm concerned, proper kitchen tools are not for convenience; they're for sanity.

In addition to what I consider the usual requirements, such as a blender and a food processor, here's a list of mostly inexpensive items that will save not just your dinner but your mental health for the next ten cooking years to come.

Food Processor

Dough Hook

Immersion Blender

Spice Grinder

Blowtorch

Truffle Shaver

Stand Mixer or Handheld Mixer

If you can't afford a stand mixer, then at the very least get a handheld mixer *that has a dough hook attachment*. The level of gluten formation in a lot of doughs out there (such as the layered paratha on page 193) is simply too difficult to be achieved by the bare hands of mortals (unless you practice using kneading pain as a sexual stimulant). Consider yourself notified.

Immersion Blender

Standard blenders are great for blending a large quantity of ingredients that have a sufficient amount of liquid in them. But when it comes to recipes in small quantities or ones that are relatively dry in nature, standard blenders fail miserably. This is when an immersion blender comes in handy. Immersion blenders usually include a narrow, deep plastic cup, and together they can make a beautiful puree of tough aromatics such as lemongrass, ginger, shallots, garlic, and more without added liquid. They can make a smooth batch of aioli, mayonnaise, or vinaigrette, no matter how little the amount. And last but not least, an immersion blender can be inserted directly into a pot to create beautiful emulsions (such as a ramen broth). I probably use my immersion blender more often than my standard blender or food processor. Once you're properly acquainted with it, you'll wonder how you ever survived without it.

Spice Grinder

This is another tool I can't live without. As mentioned earlier, I like to powderize stuff. Like, a lot. I almost always buy peppercorns and other spices whole and grind them myself. It ensures the purity as well as the freshness of my spices. But more important, I like to powderize things such as kombu (Japanese kelp) and bonito flakes to extract the maximum flavor for recipes such as my Ramen Seasoning (page 12). Powderizing ingredients also allows you to add the flavors and essences of dried mushrooms, teas, and more into dishes with the least physical trace of the item.

Spice grinders are generally affordable. Sometimes blenders will come with a spice grinder attachment, which kills two birds with one stone. But if you're buying a stand-alone spice grinder, make sure that you *choose one with a removable bowl that can be thoroughly washed,* so that the flavors from one grind don't contaminate the next.

Blowtorch

A blowtorch isn't just for crème brûlée. It adds blisters and char marks to whatever foods we like and mimics the burned aroma that we associate with food that's been grilled over high heat without our having to actually fire up a grill, all without cooking the interiors. It also finishes off areas of imperfection that may result from our inadequate home ovens and stoves. An undercharred surface on a pizza, a blond patch on a roast chicken, a missed corner on a burger patty—whatever the flaw, a blowtorch can provide a second-chance touch-up. Consider it a food airbrush. *Buy one that can be attached to a butane canister.*

Truffle Shaver

Any ingredient in this book that is "thinly shaved" is meant to be cut with a truffle shaver. In fact, I've never used a truffle shaver to shave actual truffles. I use it to create paper-thin slices of garlic and shallots and sometimes even potatoes. I prefer it to a mandoline because it's smaller, cheaper, more portable, and creates thinner slices than most mandolines.

CONDIMENTS, SAUCES, AND PASTES

On average I keep ten to twelve bottles and jars of homemade condiments and sauces in my fridge at all times. If a condiment appears in more than a couple of recipes in this book, you'll find it in this section. And please don't let the number of times it is used in recipes determine how important it is that you have it in your life. I would gladly add any or a combination of these magical things to everything I cook, but it would look suspiciously repetitive from a creative standpoint. So consider them suggested, sometimes literally at the end of some recipes. And feel free to take them beyond the boundaries of this book.

RAMEN SEASONING

This seasoning is a must if you're in the business of making good Japanese ramen at home. Don't believe me? Try seasoning the broth with just salt and be so disappointed in yourself that even your mother can't make you feel good. The only thing slightly fussy about this recipe is sourcing the ingredients, and that can be solved with a couple of clicks online. So don't go to LazyTown. Just make it, and go explore the ramen recipes starting on page 79.

MAKES 2½ CUPS, ENOUGH FOR ABOUT 24 BOWLS OF RAMEN

2 cups (480 mL) water

4 or 5 scallions, roughly sliced

6 tablespoons (18 g) mushroom powder
(see page 9)

½ cup (126 g) fine sea salt (best measured by weight, not volume)

½ cup (120 mL) fish sauce

¼ cup (60 mL) mirin (sweet Japanese rice wine)

4 tablespoons (40g) kombu powder
(see page 9)

4 tablespoons (40 g) bonito powder
(see page 9)

1. In a medium saucepan over medium heat, bring the water, scallions, and mushroom powder to a simmer and cook for 15 minutes, until the scallions are very soft, stirring occasionally. Add the sea salt, fish sauce, and mirin and simmer until the salt has completely dissolved, about 2 minutes. Stir in the kombu and bonito powders. When the mixture comes back to a simmer, immediately turn off the heat.

2. Let sit at room temperature for 30 minutes, then strain through a fine cheesecloth. Store the liquid in an airtight bottle in the fridge for up to 2 months.

VARIATION

VEGAN RAMEN SEASONING: *Omit the fish sauce and bonito powder and add 1 more tablespoon of mushroom powder and 3 more tablespoons of kombu powder. At the end, add 2 tablespoons of soy sauce.*

MAKRUT LIME LEAF OIL

The intense citrusy fragrance of makrut lime leaves is one of my favorite elements to play with. Blending the leaves into oil maximizes the flavor of every single leaf and makes it possible to infuse it into dishes that aren't a stew or soup, such as salad dressings and guacamole, and drizzle it for extra oomph on finished dishes.

I strongly recommend using an immersion blender for this recipe because of its small quantity. One ounce of makrut lime leaves is about two large handfuls, and the yield of the recipe is based on the amount that an immersion blender can effectively process. If you use a standard blender, you may have to double the recipe for it to blend properly, and that's a lot of lime leaves.

MAKES ¾ CUP

1 ounce (30 g) fresh or frozen makrut lime leaves
½ cup (120 mL) canola oil, plus more if needed

1. Remove the central tough stems of the leaves and place the tender leafy parts in the tall cup that comes with the immersion blender. Add the oil and blend for 2 minutes, scraping the sides of the cup a couple of times, until the mixture is as finely pureed as possible. If you need to add a bit more oil in order for the mixture to blend smoothly, do that.

2. Keep in an airtight container inside the fridge for up to 1 month. If you're worried you won't use it in time, freeze some and thaw before using.

GARLIC CONFIT SAUCE

There are many garlic confit recipes out there, many of which I do not understand. First of all, who needs to eat an entire clove of squishy, oil-soaked garlic? It requires so much unnecessary oil, not to mention time, for something that is only halfway there. Here's how I forge a batch of intense garlic confit in **sauce form**, *ready to wear.*

MAKES 1 CUP

2½ heads of garlic (about 35 cloves)

3 fresh bay leaves

½ cup (120 mL) canola oil

1 tablespoon fish sauce

¼ teaspoon ground white pepper

1. Gently smash the garlic cloves so they are cracked but not completely broken. Peel off the skins.

2. In a small saucepan, combine the garlic cloves, bay leaves, and oil. Simmer over low heat, stirring occasionally, until the garlic is evenly golden brown on all sides, about 12 minutes. Remove the bay leaves and transfer the rest of the mixture to a blender (or use an immersion blender). Add the fish sauce and pepper. Blend until the mixture is smooth.

3. Keep in an airtight jar in the fridge for up to 2 weeks, or 2 months in the freezer. Thaw and/or stir before use.

FRIED CHILE VERDE SAUCE

This is probably my favorite homemade chile sauce. Any chile sauce maker who knows their stuff would tell you that the point of their craft is not to burn a layer of skin off of your face and later your rear end. It is to summon and compress the sharp, mouthwateringly peppery flavors and deliver them in a condensed and powerful punch. This sauce does exactly that. Each time I make it I struggle to not devour it by the spoonful. I could add it to 80 percent of the recipes in this book but that would be weird. So consider it implied, and know that—whether smeared between layers of a sandwich, rubbed on top of a grilled steak or roasted chicken, or tossed with a green salad—it will make everything taste better.

MAKES 2 CUPS

18 ounces (about 500 g) green cayenne peppers, green goat horn chiles, Basque fryers, or green jalapeño peppers, or a combination (see Note on page 16), stemmed and cut into small dice

4 garlic cloves, 2 smashed and 2 peeled

¾ cup plus 2 tablespoons (190 mL) canola oil

2 teaspoons whole Sichuan peppercorns

3 tablespoons fish sauce, plus more as desired

1 small handful cilantro leaves (see Note on page 16)

1½ tablespoons tightly packed minced peeled ginger

1 teaspoon fresh green Sichuan peppercorns (or if unavailable, 1 tablespoon pickled green peppercorns)

2 teaspoons rice vinegar or white wine vinegar

½ teaspoon ground white pepper

1. In a medium saucepan over medium-high heat, combine the peppers, smashed garlic, oil, and whole Sichuan peppercorns. Cook until the peppers are very soft and have lost half of their volume, 10 to 13 minutes, stirring occasionally. It's important to substantially reduce the moisture inside the peppers in order to get a concentrated flavor. Add the fish sauce and cook until the liquid has completely evaporated, about 1 minute.

2. Transfer the mixture to a blender and add the cilantro leaves, ginger, peeled garlic, green Sichuan peppercorns, vinegar, and white pepper. Blend for 1 to 2 minutes, until the mixture is super smooth and creamy. Adjust with more fish sauce if needed (this is a chile sauce and thus should be robustly seasoned).

3. Store in an airtight jar in the fridge for up to 3 weeks.

NOTE ON CHILIES: *Do not use green bell peppers, poblano peppers, or any large, sweet-tasting varieties because their flavors are on the mild side. In Asia, I typically use green cayenne peppers or green goat horn chilies, but you can use Anaheim, French Basque fryers, green jalapeño peppers, or a combination of your choice to reach your preferred* spiciness. *Green peppers are younger than red and usually have thinner skins, resulting in a much creamier, less gritty texture.*

NOTE ON CILANTRO: *If you don't like cilantro, don't worry; you won't really be able to taste it aside from a nice herby note in the background.*

FRIED SHALLOTS, DRY OR IN BLENDED FAT

Fried shallots, or **crack** *as I sometimes call them, are the key component in so many Asian recipes for their intense and irreplaceable aroma that makes so many Indian, Taiwanese, and Southeast Asian dishes pop. Whether dry or stored in fat, they can sometimes be found in Asian grocery stores. But I think the homemade version is often superior in quality and fragrance. And once you're over the illogical fear of making something unfamiliar, you'll find that this is exponentially easier than baking a cake.*

For maximum flavor, use real lard or schmaltz (chicken fat) to fry the shallots. But you can (and I often do) use a combination of either one plus canola oil, depending on what is on hand. I would recommend using at least 50 percent lard or schmaltz that you render from solid pork or chicken fat (don't worry; it's so easy), especially if you're making the wet version, in which the crispy bits from the fat add a lot of flavor to the blended oil. But if you really don't want to go to the trouble of rendering your own lard or schmaltz, you can go with store-bought.

In the recipe below, you start with a base of dry fried shallots, and you have the option of turning some or all of them into wet fried shallots. I would recommend making a full batch of either dry or wet fried shallots, because the final quantity isn't a whole lot.

MAKES 2 LOOSE CUPS DRY FRIED SHALLOTS OR 2½ CUPS WET FRIED SHALLOTS

SPECIAL EQUIPMENT: *truffle shaver, mandoline, or food processor with a thin shaver blade attachment; immersion blender (preferred, for the wet version only)*

1 pound (450 g) or at least ½ pound (225 g) solid pork fat or chicken fat/skin, plus canola oil as needed

1 pound (450 g; about 25 to 30 small) shallots

1. To render lard or schmaltz, flash-freeze the pork fat or chicken fat/skin for 30 minutes to 1 hour until hardened, then cut into very small dice, *no larger than ¼ inch* (0.5 cm). Transfer to a *nonstick* saucepan 7 to 8 inches (18 to 20 cm) wide and 4 inches (10 cm) deep and set it over medium-low heat. Cook, stirring occasionally, until all the liquid lard or schmaltz has been extracted and the fat dice have become tiny, dry, crispy bits. One way to tell it's ready is when the sizzling subsides, signaling that all the moisture has evaporated. Turn off the heat. Remove the crispy bits by scooping them off the surface with a sieve and reserve them for Wet Fried Shallots (page 19).

2. Now check the lard or schmaltz level in the pan. It should be 2 inches (5 cm) deep. If you used less than 1 pound (450 g) of solid fat, you will need to add canola oil until the level reaches 2 inches (5 cm). Set the pan aside.

DRY FRIED SHALLOTS

1. Peel the shallots using a truffle shaver, mandoline, or food processor with a thin shave blade attachment. You want them in very thin slices, about ¹⁄₁₆ inch (0.2 cm). *It's important that they are all equally thick so that they cook evenly.*

2. Line a large baking sheet with paper towels and set aside.

3. Add one-third to one-half of the shallots to the lard or schmaltz; they must be fully submerged. Set the pan over *medium-low* heat and cook, stirring frequently and separating any shallots that are in clumps. Nothing too dramatic will happen in the first 10 minutes as the shallots slowly soften and lose their moisture. But after 10 minutes they will start to take on a little bit of color, and 12 to 13 minutes in, the shallots should have turned *light brown*. They might still feel soft at this point, and you may have doubts about the timing, but this light brown color means it's time to remove the shallots. They will become golden brown as they dry; any darker and they will be bitter.

4. With a webbed or spider strainer, scoop out the fried shallots and drain them over the frying oil, pressing on them with a spoon to let any excess oil drip back into the pot, then transfer them onto the paper towel–lined baking sheet. If they appear to have reclumped, fluff them up with two chopsticks or forks. Set them aside to dry and crisp. Repeat this process with the remaining shallots.

5. When the shallots are completely cooled and crisp, store them in zip-top bags in the freezer. They should be good for at least 6 months.

WET FRIED SHALLOTS

1. Place the reserved pork fat or chicken cracklings inside the tall cup that comes with your immersion blender. Add the amount of dry fried shallots that you want to turn into the wet version, along with enough frying oil to just barely cover them. Blend with the immersion blender until finely pureed.

2. Store in airtight jars in the fridge for up to 1 month (because the shallots are sort of "sealed" inside fat, they don't necessarily have to be put in the freezer). Freeze for longer storage.

MALA PASTE

If you have actually had a proper Sichuan mala hot pot in Sichuan instead of only watching it used by Anthony Bourdain as a torturing device to toy with Eric Ripert on TV, you will understand its indisputable allure. It is as close as a food can come to being narcotic, highly addictive, stupor-inducing, and mind-warping, all through perpetual tidal waves of pain and pleasure. Every Sichuan mala (ma means "numbing" and la means "spicy") hot pot restaurant creates its signature flavor profile by making a paste, a mala hot pot base. And that's where the inspiration for this recipe comes from.

Having said that, you can't use this paste as a hot pot base because, despite its seemingly long ingredient list, this recipe is still simplified compared to the real deal, which always includes more than a dozen different spices. But it will provide sufficient glory to the dishes and applications in this book.

MAKES 2 CUPS

NOTE: *This paste includes a lot of ingredients but it's totally worth it. That said, you can make some exchanges, such as using 2 tablespoons of dark miso paste instead of 1 tablespoon of Chinese fermented black beans, or skipping either the mushroom powder or kombu powder (but not both), which are there for a boost of umami. The spices are absolutely necessary.*

3½ ounces (100 g) pork back fat, diced into small cubes

3½ ounces (100 g) guanciale or pancetta, diced into small cubes

3 tablespoons Sichuan broad bean chile paste (doubanjiang; see page 8)

1 tablespoon dark miso paste

1 tablespoon Chinese fermented black beans

3 scallions, cut into 1-inch (3-cm) segments

6 garlic cloves, chopped

1 teaspoon minced ginger

4 to 6 Pickled Chilies (page 25) or pickled jalapeños, finely chopped

2 tablespoons Chinese rice wine

2 tablespoons Sichuan or Korean chile flakes

1 tablespoon mushroom powder (see page 9)

2½ teaspoons ground coriander

2 teaspoons ground cumin

1 teaspoon ground fennel

¼ teaspoon ground cinnamon

2 star anise pods

1 black cardamom pod or 2 green cardamom pods

2 fresh bay leaves

3 tablespoons ground Sichuan peppercorns

2 tablespoons toasted sesame oil

2 tablespoons soy sauce

2 tablespoons strawberry jam

1 tablespoon fish sauce

1 tablespoon kombu powder (see page 9)

1. Place the pork fat and guanciale in a medium *nonstick* saucepan and set it over medium-high heat. Cook, stirring occasionally, until all the fat has been rendered and the small dice becomes golden-brown crispy bits. Remove the crispy pork bits with a slotted spoon and reserve them. Add the Sichuan broad bean chile paste, miso paste, fermented black beans, scallions, garlic, ginger, pickled chilies, rice wine, chile flakes, mushroom powder, coriander, cumin, fennel, cinnamon, star anise, cardamom, and bay leaves to the fat in the pan. Lower the heat to medium-low and cook for 10 minutes, stirring constantly, until the mixture has darkened slightly in color. Add the ground Sichuan peppercorns and cook for 30 seconds, then turn off the heat.

2. Return the crispy pork bits to the pan and add the sesame oil, soy sauce, strawberry jam, fish sauce, and kombu powder. With an immersion blender (here it produces a smoother texture than a regular blender), blend the whole thing until extremely smooth. Transfer to an airtight container and keep refrigerated for up to 1 month until needed.

CARAMELIZED ONION POWDER PASTE

This serves as a cop-out version of fried shallots. As you can see, it's wet instead of dry, and onion instead of shallot, but it works as an acceptable substitute, sometimes. In fact, it even works better in some dishes, such as Cajun Chopped Liver Dirty Mazemen (page 121).

MAKES ⅓ CUP

½ cup (60 g) very finely ground onion powder
¼ cup plus 3 tablespoons (90 mL) canola oil
2 teaspoons fish sauce
¼ teaspoon ground white pepper

1. In a small saucepan, whisk the onion powder, oil, fish sauce, and pepper into a thick paste, then set it over medium heat. Cook, *whisking constantly* throughout the entire cooking process. When the mixture starts to simmer, turn the heat to low and cook until the paste *just starts* to turn darker in color (this will happen quite quickly). When it does, immediately take the pan off the heat and continue whisking until the paste turns the same shade of brown as caramel sauce. When in doubt, shoot for a lighter shade, because it will go from aromatic to burned from one shade to the next.

2. Transfer the paste to a cool airtight jar to prevent further cooking. Keep in the fridge for up to 1 month.

ORANGE CHILE SAMBAL

This recipe was born out of my nitpicking on sriracha. Don't get me wrong; I love sriracha just like any other reasonable earthling for its creamy and intense pepperiness, garlicky and mildly sweet heat level, and let's not forget that ingenious design of the squeeze bottle. But I wanted something more acidic and fruity that would add more zing and pop to dishes. So, out came the orange chile sambal.

MAKES 1 CUP

14 ounces (400 g) red cayenne peppers, goat horn chilies, or red jalapeño peppers, stemmed

1½ ounces (40 g) Thai hot chilies, stemmed

1 small navel orange

10 garlic cloves, peeled

2½ tablespoons fish sauce

2 tablespoons distilled white vinegar

2 teaspoons light brown sugar

1. If you like a super-smooth consistency, I suggest charring the peppers over an open flame, letting them cool, and removing the charred skins. But if you don't mind a grittier chile sauce, you can skip this step.

2. Zest the orange and place the zest in the cup of an immersion blender or in a standard blender. Cut away the pith to expose the flesh, and remove each segment from the surrounding skin with a knife. Place the segments in the cup or blender.

3. Squeeze the juice from the remaining orange flesh into the cup or blender. Add the chilies, garlic, fish sauce, vinegar, and brown sugar, and blend on high speed for a full 2 minutes, until extremely smooth.

4. Transfer the puree to a small *nonstick* saucepan and bring it to a boil over medium heat. Lower the heat to maintain a gentle simmer and cover partly with a lid to avoid splattering. Cook for about 15 minutes, stirring occasionally, until the mixture is reduced by half.

5. Let sit at room temperature for at least 24 hours before using. Store in a squeeze bottle in the fridge for up to 1 month.

MY ULTIMATE CHILE OIL

I once thought about bottling this stuff and selling it as my ticket to an early retirement in a grand château in the French countryside. It is that good. During my chile oil–sodden years in New York, Beijing, Taiwan, and Hong Kong, swimming through countless commercial brands and the versions offered in restaurants, I could always find legitimate reasons that this recipe is comparably more versatile and better tasting. And that's saying a lot.

MAKES 2½ CUPS

SPECIAL EQUIPMENT: *spice grinder*

2 tablespoons soy sauce

4 garlic cloves, grated

½ cup (50 g) Sichuan (spicier) or Korean (milder) chile flakes (I don't recommend using any other kind)

1 star anise pod

2 teaspoons ground coriander

1½ teaspoons ground cumin

¼ teaspoon curry powder

2 cups (480 mL) canola oil

3 tablespoons white sesame seeds

2 dried bay leaves

2 tablespoons finely ground Sichuan peppercorns

1. Mix the soy sauce and grated garlic together. Set aside.

2. Using a spice grinder, grind the chile flakes, star anise pod, coriander, cumin, and curry powder into a fine powder. In a large saucepan at least 6 inches (15 cm) deep, combine the spice powder with the oil, sesame seeds, and bay leaves. Set it over medium heat and bring the mixture to a gentle boil. Boil for 3 minutes, *stirring frequently,* until the chile flakes have turned maroon in color (but *not black*!).

3. When the chile flakes have turned to the desired color, *turn off the heat* immediately, then add the ground Sichuan peppercorns. Stir and let fry in the residual heat for about 30 seconds, then add the soy sauce/garlic mixture. The oil will boil up a little due to the added moisture (which is why we're using a *deep* pot). Just keep stirring until the sizzling has died down.

4. Let the chile oil sit at room temperature for at least 2 hours (or best overnight) before using. Keep in an airtight jar in the fridge for up to 3 months.

PICKLED CHILIES

*I know it's possible that you'll see the word **week** in the instructions and immediately decide not to bother and use a store-bought pickled jalapeño or something. But that would be like substituting coffee for tea—also great, just not the same fucking thing. Fermentation takes time, but it will reward you in this case with not only intensely aromatic chilies to be minced into greatness, but also a complex and deeply flavorful pickling juice that can be added to just about anything that deserves a break. I use the pickling liquid quite a lot in sauces and marinades, but if I ever have leftover liquid after the chilies are gone, I just add it to a new batch of pickles.*

Every time I buy red chilies, I wash them, pat them dry, and throw them into the freezer. I actually think frozen chilies break down faster than fresh ones, but use fresh chilies if you want.

MAKES 3 CUPS

½ cup (120 g) water

6 to 8 whole dried Thai bird's eye red chilies

1 garlic clove, peeled and cracked

2 small fresh unpeeled ginger slices

½ cup (120 mL) white rice vinegar

3 tablespoons fish sauce

2 tablespoons vodka

1½ tablespoons table salt

1 teaspoon granulated sugar

1 teaspoon Sichuan peppercorns

5 ounces (130 g) red cayenne chilies (less spicy) or Thai bird's eye red chilies (very spicy), or a combination of both

1. To make the pickling juice, in a small saucepan over high heat, combine the water, dried chilies, garlic, and ginger and bring them to a boil and cook for 30 seconds. Turn off the heat. Add the vinegar, fish sauce, vodka, salt, sugar, and Sichuan peppercorns and stir until the salt has completely dissolved.

2. Combine the pickling juice with the chilies in an airtight jar and let it sit at room temperature for at least 1 week in a hot and humid climate, or up to 3 weeks in a cool and dry climate, then transfer to the fridge. The pickled chilies should keep for up to 3 months.

SWEET SOY SAUCE

I really sort of caved in to including sweet soy sauce purely because, with the ginger sauce, it's a set for Bastardized Hainan Chicken Rice (page 225). But it's never been my favorite component of Hainan chicken. Here, in an attempt to make it more interesting, molasses is introduced, but does it measure up to the sharpness of ginger sauce or the potency of the chile sambal in the chicken rice? You can make the call.

MAKES ABOUT ⅜ CUP

¼ cup (60 mL) soy sauce

1½ tablespoons molasses

1 tablespoon dark brown sugar

In a small saucepan over low heat, bring the soy sauce, molasses, and brown sugar to a simmer and cook until the sugar has completely melted. Let cool to room temperature. This can be made the day ahead and kept at room temperature.

FRIED GARLIC POWDER

To make fried garlic powder, one has to make fried garlic chips. The best way to make perfectly even fried garlic chips is to shave the cloves with a truffle shaver. No chopping, food processing, or hand-slicing will give you pieces with such precisely equal thickness and surface area. This recipe alone is enough to justify spending a few bucks on a truffle shaver.

MAKES ½ CUP

SPECIAL EQUIPMENT: *truffle shaver; spice grinder*

Cloves from 2 garlic heads, peeled
Canola oil, for frying

1. Adjust the truffle shaver to about medium thickness and set a sieve over a medium bowl right next to the stove. Run all the cloves through the shaver, then transfer the slices to a small saucepan. Add enough canola oil to just cover the garlic and set the pan over medium-high heat. Stir frequently with a fork to loosen and separate the slices during cooking.

2. The second the chips turn honey blond (lighter than golden brown), *immediately* pour the garlic and oil into the sieve to drain. Any shade darker and the chips will be bitter. Drain well, then scatter the chips in a single layer between two paper towels and press to dry. Uncover and let cool completely.

3. Process the fried garlic in a spice grinder until finely ground. Store in an airtight jar in the fridge for up to 2 weeks. But note that fried garlic's flavor deteriorates as it sits in the fridge, so fresh is best.

HELLDUST

This condiment is actually served alongside any authentic Sichuan hot pots. Common sense would suggest that it's crazy to pull something out of what is already a pool of raging nuclear lava and then dip it into a mount of red chile flakes that clearly carry no good intention. But spiciness isn't really the point. This mixture of spices and nuts actually adds prominent aroma and a slight crunch to, well, anything! Pizza, noodles, salads, roasted meats, or vegetables— basically it should replace your boring chile flakes. I call it Helldust, but it touches everything with the kiss of god.

MAKES 1 CUP

SPECIAL EQUIPMENT: *spice grinder*

½ cup (58 g) Korean chile flakes (see page 6)

½ teaspoon fine sea salt

2 tablespoons white sesame seeds

2 teaspoons ground Sichuan peppercorns

2 teaspoons ground cumin

¼ teaspoon curry powder

⅓ tablespoon roasted skinless peanuts

2 tablespoons Fried Garlic Powder (page 27)

1. In a small skillet over medium heat, combine the chile flakes and sea salt and toast, stirring constantly, until the chile flakes turn slightly darker in color and smell fragrant. Transfer to a spice grinder and process until they resemble fine sand. Set aside in a bowl.

2. *Wipe the skillet clean* (so you don't burn leftover chile flakes) and add the sesame seeds. Toast over medium heat, stirring constantly, until each seed is light brown and plumped up. Add the ground peppercorns, cumin, and curry powder, stir, and toast for 30 seconds. Transfer to a spice grinder and process until the mixture resembles coarse wet sand. Add it to the bowl.

3. Grind the peanuts until they resemble wet sand, then add them to the bowl along with the Fried Garlic Powder.

4. Once everything is completely cooled, transfer to a zip-top bag and rub the bag to give the mixture a good massage and blend the flavors. Keep in an airtight jar in the fridge for up to 1 month. But fresh helldust tastes better.

CHINESE SOUTHERN ALMOND (APRICOT KERNEL) MILK

This recipe is used only twice in this book, but I feel that it deserves a little bit of explaining, not only because it's one of my favorite things in the world, but also because it can confuse the shit out of people.

Chinese southern almond (apricot kernel) milk? *Am I talking about almonds or apricot kernels? Despite my lifelong adoration of this ingredient, it actually took me several years to understand it.*

In Mandarin Chinese, apricot kernel is 杏仁 (杏 *is "apricot";* 仁 *is "kernel"), and it's a very common ingredient all over Asia. But where it gets confusing is that in Chinese, American almond is translated as* 美國杏仁 *("American apricot kernel"), and with reverse logic, apricot kernels in English are labeled "Chinese almonds." In fact, to buy apricot kernels on Amazon, you have to search for "Chinese almonds" or nothing will come up. So people often confuse these two ingredients, which have completely different flavors and aromas. To make matters even more confusing, almond extract, which is made from bitter almond, actually tastes* **exactly** *like apricot kernel. And amaretto, the liqueur that tastes like almond extract, is actually—yes—made from apricot kernels.*

So, when I say Chinese southern almond, I'm not talking about almonds of any kind. *I'm talking about apricot kernel—southern apricot kernel, to be exact. Because Chinese northern apricot kernel is actually poisonous.*

MAKES 3½ CUPS

1 cup (120 g) Chinese southern almond/apricot kernels (see Note)

2 tablespoons unsalted roasted peanuts

4 cups (960 mL) boiling water

1. Place the Chinese southern almonds and peanuts in a blender, add the boiling water, cover, and soak them for 2 hours. Blend on high for 2 full minutes (don't estimate—time it).

2. Pour the mixture into a large saucepan. Bring to a simmer over medium heat and cook for 5 minutes. Let cool.

3. Strain the mixture through a fine cheesecloth, squeezing on the solids to extract as much liquid as possible. Store the liquid in an airtight bottle in the fridge for up to 1 week. (Freezing almond milk is not ideal because the milk will separate after thawing. Reblending it on high speed may bring it back together, but the overall texture and taste may be affected.)

NOTE ON CHINESE SOUTHERN ALMONDS: *You can find peeled and dried southern apricot kernels in most Chinese supermarkets or online. They will usually be labeled "Chinese southern almonds" or "Chinese sweet almonds."*

1

MY DAYS AS A MA-JIANG LINE COOK

Until then, cooking was never an interest of mine.

Sometimes when I look back on my cooking addiction—like a weathered alcoholic recalling the initial spark of love from her first sip of beer, I guess—I recall a period of innocence before I started abusing it as an antidepressant. There was a time when I used to cook, purely and incandescently, for the simplest and most uncomplicated purpose.

Cash.

I started cooking at sixteen because I wanted to earn five dollars off my mother's ma-jiang table. It began as good old earnest greed for green, but little did I know that I was sowing the seeds of an obsession with cooking for the next twenty years to come. Back then, once a week (as claimed by my mother, but it was in fact closer to twice) (three times max, she says), a highly competitive assembly of four middle-aged Taiwanese housewives would gather in one of their homes and engage in the stationary sport of calculating tiles and outlasting one

another's sore asses. Sitting for ten to twelve hours straight on barely padded chairs, conducting high-risk management and gossip warfare, these aunties took their sport with all seriousness, allowing just one single meal break to fuel the fire. That's where I came in.

The rule was that each of these fine ladies would pay five dollars to fund their meal, and if I could manage to feed them on twenty dollars or less, I got to keep the change. Easy, right? I mean, how hard could it be to feed a pack of middle-aged housewives? Well, that depends on how much you know about 1990s-era Vancouver.

It wasn't just a city vibrant with Asian immigrants from Hong Kong, Taiwan, and Vietnam; at its prime it was notoriously *the* Chinatown of all North America, a renowned status earned by a supreme standard of Asian cuisine that some say superseded that of its countries of origin. It was a breeding ground for a colony of jaded connoisseurs whose taste buds were sharpened by years of immersion in top-notch ingredients—Dungeness crabs, geoducks, British Columbia sea urchins, and young, supple pigeons—the master-level preparations of which flowed through the days like breakfast cereal. These ma-jiang housewives didn't just expect to be fed. They expected to be fed *well*.

As a teenage girl whose cooking experience amounted to counting calories and microwaving face masks, I quickly realized that I was in way over my head. Either naturally or through PTSD, I have lost all recollection of the first meal I cooked for them, but a few softly spoken words from one of the aunties as she slowly lowered her chopsticks burned into my memory like a hot iron on a slab of meat: "We could also order takeout next time."

Ouch, bitch. Now you've made it personal.

Typically, I'm all about quitting at any sight of an obstacle. I'm just easygoing like that. But that day, for some reason something propelled me the other way, onto an unfamiliar path I believe they call . . . *keep trying*. I started to take cooking seriously, which is ironic because until then, cooking was never an interest of mine.

Growing up, I watched my mother, a good cook who nonetheless automated this socially imposed task apathetically, year after year, sometimes with barely concealed aversion. I thought to myself then that if I were ever to spend this amount of time doing something—anything—it wouldn't be because I should, but because I fucking *liked* it. And who knew? It turned out that cooking is just what I like.

Cooking for the aunties soon became about more than just making money: there was curiosity, perhaps, and an exhilaration at making new discoveries. Soon I found myself spending three hours meticulously nursing a clay pot of oxtails braised in soy sauce and caramel, or crisping the skins of a silver pomfret, bothered more by a missed corner of imperfection than the occasional painful splatters of oil. In the end, my net profit was nil, if not bleeding red. But at an age when the friends around me didn't even know how to avoid Hot Pockets–related explosions in the microwave, I was proud and intrigued. That said, not even remotely did I think this episode of mine would change the rest of my life.

for GETTING OUT OF BED

Look, the only thing I'd like to cook at seven in the morning—as I lie in bed with residual resentments from the day before and looming despair about the day ahead—is the people who say they love cooking breakfast. Who are these people? I imagine their breakfasts taste like denial buttered up with overcompensating enthusiasm. So, no. These recipes are not for breakfast. They are not for mornings. Both are equally and grossly overrated ideas, and thus undeserving of your efforts here.

Instead, this chapter is designed for those days when you finally get to stay horizontal until the very last second that your heart damn well pleases; for when you feel that the world owes you something for all the uncalled-for bullshit it dumped on your face the week before. Something compensatory; something corrective. Something that tastes like the very will to do it all over again.

For any other days, I do my regular coffee with a drop of laxative.

ALL-PURPOSE MOTHER DOUGH

I never thought I'd bake. Breads, especially. When it comes to cooking, I can rely on my senses to tell me the truth—a pinch of this, a splash of that, the need communicable by sight or taste. But doughs . . . doughs are strange, man. Unpredictable, mute little suckers. As far as I'm concerned, they might as well be from another universe, existing under a completely different set of physical realities. Thus I used to address them the same way as any other alien life-form: respectfully, with distance and distrust.

But as we all know, perspectives change, though usually not along the path of our choosing. About a year after my husband and I moved to Beijing, facing the choice of living off frozen bagels or something much worse, leaving the apartment, I started baking bread. And I never thought I'd say this, about bread especially, but it has been a strangely satisfying and addictive journey. To see a handful of seemingly lifeless white powder transform into a breathing sponge of microactivity is in itself transformative. These days, although I do have access to decent bread, I still prefer to bake my own.

It's generally advised that you follow baking recipes closely. But sometimes to succeed in a recipe you have to do more than simply follow it. You have to feel it, and often only through persistent repetition. Bread happens to be one of those motherfuckers.

If you are making bread for the very first time, please, don't expect it to come easy. It's not you, nor is it the recipe. It's just how it works with bread. It's a romance that should and will involve some necessary, even respectful, courtship. A dinner and a movie plus a few hour-long conversations about a rosy future and maybe—just maybe—you'll get to second base on your third date. So much of the essence of a good bread depends on variants that can't be fully transcribed in a recipe—the hand-feel of its skin and flesh, the sounds of its moans and hisses. The relationship is flirtatious and spontaneous. In a way, that's the best part.

Over the years, I've developed a bread recipe that works as the base for most of my needs: rustic country loaf, chewy crusty pizza, or puffy pita bread. I call it the **mother dough.**

This all-purpose "faux sourdough" dough is my best shot, so far, at finding that perfect balance between results and practicality. It doesn't involve keeping a jar of gas-farting bacteria—more commonly referred to as a sourdough starter or levain—as a lifelong companion. What it asks from you is at least eighteen hours of patience, most of which involve just leaving it the hell alone, plus the implementation of a couple of time-cheating tricks that make up for the rest. Ground roasted barley tea, a common tea consumed in Asia, gives the dough an extra-malty, smoky, whole-wheat-ish flavor without compromising on the texture; then a mixture of plain yogurt and water gives it faux tanginess. Shortcuts are usually not the point of why or how I cook, but in this case it's a win-win situation.

NOTE: *Please measure all ingredients by weight when it comes to the doughs in this book.*

MAKES 1 LOAF OF BREAD, 2 PIZZA CRUSTS, OR 10 PITAS

1 cup (235 g) plus 2 teaspoons water

¾ cup plus 1 tablespoon (200 g) plain yogurt

3½ cups (500 g) bread flour, plus additional flour as needed

1 tablespoon (8 g) roasted barley tea powder (see page 9)

⅓ teaspoon instant dry yeast

2 teaspoons (13 g) fine sea salt

BASE DOUGH

Autolysis: The first part of this process is called autolysis, and it starts by mixing the flour and wet ingredients without yet adding the yeast. Autolysis maximizes the gluten formation in the dough without overkneading, and the longer the autolysis, the more elastic and better-tasting your final result will be. You get a really great result for the amount of effort you put in.

The length of autolysis can be anywhere from 30 minutes to 10 hours and beyond. For best results, start the morning before you bake your bread. Then your mixture can go through 10 hours of autolysis and you can proceed with the next step that evening. Another option is starting around 6 hours before your bedtime the night before you bake, and letting the dough sit for at least 30 minutes before moving on to the next step.

1. Use an 8½-cup (2-liter) bowl or container that will allow the contents to triple in size. Whisk the 1 cup (240 mL) water and the yogurt until smooth, then add the flour and barley tea powder (do not add the yeast yet). Stir the mixture with a large spoon until a sticky, lumpy dough forms. Cover and let sit at room temperature (65° to 72°F/18° to 22°C) for at least 30 minutes and up to 10 hours.

2. *Adding the yeast:* In a small bowl, mix the yeast with the remaining 2 teaspoons of water until the yeast has dissolved (no need to wait for it to foam). Add the yeast mixture and salt to the dough, then start folding it into the dough until evenly mixed. Cover and let sit for 30 minutes.

3. *Wet your hands to prevent sticking, and don't worry about the extra moisture, because this dough can take it.* Fold the dough with a slow and gentle motion: Cup your hand around the dough from the very bottom of the bowl, bring the dough up, and fold it over itself several times. Cover and let sit for another 30 minutes, then repeat the folding two more times. (Alternatively, you can use a stand mixer or handheld mixer with a dough hook to knead the dough on high for 10 minutes just once.)

4. Proceed to make one of the bread products below. . . .

NOTE: *Room temperature means 65° to 72°F/18° to 22°C. Outside this range may result in the dough rising significantly faster or slower.*

CRUSTY LOAVES

MAKES 1 LOAF

SPECIAL EQUIPMENT: *cheesecloth*

1. *First rise:* Cover the dough with plastic wrap and let it rise for 4 to 6 hours at room temperature. The dough should about *triple* in size and look puffy and bubbly.* Generously flour the working surface, then scrape the dough out of the container onto the surface *as gently as you can* without losing too many of the air bubbles inside. Dust with flour as needed and fold the dough over itself from four different corners.

If you want to prepare the dough a couple of days in advance, or if you want a longer proofing period for better flavor and texture, let the dough expand only 200 percent (double) in the first rise and leave it in the fridge for up to 48 hours in the second rise.

2. Turn the dough over with the seam side facing down and transfer it to a surface *without flour.* Cup your hands around the dough and scoop it gently toward yourself from different directions, allowing the friction between the dough and the counter to tighten the dough and form it into a round shape.

3. Line a large bowl with a large cheesecloth (this prevents sticking), then dust it generously with flour. Transfer the dough to the bowl with the seam side down. Wrap the entire bowl all around with plastic wrap.

4. *Second rise:* Place the bowl in the fridge and let it rise overnight for 10 to 11 hours. The dough should have expanded again by about 50 percent. If the dough has doubled again inside the fridge, then that means the dough was too warm to begin with (for example, during a hot summer) and has overproofed. You might need to shorten the second rise in the fridge the next time you make the recipe.

5. *Baking:* Forty-five minutes before baking, set a lidded cast-iron pot big enough to fit the dough in the oven and preheat the oven to 500°F/250°C.

6. Lay a piece of parchment paper on the counter, then gently invert the bowl to release the dough onto the parchment. Now the seam side should be facing up. Remove the pot from the oven to a heat-proof surface, lift the parchment paper along with the dough, and set the dough and parchment in the pot. Set the lid on the pot, return it to the oven, and bake for 20 to 25 minutes. Remove the lid and bake for another 12 to 15 minutes, until the surface of the bread is deeply browned.

7. Remove the bread and set on a cooling rack for 30 minutes. Just like all breads, it's best eaten on the first day.

PITA BREADS

MAKES TEN 6-INCH (15-CM) PITAS

1. *First rise:* Cover the dough with plastic wrap and let it rise at room temperature for 3 to 5 hours, until *a little more than doubled in size* (250 percent of the original size).

2. *Second rise:* Transfer the dough to the fridge to rise overnight, 10 to 11 hours. The dough should expand by about 50 percent. If the dough has doubled again inside the fridge, then that means the dough was too warm to begin with (for example, during a hot summer) and has overproofed. You might need to shorten the second rise in the fridge the next time you make the recipe.

3. Gently scrape the dough onto a floured surface, then divide it into 10 portions. Fold the dough over itself a few times and shape each portion into a ball. Flour the top generously, then cover the balls loosely with plastic wrap and let sit for 45 minutes to 1 hour. The dough balls won't really expand much. This is just to relax the dough.

4. *Baking:* Forty-five minutes before baking, set a pizza stone or large inverted cast-iron skillet in the oven and preheat it to 500°F/260°C.

5. Transfer 1 dough ball onto a small piece of parchment paper and roll it out into a ¼-inch-thick (1-cm) disk. Slide the parchment paper onto the pizza stone or skillet and bake until the dough is puffed up into a ball and slightly brown on the edges, about 2 minutes.

6. Let cool for 10 minutes while you proceed to make the rest of the pitas.

PIZZA DOUGH

MAKES 2 PIZZA CRUSTS

1. *First rise:* Cover with plastic wrap and let rise for 3 to 5 hours at room temperature until *doubled in size* (200 percent of the original). Transfer the dough to the fridge to rest for at least 12 hours and up to 24 hours. It will do little expanding at such a low temperature, but the longer you keep it refrigerated, the better the flavor and the chewier the texture will be.

2. *Second rise:* At least 2 hours before baking, gently scrape the dough onto a floured surface, taking care not to lose too many air bubbles. Divide the dough into 2 equal portions. Working with one portion at a time, fold the corners of the dough over itself from two or three different directions, then flip it over so the seam side is facing down. Transfer to a surface without flour, then cup your hands around the dough and scoop it gently toward you from a few different directions to tighten the dough.

3. Transfer the dough to a large piece of lightly oiled parchment paper, generously flour the top, then cover with plastic wrap. Let proof for 1½ to 2 hours, until it has doubled again. To test, dust the surface with flour and gently dent the dough with your finger. If the dent stays and does not bounce back, the dough is ready.

4. For pizza recipes, see pages 216 to 222.

MOCHI CHALLAH BREAD STUFFED WITH PROSCIUTTO AND DATES

I'm aware that most respected bakers across Europe and the United States dedicate their legacies to producing the next world-shattering loaf of sourdough: the kind of bread that is years in the making, the kind that summons the power of mystically ancient yeasts shaped by the soft touches of a baker's hands to carry the messages of the gods, then unveil them to the world with the anticipation of the Second Coming of Christ. Those bakers are the legends, the worshipped, the real deal.

No one, or at least nobody worth mentioning here, gives a damn about squishy breads.

But I do. I am Team Squish. More than any crusty loaf of holey *sourdough, I care about squishy breads. Perhaps because I'm not a serious baker, or because it's a genetic mutation found in those of Asian descent, I've been on a lifelong pursuit of a perfectly soft, stringy, chewy but pillow-like squishy bread.*

You might be thinking, Oh, like a brioche? *No, dude, not like a brioche. My search began with the famous Hokkaido milk bread, which uses a cooked roux to retain the moisture inside the crumb and gave me soft and tender bread that kept me relatively happy for years. But while it excelled at softness, the chewy part—a crucial element of Team Squish that I should mention—was somewhat sidelined.*

Then, a few years ago from a Korean bakery in Beijing—who knew?—I found my ultimate squishy unicorn. How hadn't I thought of it before? A hybrid between mochi (sticky rice dough) and Hokkaido milk bread was the answer to my search for my perfect edible pillow. If you're not a fan of mochi, (a) my deepest condolences and (b) this bread does not taste like mochi, which acts only as a textural aid that gives the bread a tender chewiness. Almost an oxymoron, but it's real.

It took me several heartbreaking failures to finally arrive at this recipe, but now it's my go-to base for any squishy bread applications—in this case, a braided challah stuffed with a sweet and savory paste made from prosciutto and dates.

MAKES 1 LOAF

MOCHI BREAD DOUGH

1 cup (117 g) sticky rice flour (see page 6)

1 cup (235 g) water

3 cups (410 g) bread flour, more as needed

1 large egg, plus 1 tablespoon egg white (reserve the remaining egg white)

3 tablespoons (46 g) granulated sugar

1½ teaspoons instant dry yeast

1 teaspoon sea salt

1 tablespoon (13 g) unsalted butter

FILLING

¾ packed cup (145 g) pitted dates

¼ pound (130 g) prosciutto

2 tablespoons water

2 tablespoons honey

1 tablespoon unsalted butter

⅛ teaspoon sea salt

MAKE THE DOUGH

1. In a small saucepan, whisk the sticky rice flour and water until smooth, then cook it over medium-high heat, stirring constantly. It will appear lumpy at first, then eventually it becomes a big blob of sticky goo. When it does, turn off the heat and let it *cool completely.*

2. In the bowl of a stand mixer with a dough hook attachment, combine the cooled sticky rice goo, bread flour, egg and egg white, sugar, yeast, and salt. Knead on low speed until the mixture comes together into a sticky dough (the dough may seem dry at first, but *do not* add water).

Add the butter, scraping the sides and bottom of the bowl to help the butter incorporate evenly, and knead for 7 to 8 minutes, until the dough is extremely smooth and elastic. The dough *should be sticky,* but only sticking to the bottom of the bowl as the machine is running, leaving a thin opaque film on the sides of the bowl. If it's too wet—sticking everywhere as the machine is running—add 1 tablespoon of bread flour at a time and knead again until it looks right.

3. Cover the bowl with plastic wrap and let the dough rise at room temperature until doubled, 2 to 3 hours.

MAKE THE FILLING

4. Meanwhile, in a food processor, combine the dates, prosciutto, water, honey, butter, and salt. Pulse several times, until the mixture is ground into a thick, coarse paste. Set aside.

BRAID THE CHALLAH

5. Scrape the risen dough onto a well-floured surface and divide it by half. Dusting with flour as needed, roll out the dough into a 3 × 1-foot (90 × 30-cm) rectangle. Spread half the filling evenly across the dough all the way to the edges, then roll it into a tight log starting on the long side. Cut the log in half lengthwise. Repeat with the other half of the dough and filling. You'll then have four dough logs. Gently stretch the logs even longer, as much as you feel comfortable with without tearing them, ideally to about 18 inches (45 cm).

6. Weave the four logs together following the photos on page 45, placing one log over the next until you run out of dough. Tuck the dough ends firmly underneath the loaf, making sure you don't have any loose corners sticking out anywhere. You want a sturdy, tightly packed woven ball of challah.

7. Set the weaved challah on a parchment-lined baking sheet, then cover loosely with plastic wrap. You have two options for proofing: either leave the dough at room temperature and proof again until almost doubled, 1 to 2 hours, or set it in the fridge overnight or until doubled.

8. To bake, preheat the oven to 340°F/170°C.

9. Whip the reserved egg white until foamy, then brush it thoroughly over the challah. Bake for 20 minutes, until the surface of the challah is deeply bronzed. *Cover it loosely* with parchment paper, lower the temperature to 325°F/160°C, and bake for another 25 minutes, until a wooden skewer inserted into the center comes out clean.

10. Let cool slightly over a baking rack and tear into it while it's still warm. Store in an airtight container if not finished immediately for up to 2 days.

POACHED EGGS WITH MISO—BROWNED BUTTER HOLLANDAISE

How long does it take a person to make a new friend in a new place? Six years and 180 days? I left Beijing after six years and 179 days, so that might explain why I made zero friends and hardly ever had brunch there. Because brunch is not entirely about the food, is it? More than perhaps any other meal of the day, it's about the company. One may desire quietness and efficiency for breakfast and lunch, sometimes even dinner, but I've never heard people argue for a solitary brunch—a solemn moment alone with a mimosa, contemplating the elegance of social isolation.

So why did I make zero friends in all my six-plus years in Beijing? I have no idea. No, wait, I lied; I know exactly why. If I'd made more of this miso and browned butter hollandaise sauce, poured over jammy egg yolks and zapped with pickled shallots and capers, while (most important) keeping my mouth shut the whole time, maybe I would have made some friends.

MAKES 2 SERVINGS

SPECIAL EQUIPMENT: *immersion blender (preferred); truffle shaver*

MISO-BROWNED BUTTER HOLLANDAISE

2 tablespoons whole milk

3 large egg yolks

2½ tablespoons medium/yellow miso paste

¼ teaspoon sugar

⅛ teaspoon ground white pepper

1 tablespoon plus 1 teaspoon freshly squeezed lemon juice

1½ sticks (¾ cup/170 g) unsalted butter, cut into cubes

QUICK-PICKLED SHALLOTS

3 large or 4 small shallots, peeled

¼ cup (60 mL) juice from Pickled Chilies (page 25) or other chile pickling juice on hand, such as jalapeño

2 thick slices rustic country bread

Olive oil, for toasting the bread

2 poached eggs

Freshly ground black pepper

Drained capers, for garnish

Fresh dill or fennel fronds, for garnish

1. I highly recommend using an immersion blender for this recipe rather than a regular blender. With small quantities like this, a regular blender tends to splatter the ingredients all over the lid and nothing ends up properly blended. Heat the milk in the microwave for about 30 seconds until hot, then pour it into a tall, slender cup (one usually comes with an immersion blender) along with the egg yolks, miso, sugar, and pepper. Use the immersion blender to blend for 1 full minute, until the mixture is smooth, velvety, and foamy. Add the lemon juice and blend again until evenly mixed. Set aside.

2. In a small nonstick saucepan (so the burned butter bits end up in the hollandaise and not stuck to the pot), cook the butter over medium-high heat for about 4 minutes, swirling the pot frequently. You'll notice that the sizzling sound subsides and the butter starts to foam and smell nutty. Working quickly so the butter doesn't burn, with one hand submerge the immersion blender into the yolk mixture and *keep it on*. With the other hand, *slowly* pour the hot butter into the container. Constantly move the blender around as you pour in the butter to form a smooth emulsion. When all the butter is in and blended, the sauce should be thick and shiny. Scrape in any browned bits left in the pot and blend again until smooth. Keep the hollandaise warm in a bowl placed over a pot of hot water until needed.

3. Shave the shallots using a truffle shaver and place them in a bowl. Add the chile pickling juice and marinate for up to 10 minutes—no longer—then drain.

4. For each serving, toast a slice of rustic country bread with olive oil until crispy on the edges. Top with a poached egg, douse generously with miso–browned butter hollandaise, and scatter with the shallots, pepper, and capers. Make it pretty with nice herbs like dill or fennel fronds.

PANDORA'S BOX

I think the funny thing about growing up sandwiched between two polar-opposite cultures is that often I just couldn't tell if a particular idea that made total sense to one side would be found by the other to be equally awesome or utterly bizarre.

Take this thing called shibuya honey toast. It is an ingenious Japanese creation that basically involves cutting a whole loaf of sweet milk bread into humongous cubes, toasting them, removing the interiors, reprocessing them, then stuffing them back into the cubes and adding various toppings. To us Asians who are fanatics about milk toast—you know, those sweet, squishy, goosedown-pillow breads sold at Asian bakeries?—this is seriously genius stuff. But to the other side of me, raised to throw stones at people who eat bread that didn't bloom from a decade-old levain . . . a sweet white bread bowl? Bizarre.

So I guess this recipe is my effort to make ultimate sense of it all. It is shibuya honey toast, sort of. It is crème brûlée French toast, sort of. It even has a little bit of a custard-filled doughnut going on. The whole cube of crustless milk bread is encased in a shiny, shatteringly thin caramel shell, then filled with an enormous dollop of chamomile-infused vanilla bean custard. It's crispy, soft, pillowy, and creamy all at once, with a few pops of tart fresh berry to give it a little shout.

MAKES 2 BOXES/2 SERVINGS

CUSTARD

1 vanilla bean

2 cups (480 mL) whole milk

1 tablespoon loose chamomile tea

5 large egg yolks

¼ cup (60 mL) honey

¼ cup (50 g) granulated sugar

5 tablespoons (39 g) all-purpose flour

1 tablespoon custard powder (find online, or replace with another 1 tablespoon flour)

4 tablespoons (½ stick/54 g) unsalted butter

BOXES

1 approximately 11-inch (28-cm) loaf Hokkaido milk bread or rectangular brioche

¾ cup (180 mL) whole milk

1 large egg

2 tablespoons light brown sugar

⅛ teaspoon ground cinnamon

⅛ teaspoon salt

Granulated sugar, for coating

Unsalted butter, for frying

Tart berries—raspberries, strawberries, blueberries—to sprinkle on top

MAKE THE CUSTARD

1. Split the vanilla bean in half lengthwise, then scrape out all the seeds. Combine the pod, seeds, and milk in a medium saucepan and set it over medium-low heat, stirring occasionally to prevent scalding. When it is almost at a simmer, turn off the heat. Place a sieve over the saucepan so that it dips into the milk but doesn't sink to the bottom, then add the chamomile tea. Let steep for 5 minutes.

2. In a medium bowl, using a handheld mixer or whisk, whisk the egg yolks, honey, and sugar until thick and velvety, about 2 minutes (you should see ribbons fall from the whisk). Add the flour and custard powder, then whisk until lump-free. Remove the chamomile and vanilla pods from the milk, then slowly pour ½ cup (120 mL) of the hot milk into the yolk mixture, whisking constantly until combined. Add the yolk mixture back to the pan, then set it over medium-low heat. Whisking constantly, let the mixture bubble gently until you have a thick custard (take the pot off the heat and whisk to blend if lumps start forming on the side of the pan). Turn off the heat and whisk in the unsalted butter, one tablespoon at a time, until evenly incorporated. Let cool slightly, then transfer to an airtight container and chill in the fridge for at least 6 hours or up to overnight. The custard can be made a couple of days ahead.

MAKE THE BOX

3. With a serrated knife, remove the crust from the bread on all sides, then cut the loaf into two 5-inch (13-cm) cubes. *Try to keep the edges as straight as possible.*

4. In a large bowl, whisk the milk, egg, brown sugar, cinnamon, and salt. On a rimmed baking sheet, scatter a thin layer of granulated sugar.

Working one at a time, dip the bread cubes in the milk mixture for just a couple of seconds on each side, then place them on a baking sheet. With a spoon, scatter a generous but even layer of granulated sugar over each side (you need a good coating to get that hardened caramel shell).

5. Set a nonstick skillet over medium-low heat and add enough butter to thinly coat the surface. Use a flat spatula to gently place the coated bread cubes in the skillet, then fry on each side until the sugar is golden brown and caramelized. If you see burned sugar in the skillet as you cook, remove it with a spoon. Keep adding more butter as needed.

6. Let the cubes cool slightly on a cooling rack (the caramel needs a couple of minutes to harden). They can be made 15 minutes before serving but no longer. Right before serving, cut out a 2-inch (5-cm) hole on one side of each cube, then remove about half of the bread from the interior (chopsticks are perfect for this job). Using a piping bag or plastic bag with a cutout hole, squeeze the chilled custard inside to fill the cavity up to the top. Sprinkle with tart berries (I used blueberries because that was what I had, but more sour berries like raspberries or strawberries would work better) and a bit of powdered sugar. Dig in.

RICE CHOWDER WITH SAUSAGE CORNFLAKES

There are a few recipes from the blog that I feel are worthy of a mention in this book, and this rice-thickened "chowder" is one of them. Back when I published that recipe, my husband and I were dug deep in the trench of Dumpling's (our Maltese's) two-year battle against congestive heart failure. I was besieged by such a harsh reality that when it came to food I could think only of soft, soothing, nonconfrontational textures. There's nothing wrong with a bowl of softies, of course. Here I've made a variation on that recipe, inspired by my current hobby of using breakfast cereals in a savory way, which is (dare I say) even better than the original one. The cornflakes introduce not only pleasant crunches but a subtle sweetness that plays well against the salty sausage bits, and taken together they are the perfect topping to bite into in a bowl of thick, smooth rice chowder. I used to call it an "edible blanket," and that part still stands true today.

MAKES 4 LARGE OR 5 SMALL SERVINGS

SPECIAL EQUIPMENT: *immersion blender (preferred)*

RICE CHOWDER

½ medium onion, finely chopped

1 tablespoon chicken crackling schmaltz (see page 90) or extra-virgin olive oil

¼ teaspoon freshly ground black pepper

Pinch of sea salt

4 cups (1 quart/960 mL) chicken stock

1½ packed cups (300 g) cooked short-grain white rice

2 teaspoons fish sauce, or to taste

SAUSAGE CORNFLAKES

⅓ pound (150 g) ground fatty chicken, pork, or beef

1 garlic clove, grated

2 teaspoons fish sauce

¼ teaspoon ground white pepper

2 ice cubes

2 tablespoons extra-virgin olive oil

1 teaspoon grated ginger

1 teaspoon juice from Pickled Chilies (page 25)

½ teaspoon chopped Pickled Chilies (page 25)

¾ cup (40 g) plain cornflakes, slightly crushed

Fine sea salt

FOR SERVING

Dry Fried Shallots (page 17)

Extra-virgin olive oil, to drizzle

Freshly ground black pepper

1 Jammy Egg (page 54) per serving

MAKE THE RICE CHOWDER

1. In a large saucepan over medium-low heat, cook the onion in the chicken fat, pepper, and salt until the onion is soft and translucent but not browned, 7 to 8 minutes. Add the stock and rice and simmer for 5 minutes, until the rice is very soft. Using an immersion blender (or a regular blender), blend the mixture until very

smooth, silky, and thickened, then season with the fish sauce, adding more to taste (the amount depends on the saltiness of your stock). You can prepare the recipe up to this step the night before, refrigerate, and reheat over medium heat before serving.

MAKE THE SAUSAGE CORNFLAKES

2. We are essentially making a simple sausage here, but you can substitute with ½ pound (220 g) of any fresh sausage you like. In a medium bowl, mix the chicken, pork, or beef with garlic, fish sauce, and white pepper. Add the ice cubes and stir the mixture with a fork until the ice has completely melted. The mixture should be thick and slightly bouncy.

3. Heat the olive oil in a large skillet over medium-high heat, then add the sausage, breaking it up into small pieces with a wooden spoon, and cook until slightly browned on the edges and cooked through. Add the ginger, chile pickling juice, and chopped chilies, stir, and cook until all the liquid has evaporated, then turn off the heat.

4. You can prepare this recipe up to this stage the night before, then reheat it in a skillet over medium heat before serving.

5. *Right before serving* (to ensure the cornflakes stay crunchy), add the crushed cornflakes and a good pinch of fine sea salt. Toss evenly.

TO SERVE

6. Serve the rice-creamed chowder with a generous spoonful of the sausage cornflakes, a good dusting of fried shallots, a light drizzle of extra-virgin olive oil, and a twist of ground black pepper. There's something very playful about peeling a soft-boiled egg tableside, tearing it by hand, and adding it as a stand-alone component to the chowder. So I suggest doing that.

JAMMY EGGS

Street-named "jammy eggs" are basically eggs with yolks that hover in a physical state between goo and solid. They used to enjoy an elusive mystical status, but ever since the worldwide invasion of Japanese ramen restaurants, they've been reduced to an everyday commodity. Here's how to make them.

Choose a saucepan that will fit the number of eggs you're cooking in a loose single layer. Fill it with enough water to fully submerge the eggs, then bring the water to a boil over high heat. Slowly lower the eggs into the boiling water (the initial boiling shock will make the peeling easier later on). Turn down the heat to maintain a simmer, then set a timer for 4 minutes. When the timer goes off, turn off the heat and let the eggs sit in the pan for 5 minutes. Immediately submerge the eggs in cold water to cool completely. Set aside at room temperature for up to a couple of hours; refrigerate if you want to hold them for longer but be sure to let them come back to room temperature before using. Peel right before serving.

MAGIC 15-SECOND SCRAMBLED EGGS IN MUSHROOM CREAM

The word crisis *in Mandarin Chinese is popularly known to be made up with one character that means "danger" and another that means "opportunity."*

Cool. Sure. Seemingly insightful. But nonetheless a terribly wishful optimism that I find to be utterly untrue in most cases. Except, in the rare instance of my magic 15-second scrambled eggs, it was exactly that.

During the days when my Maltese, Dumpling, became so sick he wouldn't eat a thing, I tried to make an egg-goo thickened with cornstarch to rub on his lips and nose to trick him into licking it. Well, that didn't work. But out came this.

To appreciate the amazingness of the magic 15-second scrambled eggs, first one has to understand the intrinsic dilemma of scrambled eggs. We all know that slow, painstaking stirring over a wee flame equals creamy, decadent eggs, whereas swift cooking over higher heat leads to rubbery, soulless eggs that bleed water onto the plate. So, what if we introduce a starch that binds the excess liquid during cooking? Shouldn't that allow a thick, creamy texture even when the eggs are cooked over high heat?

Yes, it does.

The addition of potato starch and milk creates incredibly supple, soft, creamy scrambled eggs that literally take only 15 seconds to cook. And as a bonus, the high heat that is used in this technique results in patches of seared egg that exude more aroma than the slow-cooked version.

You can certainly make a case for keeping to tradition by serving the eggs with crisped bacon and sausage. But I argue, what's better to rest a softly crumpled blanket of scrambled eggs on than a salty pool of mushroom cream, where it all awaits absorption by toasted garlicky bread? Now that's what I call a crisis averted.

MAKES 2 SERVINGS

MUSHROOM CREAM

1 tablespoon olive oil

1 tablespoon mushroom powder (see page 9)

2 teaspoons water

1 shallot, peeled and quartered

1 cup (240 mL) heavy cream

2 teaspoons Ramen Seasoning (page 12) or fish sauce (or if unavailable, sea salt)

2 teaspoons Garlic Confit Sauce (page 14)

¼ teaspoon ground white pepper

⅛ teaspoon freshly grated nutmeg

⅛ teaspoon freshly ground black pepper

BAGUETTE

One 6-inch (15-cm) piece baguette

2 teaspoons unsalted butter, softened

1 garlic clove

SCRAMBLED EGGS

3 tablespoons whole milk

1½ teaspoons potato starch or cornstarch (see page 6)

6 large eggs

½ teaspoon sea salt

4 tablespoons (½ stick/54 g) butter, cut into small cubes

MAKE THE MUSHROOM CREAM

1. In a small saucepan, combine the olive oil, mushroom powder, water, and shallot over medium-low heat. Cook, stirring frequently, until the mushroom powder starts to turn darker in color, 1 to 2 minutes. Add the cream, Ramen Seasoning (you can use fish sauce or sea salt,

but seriously, make the Ramen Seasoning), Garlic Confit Sauce, white pepper, nutmeg, and black pepper. Simmer for 10 minutes on low heat until thickened, then use a slotted spoon to remove and discard the shallot. You can make the mushroom cream the day before and gently reheat it over low heat before using.

TOAST THE BAGUETTE

2. With a serrated knife, cut the baguette lengthwise into two long slabs. Spread the cut sides generously with butter, then toast them cut side down on a hot skillet over medium-high heat until crispy and browned. Cut the garlic clove through the middle and rub the cut sides thoroughly against the toasted baguette. Leave the baguette on the still-hot skillet to keep warm until needed.

MAKE THE SCRAMBLED EGGS

3. In a large bowl, whisk the milk and potato starch until smooth. Add the eggs and beat thoroughly with a whisk until you no longer see lumps of egg white floating around. Season with sea salt and set aside. Have a spatula ready on the side and heat a large *nonstick* skillet over medium-high heat (the skillet should be hot enough that the butter sizzles immediately when added). Add 2 tablespoons of the butter and swirl the pan to let it melt, *but do not let the butter brown.* Now pour *half of the beaten eggs* into the skillet but *do not stir* until you see the edges start to sizzle (this will take only a few seconds). Now, *remove the skillet from the heat* and start stirring the eggs gently with your spatula, making large circles with a *slow and thorough* movement that covers the entire skillet. Count 1 . . . 2 . . . 3. Once you get to 13 to 15 seconds, the eggs should be shiny and wet, creamy with congealed ribbons. *Immediately* transfer the eggs to a dish. Cooking any further will be considered an egg crime, punishable by death.

4. Wipe the skillet clean with a towel and repeat with the rest of the eggs and butter.

5. Reseason the scrambled eggs with more sea salt if needed. Serve them half submerged in the mushroom cream with a dusting of black pepper and a piece of garlic baguette on the side.

CLAMS OVER OATMEAL

Oatmeal . . . savory oatmeal . . . with **clams** *on top? And we're all supposed to be cool with that?*

Yes, absolutely you should be. Closely mimicking the comforting texture of rice porridge, a classic breakfast item in large parts of Asia, the oatmeal is a warm bed of counterbalance for the intensely briny sautéed clams, sharp yet soothing, stimulating yet tender type of morning call. It's not the type of breakfast that puts you back into a coma, nor the kind that tries to jumpstart your day like a pickup truck. It's the kind that lovingly kisses you on the forehead and puts a juice box in your backpack with a note that says "Alrighty then."

MAKES 2 SERVINGS

1 cup (90 g) quick oatmeal

3 cups (720 mL) water

1 tablespoon olive oil

2 garlic cloves, thinly sliced

2 Pickled Chilies (page 25), finely diced

2 teaspoons grated ginger

½ pound (240 g) small clams, such as littlenecks

½ cup plus 2 tablespoons (150 mL) cheap sake or Chinese rice wine

1 tablespoon juice from Pickled Chilies (page 25) or juice from a jar of pickled jalapeños

½ teaspoon ground white pepper

3 tablespoons unsalted butter

1 small handful of fresh mint leaves, finely chopped

Fish sauce to taste

Dry Fried Shallots (page 17), for serving

Helldust (page 28), for serving

1. In a large saucepan over medium heat, cook the oatmeal and water for 3 to 5 minutes until done (it will further thicken as it sits). Set aside.

2. In a large skillet over medium-high heat, heat the olive oil. Add the garlic, chilies, and ginger and cook, stirring often, until the garlic is *just starting* to brown on the edges, about 1 minute. Add the clams, sake, chile pickling juice, and white pepper and cook *uncovered.* Clams tend to open at various times, so I like to pick them out as they open and set them aside on a plate to prevent overcooking. When all the clams have opened, return them to the skillet and add the butter. *Turn off the heat* and stir the sauce quite vigorously to emulsify the butter with the liquid. Add the mint and season with fish sauce to taste. Aim for the heavy side because it's going to serve as a sauce for the unsalted oatmeal.

3. Divide the oatmeal between two serving bowls and pour the clams and sauce on top. Top with Dry Fried Shallots and a sprinkling of Helldust and serve immediately with an extra bowl to collect the empty shells.

SEMI-INSTANT RISOTTO WITH PORK FAT CRISPY RICE CEREAL

I was never a cereal kid. I was never a milk kid either, let alone one who dropped childishly shaped and sweetened puffs and whatnots into it and let them soak pointlessly into a curious mush.

If I were to eat breakfast cereal, it would have to be like this. Scattered over a creamy but speedy risotto made with leftover sushi rice, this crispy rice cereal is recrisped in rendered pork fat infused with fresh thyme and garlic. It acknowledges the truth in breakfast cereal that a creamy agent is made only more awesome by a contrasting crispy agent, cleverly in this case by using a single ingredient—rice—to give you two different states of texture and flavor.

And what's the other thing that people like? Breakfast for dinner? This will do, too.

MAKES 4 SERVINGS

PORK FAT CRISPY RICE CEREAL

2.3 ounces (65 g) guanciale or pancetta

4 fresh thyme sprigs

1 to 1½ cups (34 to 51 g) crispy rice cereal

¼ teaspoon freshly ground black pepper

2 garlic cloves, grated

Fine sea salt to taste

SEMI-INSTANT RISOTTO

2 tablespoons extra-virgin olive oil

½ yellow onion, finely minced

1 garlic clove, minced

Sea salt

Freshly ground black pepper

1 cup (240 mL) chicken stock, plus more as needed

¼ cup (60 mL) heavy cream, plus more as needed

2½ cups (360 g) day-old cooked sushi rice (unseasoned) or Asian short-grain rice

1 cup (80 g) Pecorino cheese, finely grated, plus more for garnish

1 tablespoon unsalted butter

MAKE THE CRISPY CEREAL

1. Finely mince the guanciale until it resembles coarse breadcrumbs. Place in a small skillet and set it over medium heat. Cook, stirring occasionally, until the pork bits are browned, about 1 minute, then stir in the fresh thyme. When the thyme stops popping, add the crispy rice cereal and black pepper and toss so that every crispy piece is evenly coated with fat. Continue to cook, stirring constantly, until the crispies are lightly browned all over. Add the garlic, making sure it is evenly mixed in, and cook for 1 minute, until fragrant. Season with salt to taste (this will depend on the saltiness of your pork). Transfer to a dish immediately (to prevent burning) and set aside.

MAKE THE RISOTTO

2. In a medium pot over medium-low heat, heat the olive oil. Add the onion, garlic, a generous pinch of salt, and ⅛ teaspoon of the black

pepper and cook until the onion is very soft and translucent. Add the stock and cream and bring to a boil, then add the rice. Separate every single grain by pressing the rice gently with a wooden spoon, then cook until the mixture has thickened (this will take only a few minutes). Stir in the cheese and butter until fully melted. You can adjust the consistency of the risotto by adding

more cream or stock. Season with more salt if desired.

TO SERVE

3. Serve the risotto immediately with the pork fat crispy rice cereal. Dust with more freshly ground black pepper and cheese.

SPELT JIANBING WITH KETTLE-COOKED POTATO CHIPS

*Nowadays, the word **jianbing** is a hashtag. But back in 2010 when we first encountered each other in front of the U.S. embassy in Beijing, nobody, including me, knew what jianbing was. I remember seeing a questionable little stall featuring a flattop crepe grill and plastic buckets of various sizes dripping over with dried-up batters and sauces from god knows how long ago.*

"Don't do it," the husband weighed in.

*But it was too late as I stood there, mesmerized as I watched this strange yet logically sound force of nature being made. A beaten egg cooking and adhering to what appeared to be a crispy-edged crepe, smeared with red sauce, sprinkled with herbs, then stuffed with a fried pastry that is all together folded into a fat square and stuffed into a paper bag? **Fascinating.** Before the husband could sound a second warning, the order came flying out of my mouth.*

Among my many regrettable life choices, that wasn't one of them, not even for the skeptical husband. Soft, chewy, eggy, spicy, savory, with the indispensable crunch in between bites, it's something you'll want to revisit time and time again. So unless you live in China (sorry) or want to spend eight to fifteen dollars to get one in New York, here's how you spin it at home.

*PS: That fried pastry turned out to be called **baocui**, and it has a texture similar to fried wonton wrappers. You could make those, or, as I have found after testing several different crispy agents (cornflakes, tortilla chips, crispy rice cereal, and so on), kettle-cooked potato chips are a most amicable substitute.*

MAKES 2 TO 3 JIANBING, DEPENDING ON PAN SIZE

SPECIAL EQUIPMENT: *immersion blender (optional); nonstick crepe pan, preferably 13-inch (32-cm); pastry scraper*

BATTER

½ cup (63 g) all-purpose flour

¼ cup (35 g) whole-grain spelt flour*

¼ cup (32 g) tapioca starch

¾ cup (180 mL) water

1 tablespoon vegetable oil

½ teaspoon light brown sugar

¼ teaspoon fine sea salt

Or substitute rye flour, buckwheat flour, mung bean flour, or whole wheat flour.

DOUBAN CHILE SAUCE

3 tablespoons Sichuan broad bean chile paste (doubanjiang; see page 8)

2 tablespoons whole milk

1½ tablespoons honey

1 tablespoon smooth peanut butter

1 garlic clove, grated

TOPPING

2 large eggs, lightly beaten

Freshly ground black pepper

2 tablespoons finely diced scallions

2 small handfuls lightly salted kettle-cooked potato chips

1. In a large bowl, whisk all the batter ingredients until smooth and lump-free. Let rest for 30 minutes at room temperature before using.

2. To make the douban chile sauce, in a small bowl, mix the Sichuan broad bean chile paste, milk, honey, peanut butter, and garlic together until smooth and set aside until needed. If the sauce is very chunky, I recommend smoothing it out with an immersion blender.

3. It's best to use a *nonstick* crepe pan about 13 inches (32 cm) in diameter, which will make 2 jianbing. If you have a smaller crepe pan, that's fine as well, and you'll probably end up with 3 smaller crepes.

4. Have a pastry scraper ready on the side. Heat the crepe pan over medium-high heat, *without oil,* for about 30 seconds, until warm. Pour half of the batter into the pan (if your pan is smaller, you'll need less), and use the pastry scraper to spread the batter outward with a circular motion until it just thinly covers the entire pan. *Don't worry* about getting it perfect in the first spread. You can keep spreading the batter over itself, and it will eventually smooth out any uneven parts. This is why you want the pan to be warm and not hot, so you'll have more time to spread

the batter out. Let the crepe cook for several minutes, until the first side starts to show a few browned spots here and there (lift the crepe up with a spatula to check).

5. Now pour one-half of the beaten egg on top (again, you'll need less if the pan is smaller) and use the pastry scraper to spread it out with the same circular motion until it covers the entire crepe. Dust with freshly ground black pepper and let cook for 1 minute, until the egg is set enough to be flipped (it should still look a bit wobbly), then *turn off the heat* and flip the crepe over. Brush a generous amount of douban chile sauce on the eggless side, enough to cover the entire crepe. Scatter 1 tablespoon of the scallions all over, then lightly crush 1 handful of potato chips in your hands and scatter them in the middle. Fold two sides of the crepe toward the middle, then the other two sides as well to make a large square pocket. Serve immediately in a paper bag.

CRACKLING PANCAKE WITH CARAMEL-CLUSTERED BLUEBERRIES

I disagree with stacked pancakes. They are juvenile nonsense for several logical (if not strictly scientific) reasons.

Reason Number 1: Gravity. *All can agree that fluffiness is the goal in pancakes. To achieve that, we use flour with the lowest possible protein content, we add buttermilk and baking powder to the batter to create air, and we fold the batter as gently as we would comb a baby's hair. We do all that just so, at the end, the pancakes can be stacked and compressed to death by the sheer weight of one fucker sitting on top of another? Frankly, it's mind-boggling.*

Reason Number 2: Texture. *Typical pancakes are underachieving in textural contrast to begin with. But to make matters worse, we further nullify whatever sad crispiness a pancake has going on at the edges by laminating them while they are still hot, and thus steaming them cheek to cheek like human sardines at a sticky, overcrowded rave party? Just saying, it's very perplexing.*

Reason Number 3: Practicality. *Let's do some simple math. Each batch of batter produces about twelve to thirteen pancakes, and each pancake takes about six or seven minutes to cook. Let's just say that you can cook two pancakes at a time—who gets a hard-on at the thought of flipping pancakes for forty-five minutes in the morning just so you can sit down, finally, with two hot pancakes and ten cold ones? Squished to death, textureless, cold pancakes. Sure, keep them warm in a preheated oven, like that's a turn-on.*

Stacked pancakes don't make sense.

What makes sense, in my reasoning, is a single-flip, stand-alone pancake that is tall and lofty with incredibly soft and airy crumbs throughout, but more important, suited in an entirely crusty, seriously golden-brown cake jacket *that emits erotic sounds when cracked open by gentle force. Better yet, it takes only thirteen minutes in its glorious entirety.*

You're welcomed, if not implored, to test this baby with your favorite fruit marmalade and fancy European butter. But here, to push our expedition further into the textural frontier, I'm pairing it with clusters of cold, sweet blueberries encased in a hardened web of shattering caramel, then drizzled with a dark, tangy, and floral balsamic and honey syrup. Hot and cold, crispy and soft, juicy and syrupy.

Pancakes don't deserve this. But you do.

MAKES 1 LARGE PANCAKE, TO SERVE 2 PEOPLE

BALSAMIC HONEY

¼ cup (60 mL) balsamic vinegar

1 tablespoon light brown sugar

⅛ teaspoon fine sea salt

3 tablespoons honey

BLUEBERRIES

Scant 1 cup (125 g) fresh (not frozen) blueberries (see Note, opposite)

⅓ cup (52 g) granulated sugar

1 tablespoon water

CRACKLING PANCAKE

1 cup (125 g) all-purpose flour

2 tablespoons light brown sugar

2 teaspoons baking powder

½ teaspoon fine sea salt

¾ cup plus 1 tablespoon (195 mL) buttermilk

2 tablespoons canola oil

1 large egg

4 tablespoons (½ stick/54 g) unsalted butter, melted, for cooking

MAKE THE BALSAMIC HONEY

1. In a small saucepan over medium heat, cook the vinegar until it's reduced by half. *Turn off the heat.* Fold in the brown sugar and salt until fully melted, then mix in the honey until smooth. The balsamic honey can be made a couple of days ahead of time and stored at room temperature.

MAKE THE BLUEBERRIES

2. Wash and gently pat the blueberries dry, then put them into a zip-top bag with a paper towel and flash-freeze them for 45 minutes to 1 hour, until frozen. This can be done the night before.

3. In a small saucepan over medium-high heat, combine the sugar and water. *Swirl gently but do not stir,* letting the sugar cook until fully melted with a deep amber-caramel color.

4. *Now turn off the heat* and add the frozen blueberries all at once. Immediately fold them into the caramel with a large spoon, *only for a few seconds,* then gently dump everything onto a plate. The caramel will be hardened by the cold blueberries, holding everything in a messy cluster. Transfer the plate to the freezer until needed.

MAKE THE CRACKLING PANCAKE

5. In a large bowl, whisk the flour, brown sugar, baking powder, and salt. In a measuring cup, mix the buttermilk, oil, and egg until smooth. Pour the wet mixture into the dry mixture, then stir gently together with a large fork until a thick batter forms. Small lumps are totally okay.

6. This recipe is just perfect for an 8- or 9-inch (20- to 23-cm) cast-iron or deep nonstick skillet. Anything too small or too big will result in a pancake that is too thick or too thin and changes in cooking time. Heat 2 tablespoons of the butter in the skillet over medium-high heat until bubbly. Pour the batter into the skillet and evenly distribute it around the skillet with a spatula. *Turn the heat down to medium-low* and cover the skillet with a lid. I prefer a glass one

so I can see what's going on inside, but any lid will do. Now let it cook for 8 minutes *without peeking*. We need the steam to be trapped inside the skillet in order for the pancake to cook through. After 8 minutes, check to see if the edges and the bottom are deeply caramelized, forming a golden brown, crusty surface. If not, continue to cook with the lid on for another couple of minutes. Flip the pancake with a wide spatula, then pour the remaining melted butter around the edges. Gently lift the edges and tilt the skillet to let the butter run underneath the pancake, then cook *with the lid off* for 5 minutes, or until the second side is golden brown as well.

TO SERVE

7. Serve the pancake with caramel-clustered blueberries straight out of the freezer. Drizzle the balsamic honey syrup over the top and eat immediately.

NOTE: *Do not use prefrozen blueberries that might have been semi-defrosted during storage and are therefore watery and contain lots of frost. The excess liquid will dilute the caramel and turn it into syrup.*

EGG IN A BLANKET WITH CREAMED GARLIC CONFIT

A great man, Harvey Dent, once said, "You either die a hero or you live long enough to see yourself become the villain." So true, as all depressing things are. And the fact of the matter is, I mostly cook by this mantra. Well, yes, but in reverse.

As far as my cooking experience goes, a recipe either dies a villain or lives long enough to see itself become a hero. When I started cooking as a recreational addiction, I would write down every single idea that came into my mind at any given moment, then I'd do the fact-checking later. Let me just tell you, the fact-checking more often than not ended in me sucking my thumb in a puddle of broken sauce on the kitchen floor.

But the thing is, the idea would be shitty only if I stopped there, at the puddle stage. Chances are that if I kept pushing on and on, again and again, I'd eventually find out that the idea wasn't shitty at all. It may have just needed a bit of technical adjustment, and through the process of trying to make it right, I'd usually learn a great deal about it.

When I first discovered Yorkshire pudding, I had an idea of this crispy, puffy, bowl-like pastry harboring a softly cooked, still-runny egg in the center. The edges would be crusty and hollow like a cream puff's and the bottom would be soft, slightly chewy, and crepe-like, lubricated with thick, runny yolk. At first, it seemed like an easy deal—that I should simply bake the pudding inside a small skillet, then slide an egg into the middle to be finished at the last step. Right?

No. The batter proved to be completely unpredictable at best, and even when it behaved according to expectation, the extra added egg would run my fragile hope into a dense, pancake-flat sadness. I kept trying, and at one point I almost stopped trying. But somewhere, somehow, it got personal. I went back to the drawing board and did my research. I learned how to handle the batter correctly (rest, my friend, rest). I tried lowering the oven temperature. And I crawled my way into finding the right timing to add that final extra egg. (Don't ask me why I couldn't just top it with a pan-fried egg. It's not my thing.)

And I'm glad I did. It's a glorious thing to make on a weekend morning with just us two.

MAKES 2 SERVINGS

EGG IN A BLANKET

4 large eggs

1 cup (240 mL) whole milk

1 cup (125 g) all-purpose flour

¾ teaspoon fine sea salt, plus more for finishing

⅛ teaspoon freshly ground black pepper, plus more for finishing

2 tablespoons rendered beef or chicken fat

CREAMED GARLIC CONFIT

2 teaspoons all-purpose flour

2 teaspoons unsalted butter

½ cup (120 mL) whole milk

½ cup (120 mL) heavy cream

1 teaspoon mushroom powder (see page 9)

½ teaspoon bonito powder (see page 9)

1 teaspoon fish sauce, plus more as needed

⅛ teaspoon freshly ground black pepper

2 tablespoons Garlic Confit Sauce (page 14)

1 tablespoon Caramelized Onion Powder Paste (page 22)

Good pinch of freshly grated nutmeg

MIXED HERB SALAD

1 large handful fresh mint leaves

1 small handful fresh parsley leaves

2 small shallots, thinly sliced

2 teaspoons extra-virgin olive oil

½ teaspoon fish sauce

½ teaspoon lemon juice

⅛ teaspoon freshly ground black pepper

MAKE THE EGG IN A BLANKET

1. In an easy-to-pour bowl, whisk 2 of the eggs and the milk until smooth. Add the flour, the ¾ teaspoon salt, and the ⅛ teaspoon pepper and whisk again to form a loose batter with tiny specks of lumps (try not to overwork the batter). Cover and let rest for at least 1 hour, or overnight in the fridge (you won't get a good rise from anything in less than 1 hour). After resting, give it a gentle stir to reincorporate the flour that has settled to the bottom. Do this before preheating the oven.

2. Preheat the oven to 375°F/190°C.

3. Crack the remaining 2 eggs into separate cups and set them aside (they need time to come to room temperature). Into two heavy-bottomed skillets that are *no bigger* than 8 inches (20 cm) in diameter, add 1 tablespoon of beef or chicken fat in each skillet. When the oven is fully preheated, place the skillets in the oven for 6 to 7 minutes to heat them well.

4. Swirl the fat in the skillets to make sure the entire surface is coated, then divide the batter between the two skillets, pouring it right in the center of each pan. The batter should be insulated in a layer of fat, which is important because even a tiny bit of sticking will sabotage a good rise.

5. Now return the skillets to the oven and bake for 30 to 32 minutes, until the batter is puffed up and golden brown. *Do not open the oven during this entire time.* It may seem ready at around 25 minutes, but it isn't. Do anything to it now and it will deflate. After 30 to 32 minutes, quickly slide 1 egg into the center of each pudding, then close the oven door immediately. Bake for another 6 minutes, until the egg is set but the yolk is still runny. Sprinkle more salt and black pepper over the eggs.

MAKE THE CREAMED GARLIC CONFIT

6. While the pudding is baking, in a small saucepan over medium heat, whisk the flour and unsalted butter together and cook for 1 minute. Add the milk, cream, mushroom powder, bonito powder, the 1 teaspoon fish sauce, and the pepper. Whisk constantly until the mixture comes to a simmer, then cook for another 2 minutes, until thickened. Add the Garlic Confit Sauce, Caramelized Onion Powder Paste, and nutmeg and simmer for 3 minutes. Season with more fish sauce if needed. Set aside.

MAKE THE MIXED HERB SALAD

7. In a large bowl, toss the mint, parsley, shallots, and olive oil to coat evenly, then set aside. Just before serving, add the fish sauce, lemon juice, and pepper and toss to combine.

TO SERVE

8. Serve each egg in a blanket with a good handful of mixed herb salad and creamed garlic confit on the side.

2

NEW YORK, NEW YORK

I came to New York utterly ignorant of food cultures outside of my immediate background. It sounds stupid but, really, TV taught me how to cook.

Some experiences cannot be transcribed. Music. Love. One's first taste of aburi kinmedai nigiri. Some emotions rattle in such complex and ecstatic frequencies that no amount of language will suffice.

I don't quite know how to describe New York.

At the age of twenty-one, I dropped out of the University of British Columbia and moved to New York to pursue an undergraduate degree in architectural design at Parsons. I landed just a week before school started. It was the very first time I had ever set foot in the city. I remember standing in the middle of the commotion of midtown Manhattan, and despite the bone-chilling temperature of January and the mediocrity of the street-vendor coffee in between my hands, I felt high as a kite. On a submolecular level, deeply seeded in my being, I knew that it was where I was meant to be. There is the place you're born, and then there is the place you're made.

I felt *made* in New York.

What a grossly unoriginal thing to say, that an unshaped, wide-eyed, and anxious young woman from a sedate suburb of Vancouver should come to New York and fall explicitly and irreparably in love with this tall dark stranger. But often the best things in life are clichés, and I feel truly lucky to be one.

However, if you assume that my subsequent seven years in New York were a booze-sodden and party-driven daze, or whatever one imagines the life of the inexhaustible youth in the city that never sleeps would be, well, you have probably never gone to architecture school.

Forget parties. Forget fun. In fact, forget about having a social life in general for the next several years of never-ending toil. In my life as an architecture student, a good day was not having to collapse underneath a drafting table in sweatpants sullied with grease from the open corpse of a sausage, egg, and cheese sandwich. A good day was not being found by the janitor as an unresponsive heap of warm body curled under the communal blanket on the abandoned futon in the hallway. A good day was not having to sleepwalk into the studio's steep stairwell only to trip on a broken pencil, and in a tragic, slow-motion tumble, debate whether I should position my skull to hit the ground first in order to save the laser-cut model that served as the only vindication of my pathetic existence.

There was the grind. And then there was the collapse. With only remorseful weeping in between.

Which was really the beginning, now looking back, of when I started cooking as a form of therapy.

Every night when I came home from school with an endless pile of projects to cry on, I'd put on cooking and travel food TV shows in the background to help scuttle the thought of ending it all. To my surprise, it worked. Thing was, having grown up in an Asian community in Vancouver in the nineties—a microcosm with sublime Cantonese and Vietnamese cuisine but sadly not much else—I came to New York utterly ignorant of food cultures outside of my immediate background. It sounds stupid but, really, TV taught me how to cook.

I was able to understand for the first time, beyond watching my mother from the kitchen counter, the explicitly technical intent behind making a roux, caramelizing, layering, pausing, speeding up, curing, and fermenting. To learn the rules, as well as to know when there is no rule, I watched each tradition being challenged and even demolished by pioneer chefs around the world. As a freshly minted proselyte, I watched them, these gods of the new, hungry for and receptive to their truths.

Sadly, my food illiteracy extended beyond just cooking. On my first date with Jason, my then-boyfriend-now-husband, he took me to a ramen joint in the East Village. "Do you like ramen?" he asked enthusiastically. "Never had ramen in my life," I replied, a little defensive but trying to maintain my dignity. Little did he know, I also hadn't had Parmigiano-Reggiano cheese, prosciutto di Parma, real pizza, a bagel, Indian food, Middle Eastern food, Thai food, French food, Ethiopian food, entire continents' worth of food. Even a properly aged steak or a glazed Krispy Kreme doughnut was a tear-inducing revelation. I felt like the girl in the movie *The Village,* crossing a wall and getting her mind blown by M. Night Shyamalan.

New York was a kaleidoscope of new cultures, flavors, questions, and answers, and I was a speck among the sparkles, enraptured in this ecstatic, spherical swirl. But perhaps the most exhilarating part was understanding for the first time that I really knew nothing at all.

They say that there's no light without darkness, no happiness without pain. But they forget to mention that such a theory works much better in that specific chronological order: a dark-and-then-light, pain-and-then-happiness situation. The thing is, you see, I did it backward. If I hadn't met the love of my life, the city of my dreams, right before I plunged into another relationship with a class-A asshole, then I guess it wouldn't suck so much. But I did. I just had to fall in love with New York before getting in bed with Dick.

for SLURPING

No one particular noodle dish is comparable to another. In fact, each is defined by and answers only to its own singular set of laws, matters, space, and time that make up its very own unique reality. If someone asks me whether I like Japanese ramen or Singaporean laksa more, that tells me they know nothing about science.

A bowl of noodles is its own little universe.

MY ALL-PURPOSE RAMEN NOODLES

Forget it, there's no point making ramen noodles at home. And by that, I'm talking about the traditional ramen noodles, which involve a combination of potassium carbonate and sodium carbonate called **kansui** *that changes the pH level of the dough, giving the noodle a snappy and bouncy texture. Not only is kansui confusing to work with, but for me it leaves a bitter medicinal taste in the noodles that often seeps into the broth. And even if you think you enjoy that taste, know that professionally made ramen noodles are often aged for at least several days and up to weeks at precisely controlled temperature and humidity levels in order to reduce it. Most ramen noodle recipes don't tell you that, and that's why they taste like shit.*

So what happens in an imperfect world in which both homemade and store-bought are no option? That's where cheating comes in.

I don't try to achieve that bouncy texture through kansui; I do it by using the underrated and dependable power of tapioca flour (aka tapioca starch). A wet tapioca flour dough cooks to a silky and chewy texture (think **pão de queijo**, *the Brazilian cheese bread balls), but a dry tapioca flour dough gives a snappy and resistant bite. A dough made in between these two extremes, and in combination with wheat flour, finds the perfect sweet spot, for a homemade noodle that achieves a highly slurpable status without any unpleasant aftertaste. I also like to add a good amount of roasted barley tea powder for that beautiful freckled look and a whiff of extra flavor, but this recipe will work wonderfully well without it.*

MAKES 4 SERVINGS

SPECIAL EQUIPMENT: *electric pasta machine (not a hand-crank machine) or stand mixer with a pasta attachment (optional)*

2 cups (224 g) tapioca flour (see page 6)

¾ teaspoon fine sea salt

¾ teaspoon roasted barley tea powder (optional; see page 9)

2 cups (250 g) all-purpose flour, plus more for rolling the dough

3 large egg yolks

Semolina flour or all-purpose flour, for storing the noodles (optional)

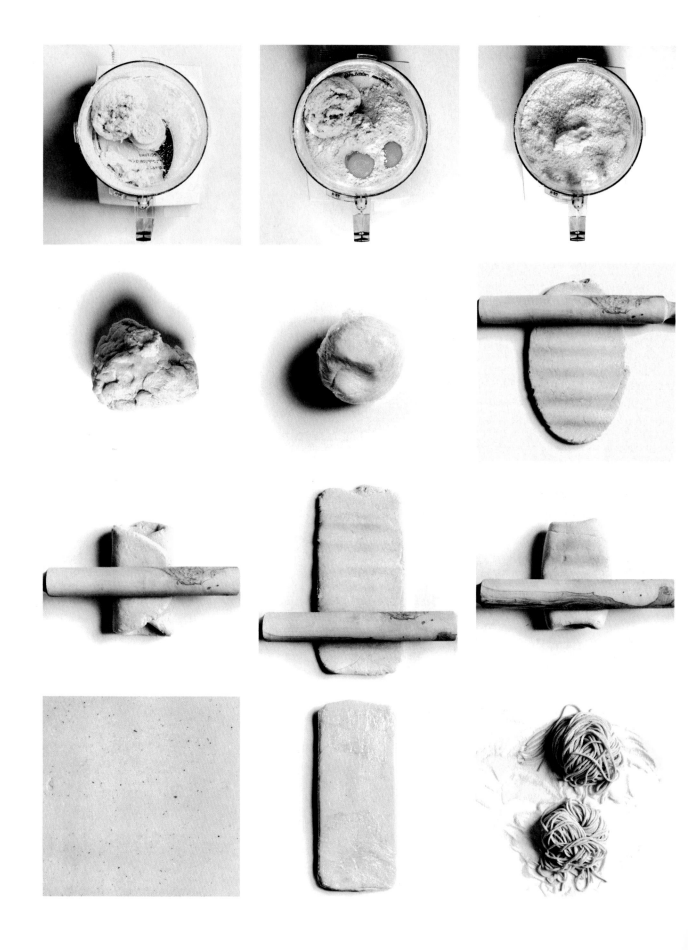

MIX THE DOUGH

1. Bring a small saucepan of water to a simmer over medium heat.

2. Meanwhile, in a food processor, combine the tapioca flour, salt, and barley tea powder.

3. When the water reaches 210°F/100°C (boiling point), pour ¾ cup (180 mL) of the water evenly into the food processor. Pulse several times, until the mixture has clumped into a wet ball; then let cool for 5 minutes.

4. Add the all-purpose flour and egg yolks and pulse until the mixture resembles fine breadcrumbs, then scrape the sides of the bowl and continue to run for *1 full minute* to blend thoroughly. The dough will look crumbly and dry, but you should be able to squeeze a large, damp lump together with your fingers. If the dough cannot come together like that, add 1 or 2 tablespoons more hot water and pulse to combine.

5. Piece two 20-inch- (50-cm-) long pieces of plastic wrap together along the long side to form an extra-large sheet. Squeeze the mixture into large lumps and transfer them onto the plastic wrap. Wrap the whole dough inside the plastic and knead it inside the wrap for 3 minutes. This is an *extremely* dry and hard dough, so put some muscle into it (the dough may still seem crumbly at first). Let the dough rest and hydrate in the wrap at room temperature for 30 minutes, then knead it again for another 3 minutes in the wrap. *As time goes by, the dough will hydrate and become softer and easier to knead.* At this stage, the dough will still look uneven, but it should not be overly crackling and dry to the touch. If it is, knead more water (a tablespoon or two; room temperature is fine) in until it isn't. Let the dough rest for another 1 hour in the plastic wrap.

METHOD 1: ROLL AND CUT THE NOODLES WITH A PASTA MACHINE

1. This is my preferred method because it obviously saves a lot of labor. Unwrap the dough and roll it into a rectangle that's just wide and thick enough to pass through the widest setting on your pasta machine or the pasta attachment on a stand mixer. Pass it through once, then fold the dough in thirds as if you're folding a letter and pass it through the machine again. *Repeat this process five to seven times, until the dough is very evenly colored, smooth, and silky.* Pass the dough through the machine, narrowing the settings as you go, until it's about ⅛ inch (3 mm) thick.

2. Switch the pasta machine to the spaghetti attachment. Feed the dough into the spaghetti attachment, lifting and moving the noodles away from the machine as it goes, so that they can stay straight and not get clumped up. Forget about any small, broken strands that fall underneath the pasta machine. I consider them collateral damage in the conflict between man and dough.

3. When the entire dough sheet has gone through, drench the noodles thoroughly with

semolina or all-purpose flour. Cut the noodles in half lengthwise and divide them into 4 equal portions. *Do not* leave the noodles hanging at room temperature for more than 1 hour or they'll stick together; if not using immediately, transfer them to a baking sheet and freeze until hard, then transfer to a zip-top bag and keep frozen until needed.

METHOD 2: ROLL AND CUT THE NOODLES BY HAND

1. Remove the plastic wrap and set the dough on the counter *without flouring the counter* (the dough won't stick). Start flattening the dough out by *pressing* it with a large rolling pin (because it's too tough to be rolled). I recommend doing this on a lower-height dining table rather than at a high kitchen counter, so that you can apply your body weight to the dough. Once flattened to about 10 × 6 inches (26 × 15 cm), fold the dough in three folds on the short side, as if you're folding a letter, then press and flatten it again with the rolling pin. *Repeat the folding and flattening as many times as you need to until the uneven dough has become even and smooth in texture and color (I've had to do it up to five times).* Wrap the dough in plastic wrap and let it rest for 15 minutes.

2. Divide the dough in half. Roll one portion out into a large, thin rectangular sheet about 1/16 inch (2 mm) thick. Rub both sides evenly and generously with flour, then fold it over itself starting on the shorter end three or four times, so the width is shorter than the length of your knife. Cut the folded sheet crosswise into thin noodles about 1/16 inch (2 mm) wide (in other words, as wide as they are thick). Don't rush it. Take your time. You want each noodle to be as even in size as possible.

3. Drench the noodles with semolina or all-purpose flour, fluff them to separate, and divide them into 2 equal portions. *Do not* leave the noodles at room temperature or they'll stick together; transfer them to a baking sheet immediately and freeze until hard, then transfer to a zip-top bag and freeze until needed. Repeat to roll and cut noodles from the other half of the dough.

CHICKEN WHITE BROTH (TORI PAITAN)

In Japanese ramen, the thick, opaque broth made from pork bones is called tonkotsu, *and its equivalent made from chicken bones is called* tori paitan, *meaning "chicken white soup." And that's what we're making here.*

Why chicken and not pork? Simply put, because it's much more practical and easier to achieve at home. The softness of chicken bones allows for blending easily with an immersion blender, a shortcut to releasing every single flavor molecule within and making it possible to forge an incredibly concentrated white broth in under six hours. Flavor-wise, it's not as consolidated and heavy as tonkotsu, but it still packs a clean yet deeply chickeny flavor. The broth will get its particular seasonings within each of the ramen recipes that follow.

Note: This recipe takes a long time, so be sure to read it through carefully and plan your attack. You can pause the recipe anywhere in the process and resume a few hours later or even the next day. For example, I've often done Step 1 the day before, then finished Steps 2, 3, and 4 on the day of serving.

MAKES 18 CUPS (4½ QUARTS/4.3 L) BROTH, ENOUGH FOR 9 OR 10 RAMEN SERVINGS

SPECIAL EQUIPMENT: *pressure cooker (optional); immersion blender (preferred) or regular blender; fine cheesecloth*

3¾ pounds (1,700 g) chicken carcasses and scraps including all bones, necks, wings, and heads

1½ pounds (700 g) chicken feet

1 extra-large or 2 medium yellow onions

18 cups (4.3 L) cold water, plus more to fill

STEP 1: FIRST BOILING

1. Remove any skin from the chicken necks and butts, but the skin on the wings and feet is fine to use (this will keep the fat level roughly appropriate). In a large stockpot, place the chicken carcasses and scraps and feet and fill with water to cover. Cook over high heat just until the water comes to a boil and you see scum and impurities floating to the surface.

2. Meanwhile, peel the onion and cut it into quarters. Place it directly over the flames on a burner and cook until the surfaces are charred, turning as needed. Set aside.

3. Discard the cooking water and rinse every chicken scrap and foot under running water until clean from any scum and impurities. Wash the pot as well.

4. Return the scraps and feet to the pot and add the onion and the 18 cups (4.3 L) of cold water. *Take note of the current water level and remember where it is, because you'll keep refilling the water back to that level.*

FROM LEFT TO RIGHT, TOP TO BOTTOM:
Blanching, after blanching, after 1½ hours of boiling, after 3 hours of boiling, blending, after second boiling, after straining, final emulsification

5. Place the pot over high heat. When the water comes to a boil, turn the heat to medium or medium-high, whatever level is needed to *maintain a very active boil*. Not a simmer, not cute bubbling, but a rolling boil. Place the lid slanted over the pot so that it covers about two-thirds of the pot. Cook for 3 hours (or you can do this in a pressure cooker for 1½ hours, as I always do).

STEP 2: BLENDING

6. After 3 hours (or 1½ hours in a pressure cooker), the water level will have gone down significantly and the bones will be very fragile. With heavy-duty scissors, snap every single bone, neck segment, and foot in half at the middle (this will help the blending go smoothly). Insert an immersion blender into the stock, taking care to avoid hot splatter, *and pulse until you have obliterated every single solid substance in the pot*. The mixture should now be creamy, slightly thick, and completely opaque.

STEP 3: SECOND BOILING

7. Add enough water to fill the pot back to the water's original level, half cover the pot, and bring to a constant and active boil. *Do not use pressure-cooking from this point on.* Cook for another 3 hours, stirring every 15 to 30 minutes so that the sediments don't settle and burn at the bottom of the pot. Refill the water back to its original level as needed, boiling for at least 30 minutes after the last refill.

STEP 4: STRAINING

8. Strain the broth through a fine cheesecloth into another large pot, squeezing out as much liquid as you can. Discard the solids. The broth is now at its optimal state of emulsification between fat, water, and protein, and is ready to be used in any of the ramen recipes that follow.

9. If you're not using the broth immediately, divide it into 2-cup portions and freeze until needed. You will notice that when the broth is reheated, the fat and liquid separate. This is totally normal; it will be boiled and beaten back into emulsion as instructed later.

CHICKEN PAITAN RAMEN

During my years in Beijing, I was unenthusiastic about pretty much everything, but especially about going outside. So when my husband told me that there was a Japanese ramen festival happening in the city, where famous ramen vendors from Japan were coming to showcase their best ramen game, I barely gave a damn. But I still went, because that's what a functional member of society does: participate.

It was an exceptionally smoggy day even by Beijing standards; the soot in the air smelled like a citywide bonfire, burning my fictitious thrill to ash. I arrived at the cornily decorated festival, tucked in between two ghastly-looking shopping centers, so packed with resentment and self-loathing that even a reasonably decent bowl of ramen might send me into a descending spiral of depression and emotional hemorrhage. Quickly, I thought to myself, frantically searching through the stalls, pleading for a slurpable Xanax to avert my melting into a sobbing mess for public entertainment.

And you, yes you, random chicken ramen in the third aisle, will have to do the job.

As we sat down, I impatiently fiddled through the oily, thick, almost yellowish broth with my chopsticks, then took a sip in desperation. A flush of unmistakably chicken aroma pumped into the cavities of my mouth and nostrils and filled the contemptuous hole in my heart, while at the back of my throat a lingering peppery fragrance wafted serpent-like, quelling my last impulse to cry. It was like taking an unexpected shot of a tranquilizer, settling me into a temporarily subdued, drowsy, but stabilized state.

What followed afterward, frankly, I can't recall from my fragmented memory. But what was certain is that this ramen rescued my day, and I want to commemorate its helpful assistance with this adaptation.

The most powerful recollection from the chicken ramen was its intense, engulfing chicken aroma and the sharp, contrasting pepperiness. So on top of the milky Chicken White Broth, here we're making schmaltz (chicken fat), rendered from frying chicken skins, which is then blended with the crispy skins on top of an exuberant amount of black, white, and pickled green peppercorns. A lot of commercial chicken ramen, to my deep bafflement, is paired with a piece of poached chicken breast. However soft and tender that chicken breast usually may be, hey, it's a **chicken breast!** *So I object in principle. I'm opting for tender, flavorful chicken meatballs that can be consumed either whole or broken up to rejoice in the intensely flavorful broth as a little sidekick to every pleasurable slurp.*

So thank you, random chicken ramen from that random day. Someday I might search for you the way people try to track down their favorite elementary school teacher on reality TV. But until then, I'll celebrate you in my own way.

MAKES 4 SERVINGS

CHICKEN CRACKLING SCHMALTZ

½ pound (220 g) chicken fat lumps and/or skins, cut into small cubes

3 teaspoons white peppercorns, coarsely crushed

1½ teaspoons black peppercorns, coarsely crushed

3 tablespoons drained pickled green peppercorns

1½ tablespoons toasted sesame oil

CHICKEN MEATBALLS

¾ pound (340 g) skinless boneless chicken thighs

¾ teaspoon sea salt

1 teaspoon toasted sesame oil

½ teaspoon ground white pepper

1 teaspoon potato starch or cornstarch (see page 6)

⅛ teaspoon light brown sugar

Unsalted butter, for cooking

FOR EACH SERVING OF RAMEN

1½ tablespoons chicken crackling schmaltz

1½ tablespoons Ramen Seasoning (page 12)

2 cups (480 mL) Chicken White Broth (page 85)

1 portion My All-Purpose Ramen Noodles (page 81), fresh or frozen

3 chicken meatballs

1 Jammy Egg (page 54)

2 tablespoons finely minced yellow onion

2 tablespoons finely diced scallions

One 5 × 2-inch (12.5 × 5-cm) sheet toasted seaweed (nori)

MAKE THE CRACKLING SCHMALTZ

1. Place the chicken fat lumps and/or skins in a small nonstick pot over medium heat. After about 3 minutes, there should be a considerable amount of chicken fat rendered. Add the white and black peppercorns and continue to cook, stirring occasionally, for another 3 minutes, until the fat bits are shrunken and crispy. Turn off the heat and let cool completely, then transfer to a tall, narrow container (like the plastic one that usually comes with an immersion blender), along with the green peppercorns and sesame oil. With an immersion blender, pulse until the mixture is finely blended. Transfer to an airtight jar and keep inside the fridge until needed.

MAKE THE MEATBALLS

2. Cut the chicken thighs into 1½-inch (4-cm) chunks, then flash-freeze on a baking sheet for 1 hour, until hardened. In a food processor, combine the chicken thighs, sea salt, sesame oil, white pepper, potato starch or cornstarch, and brown sugar, then pulse and run the processor until the mixture is finely ground, bouncy, and sticky.

3. Shape the mixture into 1¾-inch (4.5-cm) meatballs. You should have 12 meatballs. Brown them in a nonstick skillet with the butter over medium heat until evenly caramelized on the outside and cooked through on the inside, about 4 minutes.

4. Twenty minutes before serving, preheat the oven to 210°F/100°C. Place 1½ tablespoons of the chicken crackling schmaltz and 1½ tablespoons of the Ramen Seasoning in each serving bowl, then place the bowls in the oven. It's extremely crucial that the serving bowls be hot before serving.

5. Place 2 cups (480 mL) Chicken White Broth per serving inside a saucepan that's deep enough to accommodate the immersion blender. Bring the broth to a boil over high heat and keep it at an active boil until it's reduced to 1½ cups (360 mL) per serving (so, by about one-fourth).

6. Meanwhile, bring a large pot of water to a boil over high heat and have a sieve ready by the sink. Add the ramen and gently loosen the strands with chopsticks to keep them from clumping up. If the ramen is frozen, allow 30 seconds or so in the hot water for the strands to loosen before separating. Whether the ramen is fresh or frozen, it will briefly stop the water from boiling. When the water comes back to a boil, turn the heat to medium to keep the water from boiling over, and cook for 1 minute *exactly*. *Do not estimate this; time it.*

7. Transfer the ramen to the sieve and rinse it under cold water for *just a few seconds*. The purpose of this is not to cool the noodles but to remove some of the starchy water and bring back the bounce. Drain the ramen thoroughly and place it in the hot serving bowls.

8. Insert the immersion blender into the Chicken White Broth and give it several stern pulses, until the broth is emulsified and slightly foamy. Pour the broth into the serving bowls to mix with the seasonings, then top each serving with 3 meatballs, a Jammy Egg, the onion and scallions, and a seaweed sheet. Slurp immediately.

BUFFALO FRIED CHICKEN RAMEN

As a crucial part of the notoriously traditionalistic culture that is Japanese cuisine, the ramen arena is a strangely judgment-free zone that celebrates tolerance and fresh thinking. Try putting a white guy behind a sushi counter and risk expressively suspicious if not straight-up disapproving eyebrows. But when it comes to ramen, you can put a peacock behind the bar and it'd be celebrated as long as it has good ideas. I find myself relishing this rare and peculiar window of democracy and flexibility.

The flavors of Buffalo wings, for example—the delicate balance between sour, spicy, savory, and sweet—are, in my opinion, utterly wasted on generally overcooked chicken wings. Expanding that idea and expressing it with more . . . fluidity, you can create a broth that is rich and voluptuous, sharp yet nurturing, perfect as a cradle for ramen. The crucial component in a traditional ramen—the layer of fat that wraps itself around every strand of noodle—is in this case replaced with browned butter tinged with vinegary hot sauce and garlic. The flavors seep down into the rich chicken broth seasoned with an elixir made of bonito and kombu, where they're smoothed over with just a bit of blended sour cream. All in all, it's not just a happy place for noodles but also a dipping pool for juicy, crispy fried boneless chicken.

MAKES 4 SERVINGS

SPECIAL EQUIPMENT: *immersion blender*

BUFFALO RAMEN SEASONING

6 tablespoons (78 g) unsalted butter, cut into cubes

6 garlic cloves, grated

¼ cup plus 2 tablespoons (90 mL) Frank's Original Hot Sauce

¼ cup (60 mL) Tabasco sauce

2 teaspoons ground paprika

2 teaspoons honey

1 teaspoon Worcestershire sauce

⅛ teaspoon five-spice powder

CHICKEN AND MARINADE

3 or 4 (¾-pound/330-g) boneless skinless chicken thighs, cut into 2-inch (5-cm) pieces

1½ tablespoons fish sauce

1 tablespoon juice from Pickled Chilies (page 25) or juice from a jar of pickled jalapeños

1 teaspoon Dijon mustard

½ teaspoon honey

¼ teaspoon ground white pepper

BREADING AND FRYING

1 cup (125 g) all-purpose flour

1 large egg

½ cup (64 g) tapioca flour (see page 6)

2 teaspoons cayenne

2 teaspoons garlic powder

1 teaspoon baking soda

¾ teaspoon fine sea salt

½ teaspoon freshly ground black pepper

Canola oil, for frying

3 tablespoons Buffalo ramen seasoning

1½ tablespoons Ramen Seasoning (page 12)

2 teaspoons Garlic Confit Sauce (page 14)

2 cups (480 mL) Chicken White Broth (page 85)

1 serving My All-Purpose Ramen Noodles (page 81), fresh or frozen

1 tablespoon sour cream

1 tablespoon Fried Garlic Powder (page 27)

1 Jammy Egg (page 54)

One 5 × 2-inch (12.5 × 5-cm) sheet toasted seaweed (nori)

Finely diced scallions

MAKE THE BUFFALO RAMEN SEASONING

1. In a medium saucepan over medium-high heat, melt and cook the butter until it just starts to brown, about 4 minutes. Add the garlic, Frank's sauce, Tabasco sauce, paprika, honey, Worcestershire sauce, and five-spice powder, stir, and simmer for 3 minutes. Keep in an airtight container in the refrigerator until needed.

FRY THE CHICKEN

2. Combine the chicken and marinade ingredients in a bowl. Marinate for at least 2 hours, or overnight in the fridge.

3. Prepare three medium bowls: in the first, ½ cup (63 g) of the all-purpose flour; in the second, the egg (whisk it lightly); and in the third, the remaining ½ cup (63 g) all-purpose flour, the tapioca flour, cayenne, garlic powder, baking soda, salt, and black pepper, whisked to combine.

4. Coat each chicken piece evenly with the plain flour, then dip it into the egg to coat it evenly again, then transfer it to the flour mixture. Gently turn the chicken piece and press the flour mixture into it until it is tightly and thoroughly coated, then transfer the breaded chicken to a baking rack to sit for 5 minutes. *This important step lets the flour hydrate.*

5. Pour at least 2 inches (5 cm) of canola oil into a deep frying pan or Dutch oven and set it over medium-high heat. Bring the oil to 325°F/160°C (or until it bubbles up immediately around an inserted chopstick). Without crowding the pan, fry the chicken until golden brown and crispy on all sides, about 3 minutes. Let drain on a clean baking rack and set aside until needed.

TO FINISH

6. Twenty minutes before serving, preheat the oven to 210°F/100°C. Place 3 tablespoons of Buffalo ramen seasoning, 1½ tablespoons of Ramen Seasoning, and 2 teaspoons of Garlic Confit Sauce in each serving bowl and place the bowls in the oven. It's extremely crucial that the bowls be hot before serving.

7. In a small, deep saucepan (to accommodate the immersion blender) over high heat, bring the Chicken White Broth to a boil. Keep it at an active boil and cook until it's reduced to 1½ cups (360 mL; or reduced by one-fourth).

8. Meanwhile, bring a large pot of water to a boil over high heat and have a sieve ready

by the sink. Add the ramen and gently loosen the strands with chopsticks to keep them from clumping up. If the ramen is frozen, allow 30 seconds or so in the hot water for the strands to loosen before separating. Whether the ramen is fresh or frozen, it will briefly stop the water from boiling. When the water comes back to a boil, turn the heat to medium to keep the water from boiling over, and cook for 1 minute *exactly*. *Do not estimate this; time it.*

9. Transfer the ramen to the sieve and rinse it under cold water for *just a few seconds*. The purpose of this is not to cool the noodles but to remove some of the starchy water and bring back the bounce. Drain the ramen thoroughly and place it in the hot serving bowls.

10. Add the sour cream into the reduced broth, then give it several stern pulses with an immersion blender until the broth is emulsified and slightly foamy. Pour the broth into the serving bowls, then top each with Fried Garlic Powder, a Jammy Egg, the toasted nori sheet, and the diced scallions. Serve with the fried chicken on the side, available for dipping into the broth. Slurp immediately.

TRUFFLE LARD—INFUSED RAMEN WITH FENNEL PORK BELLY AND SAUERKRAUT

This ramen worships the truth that sausage, truffle, and sauerkraut are one of the holy trinities of deliciousness, if in nobody's bible but mine. And for that, we have to talk truffles.

Truffles are expensive—true for the black ones and even more so for the white. Not a lot of people can afford or even have access to fresh truffles. But you might say, wait a minute, that's not true. I, a regular Joe, have had truffle fries at my local beer hub, and pretty much everywhere else! What was that about?

Well, that brings us to something else entirely: truffle oil.

A lot of serious people have a beef with truffle oil, chefs especially, who apparently believe they're too good for this synthetically flavored olive oil that, more often than not, has nothing to do with a real truffle. Chefs sometimes even brag *about their distaste for truffle oil, righteous in their melodramatic rage, as if, somehow, their rejection of truffle oil authenticates them as legitimate cooks or serious gourmands.*

And to that I say, get over yourselves, you narcissistic pricks.

So we can't like or use stuff that's not real *now? Especially when the real shit can cost thousands of dollars per pound? So what if truffle oil has nothing to do with real truffles? Does the orange goo in Kraft Mac & Cheese have anything to do with real cheese? Does toothpaste have anything to do with fresh mint? Does soap have anything to do with real flowers? Should I be rubbing a fistful of fresh rose petals on my armpits after I shower now? Should I watch only documentaries instead of* Star Wars, *too?*

As long as you fucking like it—and the irony is that plenty of chefs liked it a lot *before they realized the facts—then what is the fucking problem?*

Sure, truffle oil does not *taste exactly like the real thing. It's more potent—perfume-like and possibly overpowering—which is why a little goes a long way. It's fine to say that you honestly don't enjoy it. But those who shit on people who may have access only to truffle oil and not real truffles don't know what the fuck they're talking about.*

So please feel free to use in this recipe whatever form of truffle or truffle flavor is available to you. Got the real deal? Good for you. Truffle oil is the only option? No problem. Have you found truffle oil that actually contains real truffles? Knock yourself out. Just keep in mind that whatever you use that's closer to real truffles, the more of it you'll need, because real truffles are a lot subtler in flavor.

MAKES 6 SERVINGS, WITH EXTRA FENNEL PORK BELLY

SPECIAL EQUIPMENT: *kitchen twine; immersion blender*

FENNEL PORK BELLY

1 shallot, grated

1 teaspoon ground fennel

1 teaspoon fine sea salt

½ teaspoon light brown sugar

½ teaspoon ground white pepper

½ teaspoon freshly ground black pepper

2 pounds (about 1 kg) skinless pork belly

TRUFFLE LARD

4 ounces (110 g) solid pork fat, finely diced

4 ounces (110 g) guanciale or fatty pancetta, finely diced

⅓ cup (75 g) mushroom powder (see page 9)

¾ teaspoon ground white pepper

¼ cup (60 mL) water

6 tablespoons (85 g) chopped black or white truffles, or 4 tablespoons (60 mL) truffle oil infused with real truffles, or 2 tablespoons truffle oil, plus more for serving if wanted

FOR EACH SERVING OF RAMEN

1½ tablespoons Ramen Seasoning (page 12)

1½ tablespoons truffle lard

2 cups (480 mL) Chicken White Broth (page 85)

1 portion My All-Purpose Ramen Noodles (page 81)

2 thin slices fennel pork belly

1 Jammy Egg (page 54)

3 tablespoons German-style sauerkraut, squeezed dry

2 tablespoons very finely minced onion

Ground white pepper

Toasted sesame seeds (see Note on page 100)

MAKE THE FENNEL PORK BELLY

1. Preheat the oven to 250°F/120°C.

2. Rub the shallot, fennel, salt, brown sugar, and white and black pepper evenly over all sides of the pork belly. Roll the belly as tightly as possible into a log *with the fat on the outside,* then tie the log with kitchen twine to secure it.

3. Heat a large *nonstick* skillet over medium-high heat and brown the pork belly until deeply caramelized on all sides. Wrap the belly tightly in two layers of aluminum foil, then place on a baking pan and roast for 3½ hours. Let it cool at least fully to room temperature or chill before slicing. (The pork can be made a few days ahead of time, wrapped tightly in plastic wrap, and kept in the fridge until needed.)

MAKE THE TRUFFLE LARD

4. Place the pork fat and guanciale or pancetta in a medium *nonstick* saucepan and cook over medium-low heat, stirring occasionally, until all the fat has been rendered and you're left with floating crispy bits in the oil. You'll be able to tell when the sizzling sound has largely subsided.

5. Remove the crispy fat bits with a slotted spoon and reserve. Add the mushroom powder, white pepper, and water to the fat in the pan and cook, stirring, over medium heat until all the water has evaporated and the mixture has darkened to a milk chocolate color, about 3 minutes. Transfer the mixture to the tall

cylinder that comes with the immersion blender and add the reserved crispy fat bits and the truffles or truffle oil. Blend with an immersion blender until smooth. (The truffle lard can be made up to 2 weeks ahead of time, kept in an airtight container in the fridge until needed.)

TO FINISH

6. Twenty minutes before serving, preheat the oven to 210°F/100°C. Place 1½ tablespoons of the Ramen Seasoning and 1½ tablespoons of truffle lard in each of the serving bowls (however many you're preparing), then place the bowls in the oven. It's extremely crucial that the bowls be hot before serving.

7. In a small, deep saucepan (to accommodate the immersion blender) over high heat, bring the Chicken White Broth to a boil. Keep it at an active boil and cook until it's reduced down to 1½ cups (360 mL; or reduced by one-fourth).

8. Meanwhile, bring a large pot of water to a boil over high heat and have a sieve ready by the sink. Add the ramen and gently loosen the strands with chopsticks to keep them from clumping up. If the ramen is frozen, allow 30 seconds or so in the hot water for the strands to loosen before separating. Whether the ramen is fresh or frozen, it will briefly stop the water from boiling. When the water comes back to a boil, turn the heat to medium to keep the water from boiling over, and cook for 1 minute *exactly*. *Do not estimate this; time it.*

9. Transfer the ramen to the sieve and rinse it under cold water for *just a few seconds*. The purpose of this is not to cool the noodles but to remove some of the starchy water and bring back the bounce. Drain the ramen thoroughly and place it in the hot serving bowls.

10. Insert the immersion blender into the Chicken White Broth and give it several stern pulses, until the broth is emulsified and slightly foamy. Pour the reduced base broth into the serving bowls, then top each with fennel pork belly (for more porky flavor, you can char the slices with a blowtorch), a Jammy Egg, sauerkraut, and onion. Sprinkle with white pepper and toasted sesame seeds. Add more black or white truffle (in whatever shape or form) if desired. Slurp immediately.

NOTE: *Toast sesame seeds in a small dry skillet over medium heat until lightly browned, stirring constantly.*

VEGAN BURNED MISO RAMEN

I have a lot of respect for people who do exactly what they say. Vegans, for whatever reasons they do what they do— whether it's health-related, or out of environmental consciousness, or simply for the love of animals—voluntarily restrict themselves to a stringent set of rules to eat by. Say what you want, but I doubt there's a single vegan who does it out of a selfish and insatiable lust for "flaxseed egg." So I respect that.

To be clear, as is evident in this book, I don't have a problem with natural food chains, bigger animals eating smaller animals, so on and so forth, and I'll also point out the potential disastrous effect on that food chain if all the predators on earth suddenly developed an emotional soft spot for their prey. However, I do struggle to find a balance between eating what I like and being a responsible earthling who understands the huge, well-documented consequences of raising and consuming livestock on an industrial scale, especially how that contributes to climate change and pollution. In one small effort, I stopped eating tuna ten years ago, and I don't have a beef with not eating steaks or burgers for long stretches. But my own choices aside, I wanted to create a recipe for people who choose to avoid animal products—and one that fully satisfies my own personal cravings.

Vegan ramen sounds as enticing as crustless pie, but it can be so much more. To compensate for the absence of richness from the bone broth, we are going to caramelize miso paste until it's the shade of dark chocolate, creating a deep and more complex flavor profile that welds wonderfully with the sweetness of a root vegetable–based stock. The addition of soy milk brings a creamy roundness, helping to create a robust, well-greased broth that happens to be 100 percent plant-based.

And if you haven't had a properly browned shiitake mushroom seasoned with good-quality soy sauce and sugar and coated in toasted sesame oil, the question of whether you prefer meat over vegetables hasn't been officially settled.

MAKES 4 SERVINGS

SPECIAL EQUIPMENT: *pressure cooker (optional)*

ROASTED ROOT VEGETABLE BROTH

1 jumbo scallion or regular leek (well rinsed), cut into 2-inch (5-cm) segments

1 carrot, cut into small chunks

1 yellow onion, quartered

½ medium daikon (Japanese white radish), cut into small chunks

Six 3-inch (8-cm) ginger slices

Olive oil

6 cups (1½ L) packaged vegetable broth

1 cup (240 mL) cheap sake or Chinese rice wine

2 tablespoons mushroom powder (see page 9)

BURNED MISO PASTE

½ cup (160 g) medium/yellow miso paste

¼ cup (60 mL) toasted sesame oil

¼ cup (60 mL) canola oil

2 tablespoons grated ginger

4 garlic cloves, grated

1¼ teaspoons light brown sugar

⅛ teaspoon curry powder

UMAMI SHROOMS

Canola oil, for cooking

20 shiitake mushrooms, cleaned and cut in half vertically through the cap and stem

1 tablespoon plus 1 teaspoon toasted sesame oil

1 tablespoon plus 1 teaspoon soy sauce

1 heaping teaspoon light brown sugar

Freshly ground black pepper to taste

FOR EACH SERVING OF RAMEN

1½ cups (360 mL) vegetable broth

2½ tablespoons burned miso paste

1 teaspoon Caramelized Onion Powder Paste (page 22)

1 tablespoon Vegan Ramen Seasoning (page 12)

A thin wedge of cabbage

¼ cup (60 mL) unflavored soy milk (no vanilla, no nothing), preferably an Asian brand

1 portion My All-Purpose Ramen Noodles (page 81)

5 to 6 pieces umami shrooms

2 tablespoons finely diced scallions

2 teaspoons Fried Garlic Powder (page 27)

Orange Chile Sambal (page 23), for serving

Two 5 × 2-inch (12.5 × 5-cm) sheets toasted seaweed (nori)

MAKE THE BROTH

1. Preheat the oven to 425°F/220°C.

2. Scatter the scallion or leek, carrot, onion, daikon, and ginger on a large rimmed baking sheet and drizzle with a little olive oil, just enough to thinly coat the vegetables. Roast for 30 to 40 minutes, flipping once during that time, until the vegetables are deeply browned on the edges and softened.

3. Transfer the vegetables to a pressure cooker (or regular stockpot) and add the vegetable broth, sake, and mushroom powder. Cook according to the pressure cooker's instructions for 30 minutes (or over medium heat in the stockpot, *partially covered,* for 1 hour).

4. Strain the stock through a fine sieve, pressing on the solids to extract as much liquid as you can. Discard the solids. The broth can be made 3 or 4 days ahead of time and kept in the fridge.

MAKE THE BURNED MISO PASTE

5. In a medium saucepan, combine the miso, toasted sesame oil, and canola oil. Cook over medium-low heat, using a wooden spoon to stir constantly and press on the miso paste to break it up evenly, until the paste has turned the shade of dark chocolate (the time will vary depending on how dark your miso is to start with). Turn off the heat and stir in the ginger, garlic, brown sugar, and curry powder. The paste can be made several days ahead and kept in an airtight container in the fridge.

MAKE THE UMAMI SHROOMS

6. *You may have to work in 2 or 3 batches, depending on how big your skillet is.* Heat a large, flat skillet over high heat, then add enough canola oil to generously coat the entire surface of the skillet. Add just enough mushrooms to *loosely* fit the skillet and set them *cut side down. Do not move the mushrooms until the first side is deeply caramelized and browned,* about 2 minutes. Turn the mushrooms over and again *do not move them* until that side is deeply browned as well. The mushrooms should have shrunk significantly at this point. Remove them to a large bowl and repeat to caramelize the rest of the mushrooms, adding more canola oil to the skillet for each batch.

7. Wipe the skillet clean and return the mushrooms to it over low heat. Add the sesame oil, soy sauce, brown sugar, and a few turns of black pepper. Toss the mushrooms until all the liquid is *fully absorbed* and they are shiny and slightly thickened. Set aside until needed.

TO FINISH

8. In a saucepan over medium heat, bring the roasted root vegetable broth, burned miso paste, and Caramelized Onion Powder Paste to a gentle boil. Whisk to dissolve the pastes, then cook for 10 to 15 minutes, until reduced just slightly. Whisk in the Vegan Ramen Seasoning and add the cabbage wedge(s). Cook the cabbage until it's softened but still retains its crunch, flipping it once, then remove it from the broth and set aside. Add the soy milk and cook *just until the broth comes back to a simmer.*

9. Meanwhile, bring a large pot of water to a boil over high heat and have a sieve ready by the sink. Add the ramen and gently loosen the strands with chopsticks to keep them from clumping up. If the ramen is frozen, allow 30 seconds or so in the hot water for the strands to loosen before separating. Whether the ramen is fresh or frozen, it will briefly stop the water from boiling. When the water comes back to a boil, turn the heat to medium to keep the water from boiling over, and cook for 1 minute *exactly. Do not estimate this; time it.*

10. Transfer the ramen to the sieve and rinse it under cold water for *just a few seconds*. The purpose of this is not to cool the noodles but to remove some of the starchy water and bring back the bounce. Drain the ramen thoroughly and place it in the hot serving bowls.

11. Pour the broth over the noodles, then top each bowl with the poached cabbage, umami shrooms, diced scallions, and Fried Garlic Powder. Serve with Orange Chile Sambal sauce and the nori sheets.

CHILLED RAMEN IN CHINESE ALMOND MILK SLUSH, SERVED WITH GRILLED PORK BELLY

If you ask me now, like right this moment, months after I've written this recipe, which one particular dish from this cookbook I would like to eat, it's still this one. Maybe it's my lifelong infatuation with the distinctly floral fragrance of Chinese almond milk (see page 29 for the discussion of its true nature); or maybe it's the surprise at how brilliantly it performs as a savory element when it's usually underutilized in desserts only; or maybe it's because the ramen noodles contract in this ice bath of intensely seasoned nut milk and toasted sesame oil into strings of chewy, bouncy, textural delight; or maybe it's because all these refreshingly arctic sensations are further brought into focus by pairing them with the sizzling, greasy, caramelized wonder of grilled pork belly on a stick. All of the above, perhaps?

MAKES 1 SERVING

GRILLED PORK BELLY

1 slice skinless pork belly, about 4 × 2 × ½ inches (10 × 5 × 1.5 cm)

1 tablespoon juice from Pickled Chilies (page 25) or other chile pickling juice

¼ teaspoon sea salt

RAMEN

1¼ cups (300 mL) Chinese Southern Almond (Apricot Kernel) Milk (page 29)

1½ tablespoons Ramen Seasoning (page 12)

1 portion My All-Purpose Ramen Noodles (page 81)

1 tablespoon juice from Pickled Chilies (page 25) or juice from a jar of pickled jalapeños

1 Onsen Egg (recipe follows)

3 tablespoons finely chopped chives or scallions

1 tablespoon toasted sesame oil

Ground white pepper to taste

1. Marinate the pork belly in the pickling juice and sea salt for 2 hours, or up to 6 hours in the fridge, flipping occasionally.

2. Thirty minutes before serving, in the serving bowl, mix and chill the almond milk and Ramen Seasoning. Freeze until the top surface is frozen.

3. Bring a large pot of water to a boil and prepare a large bowl of ice water. Place the noodles into the water and gently separate each strand with chopsticks to prevent clumping up. If the ramen was frozen, allow 30 seconds or so in the hot water for it to loosen before separating. When the water comes back to a boil, cook for 3 minutes (*do not estimate—time it*), then transfer the ramen to the ice-water bath to cool completely. *We are cooking the noodles much longer here than in recipes with hot soup, because otherwise the noodles would be too rubbery in the icy sauce.*

4. Meanwhile, either in a skillet over medium heat or on a grill, cook the pork belly until evenly caramelized on both sides. *You want to finish cooking the pork belly right before serving, so that you get the contrast of the hot meat and cold noodles.*

5. Remove the almond milk from the freezer and crack the frozen surface into small icebergs. Drain the noodles and place them inside the almond milk slushy. Drizzle in the chile pickling juice, crack the Onsen Egg inside, and top with the chives, sesame oil, and a dash of white pepper. Serve immediately with the grilled pork.

ONSEN EGG

Onsen egg, aka hot spring egg, aka sous-vide egg, is an egg that is cooked at a constant low temperature until its entirety has reached an ethereal state between liquid and solid. When the shell is cracked open, the entire egg slides out intact, with a texture that's half Jell-O, half lava. It's like an oval jewel—shiny and elegant, with the yellow yolk glowing through the translucent egg white. There is no more sophisticated way for an egg to go down.

1. Let your egg(s) come to room temperature. Fill a bowl with cold water and set aside.

2. Fill a cast-iron pot (which retains heat better) with water (the amount of water *must be at least four to five times* the volume of the eggs you're cooking) and insert a cooking thermometer into the pot. Bring the temperature of the water to 167°F/75°C, then turn the heat down to the *lowest* setting your stove can manage (a whiff of flame only; use a flame tamer if necessary). Carefully lower the eggs into the water, which will lower the temperature of the water to approximately 158°F/70°C. The *second* you lower the eggs into the water, set the timer for 22 minutes.

3. Now you *must* maintain the temperature of the water at 158°F/70°C for the entire duration (fluctuation by a couple of degrees is acceptable), gently stirring the water to ensure evenness. If the temperature drops, turn up the flame ever so slightly, and if it increases, add some cold water to bring it down (you'll get the hang of it quickly).

4. When the timer goes off, immediately transfer the egg(s) into the cold water bowl and let sit until *completely cooled down*. You can refrigerate the eggs for up to 4 days until needed and bring them back to a warmer temperature by submerging them in hot tap water for a few minutes.

MALA HOT POT TSUKEMEN

How shall I explain this? There lives a faulty chromosome inside the genome of every single Homo sapiens that walks this earth. Whether dormant or active, that chromosome stands firm, carrying a single mark that propels the human species toward an unwinding, unrelenting pattern of self-torture and self-destruction. Left unmanaged, it drives humans to date mean people, eat an ungodly amount of beef, burn fossil fuels, litter on the beach, make war, and ultimately burn Earth down to a tragic pile of ash. This single chromosome may be the loose end of a skein of yarn that unravels the entire fabric of modern civilization, toward the inevitability of self-extinction.

The gods saw this—and responded with mala hot pot.

Ma means "numbing," and la means "spicy" and "heat." It's a flaming red Jacuzzi of pain, delivering an excruciatingly deep burn while engulfing one's entire sensory system in a delirious high. This Sichuan creation is a highly engineered gift for the human species to satisfy our constant inner urge for self-inflicted suffering, the gods' loving way of saying, "If you really must hurt yourself, then do it with this. Leave my other shit alone."

For those who haven't yet found this gift, I implore you to repent and do so immediately. And if you already have, then you know about the best part of all.

At the end of every mala hot pot meal, the humans rejoice and show their gratitude by performing a final, climactic ritual in which they dunk starchy, chewy noodles into the remaining face-scorching broth. This ingenious finale sucks up every brain-hurting molecule of the roiling chile oil, plus the essence of every other ingredient that had previously given its tender soul to this godly creation, tempering our last impulse to shoot a polar bear down to a mild tinge of contentment.

Sadly, this gift from the gods has not yet been properly preached to the less fortunate. So, combined with a Japanese delivery system called tsukemen ("dipping noodle"), here's my effort to exercise my holy responsibility to do so.

MAKES 4 SERVINGS

BRAISED SHORT RIBS

1 tablespoon canola oil

1 pound (450 g) whole boneless beef short ribs

2 scallions, roughly chopped

Two 3-inch (8-cm) slices ginger

3 garlic cloves, chopped

1 tablespoon mushroom powder (see page 9)

1½ teaspoons fine sea salt

2 cups water

FOR EACH SERVING OF TSUKEMEN

2 cups (480 mL) Chicken White Broth (page 85)

½ teaspoon unflavored gelatin

1 portion My All-Purpose Ramen Noodles (page 81)

1 teaspoon toasted sesame oil

1 Jammy Egg (page 54)

One 5 × 2-inch (12.5 × 5-cm) sheet toasted seaweed (nori)

2 tablespoons Mala Paste (page 20)

1 tablespoon Ramen Seasoning (page 12)

2 tablespoons finely diced scallions

2 teaspoons Fried Garlic Powder (page 27)

1 teaspoon juice from Pickled Chilies (page 25)

½ teaspoon ground Sichuan peppercorns

My Ultimate Chile Oil (page 24) to taste

MAKE THE SHORT RIBS

1. I prefer cooking these in a pressure cooker, but you can use a large saucepan or Dutch oven. In the pot that you choose to use, heat the oil over high heat, then cook the whole chunk of meat until browned and caramelized on all sides, 5 to 7 minutes total. Add the scallions, ginger, garlic, mushroom powder, sea salt, and water and cook for 40 minutes in the pressure cooker (follow the manufacturer's instructions) or 2 hours in a covered pot over low heat. Either way, the meat should be very tender. To serve, cut into ½-inch (0.5-cm) cubes.

TO FINISH

2. I highly recommend choosing serving vessels that preserve heat well for the tsukemen dipping sauce, such as mini cast-iron pots, mini clay pots, or stone bowls. If you're using mini cast-iron or clay pots, you can cook the dipping sauce right in there and serve directly. But if you're using other noncooking vessels to serve it, prepare the sauce in another pot while you preheat the serving bowls in a 400°F/200°C oven.

3. In a saucepan, combine the Chicken White Broth and gelatin (this increases the thickness of the dipping sauce and its ability to cling onto noodles) and bring to a boil over medium heat. Cook until the broth is *reduced to 1 cup (240 mL) per serving.*

4. Meanwhile, bring a large pot of water to a boil over high heat and have a sieve ready by the sink. Add the ramen and gently loosen the strands with chopsticks to keep them from clumping up. If the ramen is frozen, allow 30 seconds or so in the hot water for the strands to loosen before separating. Whether the ramen is fresh or frozen, it will briefly stop the water from boiling. When the water comes back to a

boil, turn the heat to medium to keep the water from boiling over, and cook for 1 minute *exactly. Do not estimate this; time it.*

5. Transfer the ramen to the sieve and rinse it under cold water until completely cooled down. Drain the ramen thoroughly and place it in the hot serving bowls, then toss with the sesame oil to prevent sticking.

6. Top each bowl with braised short rib chunks, a Jammy Egg, and a sheet of toasted seaweed. Set aside.

7. To finish the mala dipping sauce, when the broth is reduced, whisk in the mala paste and cook for 1 minute, then turn off the heat. Mix in the Ramen Seasoning and top with finely diced scallions, Fried Garlic Powder, chile pickling juice, Sichuan peppercorns, and as much chile oil as you see fit. If the dipping sauce isn't already in its serving bowl, transfer it into the preheated serving bowl.

8. Serve, dipping the ramen, short ribs, and eggs into the mala sauce as you go.

CRAB BISQUE TSUKEMEN

I'm scared to go to France. I'm scared to go to France because, as if I need any more reasons, it makes me hate my life. In 2016, we took a cross-country road trip starting from Paris, cutting through Lyon, and ending on the French Riviera around Marseille. As a result, in the airport waiting to leave this beautiful place, I almost shot myself. Okay, I kid, I kid. I just kept a folding knife in my purse as we went through airport security and waited for them to finish the job (based on a true story).

On top of its infuriating beauty, France had enlightened me to the pleasures of the simplest things in life—a croissant, bread and butter, a peach, and a picnic under a tree—and when I thought I couldn't possibly be more obsessed about anchovies than I already was, imagine my true wonder at tasting a fresh *one.*

Take this thing, for example: bouillabaisse.

Before tasting the bouillabaisse in Marseille, I thought of it as a watery seafood soup floated with ambiguous, flavorless oceanic body parts, tainted with an emotionally insulting incense of stale dried herbs. But it certainly is not that in Marseille, where bouillabaisse is a consolidation of intense seafood flavors, the central bank of all currencies trafficking in the Mediterranean Sea—fresh, briny, creamy, roe-y, and unbelievably rich. Even more astonishing, the bouillabaisse was served not as a thin soup but more appropriately as a thickened and condensed stew. *And as I mopped the last drop of that earthy brownish orange brew with my aioli-coated bread, I couldn't help thinking,* If only I had me some noodles right now.

And so, here we are. A triple-condensed tori paitan (Japanese chicken white broth) welded together with the maximum saturation of flavors from various crustaceans. The shells, heads, roe, and meat of fresh crab and shrimp are completely obliterated with an immersion blender and release inside the soup the entirety of their deepest, darkest, most sinister ambitions. The result is a thickened reduction infused with heavy cream and cognac and tinged with kombu and bonito seasoning.

Last but not least, the French may know their bouillabaisse, but what they don't know is that when you dip a wafer-like, thinly sliced pork belly char siu *into a condensed and creamy seafood sauce, your head explodes.*

MAKES 4 SERVINGS

OLD BAY OIL

2½ ounces (70 g) solid chicken fat/skin or pork fat, diced

One 2-inch (5-cm) piece ginger

2 garlic cloves, chopped

1½ tablespoons Old Bay seasoning

1 tablespoon bonito powder (see page 9)

CRAB BROTH

¾ pound (350 g) small blue crabs or other seasonal varieties (see Note)

⅓ pound (150 g) shrimp shells and heads

3 tablespoons canola oil

½ carrot, chopped

6 garlic cloves, chopped

2½ tablespoons chopped ginger

3 fresh bay leaves

2 tablespoons tomato paste

1½ teaspoons ground paprika

⅛ teaspoon freshly ground black pepper

⅛ teaspoon freshly ground white pepper

¼ cup (60 mL) cognac

8 cups (1.88 L) Chicken White Broth (page 85)

FOR EACH SERVING OF TSUKEMEN

1 portion My All-Purpose Ramen Noodles (page 81)

1 cup crab broth

2 tablespoons heavy cream

1 tablespoon Ramen Seasoning (page 12)

½ teaspoon Dijon mustard

Suggested toppings: cooked lobster meat or sea urchin, soft-boiled egg, thinly sliced fennel pork belly (see page 99)

1 tablespoon grated ginger

2 tablespoons minced shallots or scallions

NOTE: *Because we are blending the shells, I would recommend using smaller blue crabs, which have softer shells than, say, lobsters or other types of crustaceans. Besides, small blue crabs are generally much cheaper.*

MAKE THE OLD BAY OIL

1. In a small *nonstick* saucepan, cook the chicken or pork fat and ginger over medium heat until all the fat is rendered and you're left with crispy bits. Add the garlic and Old Bay and cook for 30 seconds, until fragrant. Turn off the heat, then add the bonito powder. Blend the mixture in a blender or with an immersion blender until smoothly pureed. The Old Bay oil can be made several days ahead of time and kept in the fridge. Warm through before using.

MAKE THE CRAB BROTH

2. *Because of the nature of seafood broth, I would strongly recommend making the crab broth on the day it is going to be served.* Place the crabs in a large saucepan, then pound them with the tip of a rolling pin until the shells are smashed into pieces as small as possible. Set the pan over high heat, then add the shrimp shells and heads, oil, carrot, garlic, ginger, and bay leaves. Stir frequently and cook until the liquid has evaporated and the shells are starting to brown on the edges. Add the tomato paste, paprika, and black and white pepper and cook, stirring, for 2 minutes, until the tomato paste starts to

caramelize on the sides and bottom of the pan. Add the cognac, scraping the sides and bottom of the pan to release any browned bits, and cook until the alcohol has evaporated. Turn off the heat and add the Chicken White Broth.

3. With an immersion blender (or you can use a regular blender, but you'll have to blend in batches and all the transferring back and forth is a hassle), pulse and blend the mixture as finely as you can. You'll probably be left with small bits of shell here and there, and that's fine.

4. Return the pot to medium heat, cover it halfway, and simmer until the liquid is reduced by half, 25 to 30 minutes. Strain the broth through a fine sieve, pressing on the solids to extract as much liquid as you can, then discard the solids.

MAKE THE TSUKEMEN

5. Bring a large pot of water to a boil over high heat and have a sieve ready by the sink. Add the ramen and gently loosen the strands with chopsticks to keep them from clumping up. If the ramen is frozen, allow 30 seconds or so in the hot water for the strands to loosen before separating. Whether the ramen is fresh or frozen, it will briefly stop the water from boiling. When the water comes back to a boil, turn the heat to medium to keep the water from boiling over, and cook for 1 minute *exactly. Do not estimate this; time it.*

6. Transfer the ramen to the sieve and rinse it under cold water until completely cooled down. Drain the ramen thoroughly and place it in hot serving bowls, along with the toppings of your choice.

7. I highly recommend choosing serving vessels that preserve heat well for tsukemen dipping sauce, such as mini cast-iron pots, mini clay pots, or stone bowls. If you're using mini cast-iron or clay pots, you can cook the dipping sauce right in there and serve directly. But if you're using other noncooking vessels to serve it, prepare the sauce in another pot while you preheat the serving bowls in a 400°F/200°C oven.

8. Bring the broth to a simmer, then whisk in the cream, Ramen Seasoning, and mustard. Transfer the broth to the serving bowls, and top each with your choice of protein, the ginger, minced shallots or scallions, and 1 tablespoon of the Old Bay oil. Dip the ramen and toppings in the bisque as you go and slurp away.

DANDAN MAZEMEN

If you order dandan noodles in China, depending on the cities where they're served, chances are that they will come with a substantial amount of soup, a bit different from the dry version that I often find in the United States. But I've grown increasingly fond of the dry version because it's a snuggly gray area in between a dandan noodle and a cold noodle in peanut sauce. It's not quite hot, but not quite cold, and it has just the right balance between heat and sweetness, with the nuttiness of the sesame and peanuts injected with a deep, complex aroma from Caramelized Onion Powder Paste. It stings you as it loves you, the definition of an abusive relationship, but in this case, a very welcome one.

MAKES 2 SERVINGS

4 to 6 scallions

½ cup (120 mL) chicken stock

¼ cup (76 g) Mala Paste (page 20)

¼ cup (60 g) tahini

2 tablespoons smooth peanut butter

2 teaspoons Caramelized Onion Powder Paste (page 22)

2 teaspoons juice from Pickled Chilies (page 25) or juice from a jar of pickled jalapeños

2 Pickled Chilies (page 25) or pickled jalapeños, finely diced

2 garlic cloves, grated

Ramen Seasoning (preferred, page 12) or soy sauce to taste

2 portions My All-Purpose Ramen Noodles (page 81)

Toasted sesame oil to taste

Chile flakes to taste

Ground Sichuan peppercorns, for dusting

My Ultimate Chile Oil (page 24), if you want more heat

1. Cut the scallions into strips as thin as humanly possible and about 3 inches (8 cm) long. Soak them in cold water. (This softens the sharpness of the raw scallions, so that they won't overpower the dish.) Set aside.

2. In a medium saucepan, combine the stock, Mala Paste, tahini, peanut butter, Caramelized Onion Powder Paste, chile pickling juice, Pickled Chilies, and garlic. Bring to a simmer over medium heat and whisk until smooth. Season with Ramen Seasoning or soy sauce if needed, then transfer to serving bowls.

3. Meanwhile, bring a large pot of water to a boil over high heat and have a sieve ready by the sink. Add the ramen and gently loosen the strands with chopsticks to keep them from clumping up. If the ramen is frozen, allow 30 seconds or so in the hot water for the strands to loosen before separating. Whether the ramen is fresh or frozen, it will briefly stop the water

from boiling. When the water comes back to a boil, turn the heat to medium to keep the water from boiling over, and cook for 1 minute *exactly. Do not estimate this; time it.*

4. Transfer the ramen to the sieve and rinse it under cold water for *just a few seconds*. The purpose of this is not to cool the noodles but to remove some of the starchy water and bring back the bounce. Drain the ramen thoroughly and place it in the hot serving bowls.

5. Drain the scallions well, then add in a little sesame oil and some chile flakes and toss until thoroughly coated. Place them on top of the noodles. Dust the bowls with ground Sichuan peppercorns, add some chile oil if you want to dial up the heat, and serve.

CAJUN CHOPPED LIVER DIRTY MAZEMEN

A long, long time ago, in a kingdom far, far away, a young girl was having her first chopped liver toast at the Spotted Pig on West 11th Street in New York City. Astonished by the creamy, pinkish, and fantastically complex flavors of what she ate, she asked the gods to give her the knowledge to re-create it for herself, and in return, she was willing to offer something that is dear and beloved to her heart. But what she didn't expect was that the gods would then remove her from the kingdom and banish her to a land filled with treachery and oppression on Xiangheyuan Street in Beijing, China.

Shit. That was totally not the agreement. She thought it'd be like quitting sugar for a month or something.

So there she sat in her tower, looking up into a sky severed from heaven—or blocked by smog, it was hard to tell—asking the gods to forfeit their contract, especially since, as she soon realized, kicking herself, the recipe had all this time been free and available in a place up in the clouds called the Internet. What could she do to make the gods undo their wrath? she asked herself, day and night. And finally, on a particularly hellish day in Beijing, she offered them her delicious variation on this infamous dish, spinning it into a slurpable delight worthy of the gods, tingling with Cajun charm and spices.

Maybe it's the firewall or whatever; the gods haven't replied. But they totally should.

MAKES 2 SERVINGS

SPECIAL EQUIPMENT: *immersion blender (preferred)*

CHOPPED LIVER

½ pound (220 g) chicken livers

3 tablespoons olive oil

¼ cup plus 3 tablespoons finely minced shallots

2 garlic cloves, finely minced

¼ cup (60 mL) Shaoxing wine

2 teaspoons fish sauce

½ teaspoon ground white pepper

¼ teaspoon freshly ground black pepper

1½ teaspoons Dijon mustard

1 tablespoon chicken crackling schmaltz (see page 90)

2 tablespoons finely chopped celery leaves

CAJUN MAZEMEN SAUCE

2 tablespoons canola oil

2 tablespoons all-purpose flour

⅓ cup finely diced celery

⅓ cup finely diced poblano pepper (or green bell pepper)

2 garlic cloves, chopped

1 tablespoon diced pickled jalapeño

2 teaspoons tomato paste

1 teaspoon garlic powder

1 teaspoon ground paprika

¾ teaspoon dried oregano

¼ to ½ teaspoon cayenne

½ teaspoon ground cumin

½ teaspoon freshly ground black pepper

1½ cups (360 mL) Chicken White Broth
(page 85)

2 tablespoons Caramelized Onion Powder Paste
(page 22)

1½ tablespoons Garlic Confit Sauce (page 14)

2 fresh bay leaves

1 tablespoon Ramen Seasoning (page 12)

¾ teaspoon red wine vinegar

OLD BAY OIL

1 tablespoon Old Bay seasoning

2 tablespoons canola oil

TO FINISH

2 portions My All-Purpose Ramen Noodles
(page 81)

¼ cup finely minced scallions

2 Jammy Eggs (page 54)

MAKE THE CHOPPED LIVER

1. Soak the chicken livers in ice water in the fridge for at least 2 hours or up to overnight, after which the livers should become slightly pale in color. Dab them completely dry with a paper towel and set aside.

2. In a large skillet over high heat, heat 1 tablespoon of the olive oil until it starts to smoke. Add the livers, gently spacing them apart from each other (you may want to wear a mitt when you do this, because livers love to splatter), then partially cover the skillet to avoid splattering. Cook for 1 minute *undisturbed.* Use tongs to turn the livers *once,* then cook for 1 minute more. They should be deeply caramelized on the outside but still lightly pink on the inside. Transfer to a dish and set aside.

3. In the same skillet, add the remaining 2 tablespoons olive oil, the ¼ cup of shallots, and the garlic. Cook until the shallots are soft, about 1 minute, then add the wine, fish sauce, and white and black pepper, scraping the bottom of the pot to remove any brown bits. Simmer, whisking often, until you have about 3 tablespoons of liquid left in the skillet. Return the livers to the pan, stir gently, and cook until there are about 2 tablespoons of liquid left. Transfer the ingredients of the pan to a large bowl.

4. Add the remaining 3 tablespoons of shallots, the mustard, and chicken crackling schmaltz to the bowl. With a large spoon, mash the livers until creamy but still partly chunky and mix to combine all the ingredients. You can prepare this several hours ahead of time and keep covered in plastic wrap at room temperature. Before using, stir in the celery leaves. There's no need to reheat it.

MAKE THE CAJUN MAZEMEN SAUCE

5. Preheat the oven to 350°F/175°C.

6. To make a dark roux, in a small ovenproof saucepan, whisk the oil and flour until smooth. Bake for 35 to 45 minutes, until the mixture takes on the color of dark caramel. Set the pan over medium heat and add the celery, poblano pepper, garlic, and pickled jalapeño. Whisk to combine and cook until the vegetables are soft, about 1 minute. Add the tomato paste, garlic powder, paprika, oregano, cayenne, cumin, and black pepper and cook for 1 minute, then add

the Chicken White Broth, Caramelized Onion Powder Paste, Garlic Confit Sauce, and bay leaves. Simmer until the mixture is reduced by two-thirds, stirring occasionally, about 10 minutes. Add the Ramen Seasoning and vinegar and remove the bay leaves.

7. Using either an immersion blender (easier because you can do it right in the pan) or a regular blender, blend the sauce until smooth and thickened. You can prepare the sauce the day before and reheat before use.

MAKE THE OLD BAY OIL

8. In a small saucepan over medium-low heat, whisk the Old Bay seasoning and the oil. Bring to a simmer and cook for about 30 seconds or so. You can prepare this ahead of time and keep it at room temperature in an airtight container for up to 2 weeks, or longer in the fridge.

TO FINISH

9. Bring a large pot of water to a boil over high heat and have a sieve ready by the sink. Add the ramen and gently loosen the strands with chopsticks to keep them from clumping up. If the ramen is frozen, allow 30 seconds or so in the hot water for the strands to loosen before separating. Whether the ramen is fresh or frozen, it will briefly stop the water from boiling. When the water comes back to a boil, turn the heat to medium to keep the water from boiling over, and cook for 1 minute *exactly. Do not estimate this; time it.*

10. Transfer the ramen to the sieve and rinse it under cold water for *just a few seconds*. The purpose of this is not to cool the noodles but to remove some of the starchy water and bring back the bounce. Drain the ramen thoroughly.

11. Divide the mazemen sauce into two serving bowls. Top with noodles, then divide the chopped liver into each bowl. Add 2 tablespoons finely diced scallions to each and top with halved Jammy Eggs and a drizzle of Old Bay oil. Slurp immediately.

PEKING DUCK RAMEN

I had long suspected that I wasn't that big of a fanatic when it comes to Peking duck. The crispy slices of duck skin wrapped in thin Chinese crepes with a smear of sweet bean paste and thinly sliced garnishes, it pains me to report, had always dazzled more in expectation than in reality. And the six years in Beijing, where these ducks are sold in restaurants like cereal in a supermarket, had only further proved such an unfortunate theory. But I keep going back to it anyway.

Why? Not for the crispy but often slightly bland duck skin or the overcooked and even blander shreds of meat, but for the pot of duck soup that they serve at the end of the meal, as I sit in jittery anticipation. Forged upon layers and layers of Peking duck carcasses they collect after the skins and meat are removed, the soup is an opaque, milky–white essence of this glorious but underutilized bird. So it only seemed just to refocus the attention on the true hero of a Peking duck and turn it into a bowl of noodle soup.

But of course, we don't have twenty Peking duck carcasses at our disposal, so instead, we're going to use just one duck and make up the rest with lots of deeply caramelized chicken feet. The caramelization on the duck skin and chicken feet is the key to the unique flavor profile of this dish, so don't try to substitute roast chicken carcass (because chicken, won't, taste, like, duck*). And don't expect any crispy duck skin (achievable only on predehydrated skin) to come out of this recipe, because again, that's not the point.*

MAKES 5 SERVINGS

SPECIAL EQUIPMENT: *pressure cooker (optional); immersion blender (preferred; or use a regular blender and work in batches)*

DUCK BROTH

1 whole 5-pound (2.5-kg) Peking duck, preferably with the head attached

11 or 12 (1.1 pounds/500 g) chicken feet

3 (8.5 ounces/240 g) jumbo scallions, or the equivalent weight of standard scallions, cut into 3-inch (8-cm) chunks

1 tablespoon honey

1 tablespoon water

5 ounces (150 g) daikon (Japanese white radish), peeled and cut into small chunks

10 cups (2.4 L) water

¾ cup (180 mL) sake or Chinese rice wine

DUCK BREAST CHAR SIU

2 duck breasts (from the whole duck above)

1½ tablespoons soy sauce

½ tablespoon honey

⅛ teaspoon freshly ground black pepper

⅛ teaspoon five-spice powder

FLAVORED OIL

⅓ cup (80 mL) broth fat from the duck broth

2½ teaspoons onion powder

2 teaspoons white sesame seeds, toasted (see page 100)

1½ tablespoons tian mian jiang (Chinese sweet bean paste)

FOR EACH SERVING OF RAMEN

1½ tablespoons Ramen Seasoning (page 12)

2 cups (480 mL) duck broth (above)

4.2 ounces (120 g) dragon beard noodles (or any super-thin Asian wheat noodles)

1 Jammy Egg (page 54), halved

1 small handful bean sprouts, with root ends trimmed

Finely diced scallions

Ground white pepper

PREP THE DUCK

1. Preheat the oven to 350°F/180°C.

2. Remove any organs from the cavity of the duck, if included. Rinse the duck thoroughly inside and outside to get rid of any blood lumps. With a sharp paring knife, remove the breasts (including the skin) and reserve (you can also ask your butcher to do this). Pat the duck dry with a clean towel. Wash the chicken feet and trim the nails (if any) with kitchen scissors. Pat dry.

MARINATE THE DUCK BREASTS

3. Place the duck breasts in a large zip-top bag and add the soy sauce, honey, black pepper, and five-spice powder. Rub the bag around the breasts to evenly distribute the marinade, then seal and leave in the fridge to marinate while the broth is being made (at least 2 or up to 6 hours if you're making the broth in advance).

MAKE THE DUCK BROTH

4. Lay the duck carcass on a large rimmed baking sheet with the breast side down and surround it with the chicken feet and one-third of the chopped scallions. Mix the honey with the 1 tablespoon of water and brush it evenly over every surface of the duck and chicken feet. This will help them caramelize as they roast.

5. Roast for 1½ hours, occasionally turning the chicken feet over with tongs. Turn the duck breast side up and roast another 30 minutes. All the elements should then be colored a deep amber brown.

6. With tongs in one hand and kitchen scissors in another, hold the duck and dismantle it from limb to limb, cutting every bone right through the middle. Process the chicken feet the same way. Think of this as opening the gate to a heaven of flavors. As you work, put the bones and chicken feet into a pressure cooker or large stockpot. Transfer everything left on the baking sheet, including the fat drippings, to the cooker or pot as well (except any burned bits sticking on the sheet). Add the remaining scallions, the daikon, and the 10 cups (2.4 L) water. *Remember the level of the water at this stage, because you'll need to keep filling the pot back to this level.*

7. If you're using a pressure cooker, close the lid and cook for 1 hour according to the manufacturer's instructions. This time in the pressure cooker is meant only to give a head start in breaking down the bones, but the real grunt work of making the opaque, dense broth has to be done in the traditional way. (If you're using a stockpot, cook over medium-high heat

for 2 to 3 hours; see page 85 for note on making Chicken White Broth.)

8. After the pressure is released (or, if using a stockpot, when 2 hours have passed), remove the lid and check the bones. By now they should be vulnerable to the squeeze of your tongs (if not, simmer the broth for up to another hour). Now, with an immersion blender, pulse the broth and bones to completely obliterate any solids inside. The liquid should now look opaque and slightly thick. Add more water to return it to the original water level. Turn the heat to medium-high, cover halfway with the lid, and bring the broth to a constant boil (not a simmer!). Because the liquid will evaporate quite quickly at a heavy boil, check the liquid level every 30 minutes or so and refill it to the original level. Continue this process for 3 hours, until the fat, liquid, and protein have achieved emulsification, becoming completely milky. Add the sake with the last addition of water and boil for another 30 minutes.

9. When it's ready, the broth will have turned opaque and dark beige in color. You will see small bits and lumps of fat floating at the surface. These are important flavor and textural elements in ramen that we don't want to lose during straining, so remove them with a ladle into another bowl and reserve. Strain the liquid through a large sieve into the same bowl, pressing on the solids to get out as much precious liquid as you can, then discard the solids. Skim off about ⅓ cup (80 mL) of the fat from the surface of the liquid (it will seem milky and cloudy at this point) and set it aside in a small bowl. This is for making the flavored oil; leave the rest of the fat in the broth.

10. You can prepare the broth ahead of time. Divide it into 2-cup (480-mL) portions and freeze until needed.

COOK THE DUCK BREASTS

11. Rinse the duck breasts under water to get rid of the excess marinade, then pat them *really really* dry with a clean towel. Place them skin side down in a medium nonstick skillet and set it over medium heat. When you start to hear a sizzling sound, reduce the heat to low and cook for 15 to 16 minutes, until the skin side is darkly caramelized. Periodically check to see if there are any hot spots, move the breasts around, and press down on certain areas to get even browning. Flip and cook the meat side for just 2 minutes, then turn off the heat and leave the breasts in the pan for 5 minutes to finish cooking. Just before serving, cut the duck breasts crosswise into ¼-inch (3-mm) slices, taking care to keep fat and meat in each slice.

MAKE THE FLAVORED OIL

12. In a small saucepan over medium heat, combine the reserved ⅓ cup (80 mL) fat from the broth with the onion powder and sesame seeds. Cook, stirring constantly, until the onion

powder starts to turn into browned bits, 1 to 2 minutes. Turn off the heat, then stir in the tian mian jiang. Set aside.

TO FINISH

13. Preheat the oven to 210°F/100°C.

14. Place 1½ tablespoons of Ramen Seasoning in each serving bowl (however many you're preparing), then place the bowls in the oven. It's extremely crucial that the serving bowls be hot before serving.

15. Pour 2 cups (480 mL) of the duck broth per serving into a deep saucepan (to accommodate the immersion blender) and bring it to a boil over medium-high heat. Simmer until the broth has reduced by one-fourth, or to 1½ cups (360 mL) per serving.

16. Meanwhile, bring a large pot of water to a boil, then add the ramen and gently loosen the strands with chopsticks to keep them from clumping up. If the ramen is frozen, allow 30 seconds or so in the hot water for the strands to loosen before separating. Whether the ramen is fresh or frozen, it will briefly stop the water from boiling. When the water comes back to a boil, turn the heat to medium to keep the water from boiling over, and cook for 1 minute exactly. *Do not estimate this; time it.*

17. Transfer the ramen into a sieve and rinse under cold water for just a few seconds. The purpose of this is not to cool the noodles, but to remove some of the starchy water and bring back the bounce. Drain the ramen thoroughly and transfer to the serving bowls.

18. Use the immersion blender to give a few pulses in the duck broth to make it creamy and slightly foamy. Pour the broth over the noodles, then top with sliced duck, Jammy Egg, bean sprouts, and scallions. Drizzle 1 tablespoon of the flavored oil over the dish and dust with white pepper. Serve immediately.

MY PHO BO

I once hired a taxi driver to take my husband and me to pet cows in the farmland on the outskirts of Hanoi.

Actually, correction, I asked my husband, who doesn't speak a word of Vietnamese, to hire a taxi driver, who didn't speak a word of English, to take us to pet cows in the farmland on the outskirts of Hanoi. It was our last day in Vietnam, and we arrived at the airport about one hour too early. So, cow petting, obviously, was the solution to the problem. But as expected, the husband's efforts failed to establish clarity with the taxi driver, which was when, as always, I had to step in. With exuberant confidence—chest up, two index fingers sticking above my forehead—I leaned forward with one leg firmly swooping the ground and performed what could only be taken as an articulate impression of a Southeast Asian bovine.

"We [pointing at us] want to see [pointing at my eyes] cows [kicking, kicking]— moooooo . . . !" Oscars.

The driver's face lit up, and he nodded in a way that I could only imagine meant we'd had a successful cross-linguistic communication. "See! How hard was that?" I boasted as I swooped the husband and luggage into the taxi with celebratory verve, certain of my imminent cuddling with a baby cow as she suckled on a bottle in my arms and I sang her a lullaby.

But twenty minutes into our seemingly aimless wandering on the highway, something didn't feel right.

"Hm, excuse me, could you pull over for a sec? Are you taking us to cows?" Then I did my cow thing again, just as a bonus round, but this time the driver responded to my flawless performance with a deeply perplexed stare.

"Cow?" I said.

"Hm?" he said, staring.

Gasp! So he hadn't understood me this whole time?! How was that possible, as I'd clearly conveyed the spiritual embodiment of a living cow?! I was practically the Meryl Streep of cows! Unbelievable! I turned to the husband, looking for an ally in dismay but found rather that he shared it with the taxi driver.

At this point the situation had taken a deeply personal turn. Hear me, Zeus! Either I make my physical and emotional connection with a beautiful cow today, or nobody—I mean nobody—is going home. Two minutes into our standoff, the driver finally decided to call an English-speaking friend. He handed the phone to me.

"Cows . . . I want to see cows. . . . Moo." My voice was starting to crack.

"Cows? Cows the animal?"

"Yes, cows! Mooo!"

I returned the phone to the driver, and almost instantaneously his mouth widened and curled up at the corners in enlightenment.

"Aah, bo!" he said.

"Um, no no, moo," I said.

"No, bo!!" he said.

Wait. Bo! As . . . as in pho bo! Of course, because in Vietnamese, bo means "cow"!

This beautiful day ended with me almost getting trampled by a frantic cow who was in disagreement with my choice of a rainbow-striped dress. But at least I'd learned a new word.

It's not just called pho. It's pho bo—yes, the cow.

This is how I make mine.

1. The commonly enjoyed pho bo in North America is closer to the versions found in Saigon/Ho Chi Minh City, which emphasize fresh herbal fragrances, than those in Hanoi, which are heavier on dried spices. This is a reconciliation of the two.

2. Many people have come to believe that a proper pho bo broth is "clear," as in consommé clear, as in pissing clear. This is bullshit. It's a dumb idea that the poor Vietnamese people were, I believe, bullied into adopting during the French colonial era. Look, none of the best pho bo I had in Vietnam was ever truly clear. Sure, there were some versions that came as clear as water—and tasted like it, too. But not the good ones. Those often appeared to be slightly cloudy, evidence suggesting that the broth was forged at a healthy boil, not a sleepy simmer—certainly not as intense as Japanese tonkotsu ramen, but far from as boring as consommé, sitting somewhere rightly in between. These ideal broths had enough body to satisfy and enough lightness to make room for the herbal fragrance.

3. I use lemongrass in my pho bo. It's not typical, but that's how I like it. I also use a smear of shrimp paste to add a trace of complexity to the broth. And instead of whole spices, I grind them before use, which is infinitely more efficient in terms of releasing flavors.

4. Why brisket when we can have short ribs? Think about it.

5. Paper-thin lean beef tastes like paper. Do you like eating paper? Vietnamese people certainly don't, which is why they use beef that is pounded by brute force until flattened, ready for gentle poaching in the hot broth, resulting in meat that is superior in texture and taste.

6. Repeat after me. It's not you, it's MSG. If somehow after considerable effort your pho bo still does not match those found on the streets of Vietnam, it's safe to assume that you've forgotten a sacred essential ingredient, and thus offended the gods: MSG. If you want to be a pussy about it, go to a restaurant where you don't have to add it yourself, but be sure that it's in there.

MAKES 6 SERVINGS

PHO BROTH

1¾ pounds (800 g) beef bones (rib bones, spine, or leg bones), cut by the butcher into 2-inch (5-cm) chunks

12 cups (2.85 L) water

1½ yellow onions, quartered

2 ounces (60 g) ginger, smashed

5 lemongrass stalks, smashed

1 tablespoon shrimp paste (Lee Kum Kee brand or similar; see page 8)

6 bone-in beef short ribs (about 3.3 pounds/1.5 kg total; each about 3 inches/8 cm; you can ask the butcher to cut yours)

PHO SPICE *(see Note on page 138)*

6 star anise pods

30 whole cloves

1 tablespoon fennel seeds

1 tablespoon ground cinnamon

POACHED BEEF

½ pound (220 g) beef bottom round or eye of round steak

2 tablespoons fish sauce

1½ teaspoons vegetable oil

¼ teaspoon ground white pepper

⅛ heaping teaspoon baking soda

FOR EACH SERVING OF PHO BO

2 beef balls (optional but easily found in the freezer section of an Asian grocery)

1 serving (3 ounces/85 g) pho/Vietnamese rice noodles

1 small handful bean sprouts

1 shallot, thinly sliced

2 tablespoons finely minced scallions

1½ tablespoons fish sauce, plus more as desired

¼ to ½ teaspoon MSG

Black and white ground pepper

Lime wedge

Fresh Thai basil, mint, and cilantro sprigs

Orange Chile Sambal (page 23)

Hoisin sauce

MAKE THE PHO BROTH

1. Place the beef bones in a large stockpot and fill it with enough cold water to *completely submerge the bones.* Set the heat to high and bring the water to a boil. Cook for 1 minute at a full boil, until there are no visible pink spots on the bones. Drain and rinse the bones under cold water, attentively removing any scum and impurities.

2. Place the bones and the 12 cups (2.85 L) of water in a pressure cooker or a regular stockpot. *Remember the water level at this point, because you'll refill the pot to this level later on.*

   If using a pressure cooker, cook according to the manufacturer's instructions for 1½ hours. When the pressure is released, open the lid and refill the water to its original level.

   If using a stockpot, bring the water to a boil over medium-high heat. Lower the heat to maintain a medium boil and cook, partially covered, for 3 hours. Once or twice in between, refill the water to its original level. The goal is to end up with the same amount of liquid as when you started.

3. While the broth is cooking, make the other elements of the pho bo. Place a grilling rack

directly over the stovetop over high heat. Lay the onions, ginger, and lemongrass on the rack over the flames and char them evenly all around, turning with tongs as needed. Smear the shrimp paste on the surface of a charred onion piece and toast for a few seconds until it smells pungent.

4.   Place the short ribs in a medium saucepan and fill it with enough cold water to *completely submerge the short ribs.* Bring to a boil over high heat and cook for 1 minute, until there are no visible pink spots on the short ribs. Drain and rinse them under cold water, carefully removing any scum and impurities, and set aside.

5.   To make the pho spice, place the star anise pods, cloves, and fennel seeds in a small skillet over medium heat. Toast, stirring often, until the fennel seeds start to pop and smell fragrant. Transfer the spices to a spice grinder and add the cinnamon. Grind until powdered and set aside.

6.   When the broth is ready, remove the bones, *but preserve any bone marrow and fat that is stuck on the bones and return them to the broth.* Treasure these precious little flavor bits as you would your mother's pearls. Discard the bones.

7.   Add the short ribs, charred aromatic vegetables, and *half* the pho spice (not all!). *Take note of the water level.* It will be different from before because the solid mass has changed.

If using a pressure cooker, cook for 30 minutes. Release the pressure, add water to reach the initial level, bring to a boil over medium-high heat, and adjust to cook at a medium boil for 20 minutes.

If using a stockpot, bring the broth to a boil over high heat and adjust the heat to maintain a medium boil for 90 minutes. Add water once or twice during the boiling to reach the initial level, but always cook for another 30 minutes more after your last addition of water. Again, the goal is to end up with the same amount of liquid as when you started.

8.   We're almost there. With tongs, carefully transfer the short ribs to another stockpot. You should see a remaining thick layer of top fat freckled with loose bone marrow. The marrow is light in weight and will float to the surface, making it easy to capture. Ladle the fat and marrow bits into the pot with the short ribs. When you think you've caught all the marrow, strain the broth through a fine sieve into the pot with the short ribs. Press on the solids to extract as much liquid as you can, then discard the solids. You can skim off some of the excess fat from the broth at this point, but don't overdo it! Good, authentic pho bo always has a healthy amount of fat for flavor.

9.   Technically the pho bo broth is done, but I would encourage you to let it sit in the fridge overnight for the flavors to meld. You can prepare it up to 3 days ahead of time, or freeze it in advance.

PREP THE POACHED BEEF

10. Two hours before serving, slice the bottom round or eye of round into 6 thin steaks about ⅓ inch (1 cm) thick and 3 inches (8 cm) wide, making sure to cut it against the grain. Rub the slices evenly with the fish sauce, vegetable oil, white pepper, and baking soda (which works as a tenderizer). Set aside.

11. Shortly before cooking, place each steak in between two pieces of parchment paper and pound it with a meat pounder until it is as thin as it can be without tearing.

TO FINISH

12. Bring the broth back to a medium boil and add the beef balls, if using.

13. Bring another pot of water to a boil and cook the noodles according to instructions, then at the end, add the bean sprouts and cook for 10 seconds more. Drain well and transfer to individual serving bowls.

14. Drape the beef slices over the noodles and scatter with the shallots and scallions. Add fish sauce to taste, MSG (¼ teaspoon if you're scared, ½ teaspoon if you're legit), and a good dusting of ground black and white pepper. To extract more aroma, you can dust with a whiff more of pho spice before serving. Ladle 2 cups of hot broth directly over each bowl, which will gently poach the pounded beef on top.

15. Serve with a plate full of lime wedges and Thai basil, mint, and cilantro sprigs ready to be hand-torn, plus little bowls of my Orange Chile Sambal and hoisin sauce, for dipping.

NOTE ON PHO SPICE: *If you have extra, use it in the Vietnamese-Style Chopped Liver Toast recipe on page 278.*

FRESH RICE VERMICELLI IN CHILLED SPICY SAUCE

The first time I visited Vietnam, I was mind-boggled. I couldn't understand how I, an Asian who had been properly baptized by Vancouver's exceptional Vietnamese food culture, could be so blown away by the exponentially more complex and diverse wonderland that is real Vietnamese food in Vietnam. I felt stupid. I felt left out. And I left the country so drenched in wounded pride and embarrassment that I didn't even think about buying an authentic Vietnamese cookbook there.

I regretted this foolishness tremendously, and it certainly came back to haunt me a few years later when I tried to re-create a Vietnamese dish called chả cá Lã Vọng. The main dish itself—turmeric-marinated catfish fried in an exuberant amount of oil with scallions and dill—was not the real issue. I'd come to realize that a crucial element that makes this and many other Vietnamese dishes so tantalizing—along with the unique and incredibly fresh herbs in them—is freshly made rice vermicelli noodles, which couldn't be easily found in Beijing. I stood, lost and sulking, as I tried to capture the essence of this memorable dish at home.

If only I had a book that told me exactly what to do . . .

And now, almost a decade after my trip to Vietnam, I've finally found closure. In order to create a satisfying recipe for homemade rice vermicelli, I drew inspiration from a very similar variety in Taiwan called mitaimu, a tender, mildly bouncy noodle made with both rice and tapioca flours. The rice flour provides a subtle fragrance, while the tapioca flour brings springiness. Brought together in the proper proportions, they reconnect me to that time I was sitting on a plastic stool in Hanoi, fuming with amazement.

There are plenty of chả cá Lã Vọng. recipes out there, so I'm suggesting a different application for this widely versatile noodle: a quick, refreshing, summery sauce that is spicy, tangy, sweet, herby, and savory all at the same time, the embodiment of the profound wisdom that is Vietnamese food. But you could also serve the noodles with hot soup, or even, as is often done in Vietnam, as a slippery, chewy delight in shaved ice desserts.

MAKES 2 MAIN-COURSE SERVINGS OR 4 SNACKS

SPECIAL EQUIPMENT: *stand mixer with a whisk attachment; potato ricer or pastry piping bag with a small hole*

CHILLED CHILE SAUCE

1 cup (240 mL) packaged chicken stock (it won't contain much gelatin and will stay liquid when chilled)

3 tablespoons freshly squeezed lemon juice

Zest of 1 lemon

1 tablespoon minced ginger

2 garlic cloves, peeled

1 large shallot, peeled

2½ tablespoons fish sauce

2 tablespoons light brown sugar

1½ teaspoons ground paprika

1 teaspoon Dijon mustard

¼ teaspoon freshly ground black pepper

3 tablespoons extra-virgin olive oil

RICE VERMICELLI

1 cup (123 g) rice flour (see page 6)

½ cup (64 g) tapioca flour (see page 6)

¼ teaspoon fine sea salt

¾ cup (180 mL) simmering water (210°F/100°C)

6 tablespoons (90 mL) cold water

Canola oil, to coat

FOR SERVING

Dry Fried Shallots (page 17)

Thinly sliced fresh Thai basil and mint leaves

Helldust (page 28) or Orange Chile Sambal (page 23), for more heat if desired

MAKE THE CHILE SAUCE

1. In a blender, combine the stock, lemon juice and zest, ginger, garlic, shallot, fish sauce, brown sugar, paprika, mustard, and pepper. Blend until the mixture is smoothly pureed. While the machine is running, slowly drizzle in the olive oil. Cover and chill for 2 hours before use.

MAKE THE RICE VERMICELLI

2. In the bowl of a stand mixer with a whisk attachment, combine the rice and tapioca flours and the salt. Pour in the simmering water and mix on low speed until the mixture is crumbly. With the machine running, add the cold water 1 tablespoon at a time, turning to high speed until the dough is extremely smooth, shiny, and thick.

3. Bring a saucepan of water at least 5 inches (12.5 cm) deep to a full boil over high heat (you need enough space for the noodles to move around; otherwise they will clump up). Have a large bowl of ice water ready on the side.

4. There are two ways to form the batter into noodles, and my favorite is to use a potato ricer (Method 1). You can also use a pastry piping bag with a small hole (Method 2), but it's much more labor-intensive.

Method 1, potato ricer: There are usually holes on the sides of a potato ricer. Simply seal them with tape on the inside, leaving only the bottom holes open. Feed half of the batter into the ricer at a time. Scrape the bottom of the ricer with a knife to remove any clumps, then hold the ricer as close to the water as possible without touching it (because you want the strands of batter to cook immediately once they leave the ricer, so they don't stick to each other) and slowly press down to release the batter into the boiling water. When all the dough is through the ricer, gently shake it to fully release the noodles into the water. The noodles should float to the surface within 10 seconds; that's how fast they cook. Use a slotted strainer to transfer them into the ice water to stop the cooking (they can stay in the water while you finish making the rest of the noodles). Repeat with the second half of the batter, making sure that you scrape the bottom of the ricer again before you press.

Method 2, pastry piping bag: Transfer the batter into a pastry piping bag with an approximately ⅛-inch (0.3-cm) round metal hole. Squeeze a single strand of the batter into the boiling water (it will break occasionally and that's fine). The batter is thick, so you'll have to put some muscle into it. As soon as the vermicelli float to the surface, transfer them into the ice water with a slotted spoon.

5. Whichever method you use, drain the chilled rice noodles well, then transfer them to a large bowl and gently toss them with a small amount of canola oil, to prevent sticking. Cover with plastic wrap and keep at *room temperature* (do not chill in the fridge or the noodles will toughen) until needed.

TO FINISH

6. Pour the chilled sauce over the rice vermicelli and garnish with Dry Fried Shallots and Thai basil and mint. Helldust it (or Orange Chile Sambal it) and serve.

SEMI-INSTANT LAKSA MIX

I've always wanted to make my own instant noodle packets. How cool would it be to give them out to friends I don't have? And if I'm going to do it I might as well go after the best. They say, almost unanimously, that the best instant noodle in the world is Prima's laksa from Singapore. So that's the one I did.

This paste can be divided into individual packets, so that when the craving hits, you can almost immediately enjoy a coconutty, creamy, and spicy slurpable snack packed with shrimpy flavor. In order to stay true to its calling as an "instant noodle," I'm keeping it free from any fancy additional seafood that most restaurant laksa comes with. But go ahead and ignore my childishness completely.

MAKES 10 OR 11 SERVINGS

SEMI-INSTANT LAKSA PASTE

1 cup (240 mL) water (or coconut cream, for a richer, oilier paste)

5 or 6 (105 g) lemongrass stalks, cut into ½-inch (0.5-cm) chunks

2 ounces (60 g) belacan shrimp paste (see page 8)

3 ounces (85 g) galangal, cut into ½-inch (0.5-cm) chunks

½ cup (120 mL) canola oil

1¼ cups (140 g) dried shrimp (see page 6)

6 to 8 small shallots (125 g), peeled

10 garlic cloves (30 g), peeled

3 tablespoons packed dark brown sugar

1 tablespoon ground paprika

1 tablespoon cayenne

2 tablespoons curry powder

1 teaspoon ground coriander

½ cup (120 mL) shrimp and chile coconut oil (see page 258)

FOR EACH SERVING OF LAKSA

½ cup (120 ml) coconut milk

⅔ cup (160 mL) chicken stock

¼ cup (76 g) semi-instant laksa paste

¼ teaspoon freshly ground black pepper

Chile flakes

Any type of rice noodles, a brick of instant noodles, or even macaroni can work!

Suggested toppings: shrimp, cockles, fish cakes, fish balls, fried tofu, bean sprouts, laksa leaf, store-bought sambal

MAKE THE LAKSA PASTE

1. It is important to blend the most fibrous ingredients first, so as to get the smoothest consistency for the paste. In a blender, combine the water, lemongrass, and belacan (the salt in the shrimp paste helps break down the ingredients). Blend on high for 1 minute, until the mixture is extremely smooth. Add the galangal and blend for 1 minute, until smooth. Add the canola oil and shrimp and blend for 1 minute, until smooth. Add the shallots, garlic, brown sugar, paprika, cayenne, curry powder, and coriander and blend until very smooth.

2. Transfer the mixture to a medium *nonstick* saucepan (please, it has to be nonstick or you'll seriously regret it) and cook over medium heat, stirring every 2 or 3 minutes, for about 20 minutes. Lower the heat to medium-low and cook, stirring every minute or so, for 10 minutes. The first 20 minutes are to evaporate any excess water from the paste and the last 10 minutes are for "toasting" the paste, if you will. By the end, the paste will have lost almost half of its volume and will have darkened in color considerably.

3. Turn off the heat and mix in the shrimp and chile coconut oil. Let cool completely. Divide into ten or eleven ¼-cup portions in small zip-top bags. The paste will keep in the fridge for up to 1 month, or 3 months in the freezer.

TO FINISH

4. Combine the coconut milk, stock, laksa paste, and pepper in a small saucepan and bring to a simmer. Use a whisk to dissolve the paste into the liquid and simmer for 10 minutes, until the broth is slightly thickened and a thin film of oil has floated to the surface. While the broth is cooking, taste and adjust the heat by adding chile flakes.

5. Cook separately the noodles of your choice according to the package instructions. Pour the broth over the drained noodles. (If you're using a brick of instant noodles, you can cook it directly in the broth.)

6. Add toppings of your choice, if using. Serve immediately.

THE SOLOIST

We all love Xi'an-style Biang Biang noodles, as popularized in the United States by Xi'an Famous Foods in New York City. We all love that slick, full-body chewiness that defines what success should taste like when it comes to Asian wheat noodles. As a silver lining, Beijing happens to be a loving cradle of this type of noodle. Even in times when I've had to list Beijing as my permanent address—in what can only be described as a bone-chilling reckoning of regrettable life choices—I could look down on my proper bowl of Biang Biang noodles and say, "This doesn't fucking cut it, but it makes it better."

You can make great Biang Biang noodles at home. In fact, I've published recipes for them on my blog, twice. But a nagging imperfection remains—not within the recipes but in the flow of execution. To stretch the noodles uniformly one after another and drop them into the boiling water as you go—which is usually how it's done in restaurants—requires skills not possessed by most home cooks, including myself. And to prestretch each noodle beforehand and let it lie flat and separate from other noodles to prevent sticking occupies too much counter space.

So ladies and gents, let me introduce you to The Soloist.

One noodle, one serving: a single super-wide and super-long flap of perfect chewiness all lubed up in a thick and spicy smoky eggplant sauce, then swathed in the indispensable My Ultimate Chile Oil. To go from tip to end, or divide and conquer? That's about as much freedom as one will enjoy in China.

MAKES 4 SERVINGS

SPECIAL EQUIPMENT: *stand mixer with a dough hook*

DOUGH (I strongly recommend measuring by weight)

2½ cups (363 g) flour with 10 to 11 percent protein (I like to combine 1¼ cups all-purpose flour and 1¼ cups bread flour)

¾ teaspoon (6 g) table salt

¾ cup plus 1½ tablespoons (200 g) water

Canola oil, for the dough

SMOKY EGGPLANT AND SPICY MISO SAUCE

2 medium (500 g) Asian eggplants

¼ cup (60 mL) canola oil

Loose ¼ cup (38 g) sun-dried tomatoes in olive oil, drained

3 garlic cloves, peeled

2 small shallots, peeled

¼ cup (75 g) medium/yellow miso paste

2 tablespoons gochujang (Korean chile paste)

¼ teaspoon ground cumin

¼ teaspoon freshly ground black pepper

2 tablespoons rice wine

¼ cup (60 mL) packaged chicken stock

1 tablespoon fish sauce

¾ teaspoon light brown sugar

2 teaspoons unflavored gelatin

Pickled Chilies (page 25), diced

TO FINISH

My Ultimate Chile Oil (page 24)

Finely diced scallions

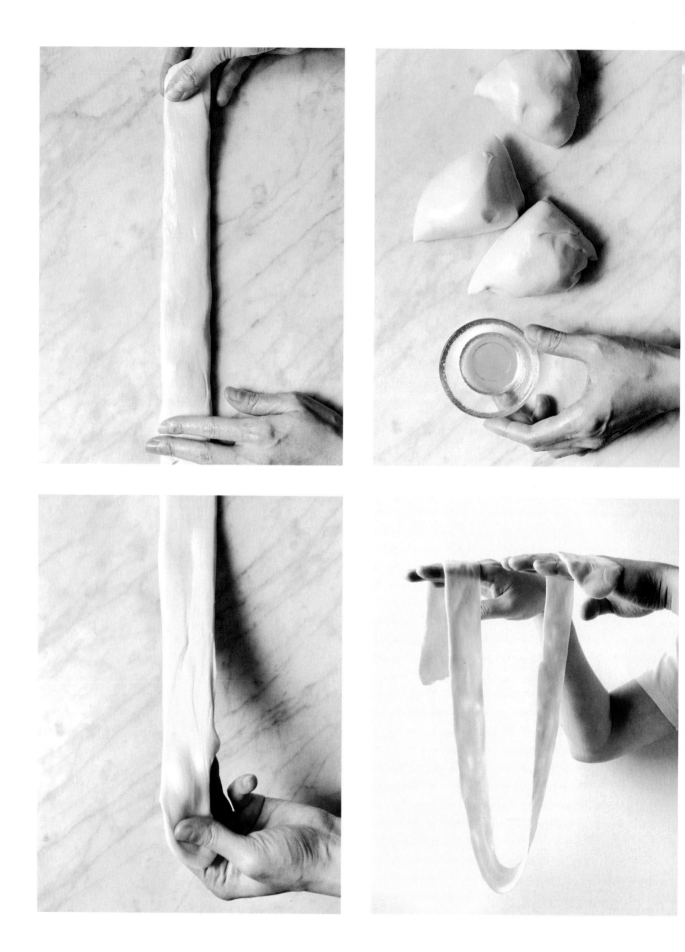

MAKE THE DOUGH

1. In a stand mixer with a dough hook attachment, combine the flour, salt, and water and knead for 10 minutes on medium-high speed, until a soft, supple, and elastic dough has formed. The dough should be just dry enough to pull away cleanly from the bottom and sides of the bowl while the machine is running but still slightly tacky to the touch and very soft. Cover the bowl with plastic wrap and let it rest for *at least 2 hours*.

2. After resting, divide the dough into 4 equal portions and rub each generously with canola oil. Shape each piece of dough into a long, flat rectangle (about 6 x 2 inches/15 x 5 cm), rub it generously again with oil, and cover it with plastic wrap. The dough should rest for at least another 30 minutes to let the gluten relax again, or it won't stretch properly and will tear during cooking. (You can also prepare the dough up to this stage the day before and leave it covered with plastic wrap in the fridge, but be sure to let the dough come back to room temperature before stretching. Unused dough can be kept in the fridge for up to 2 days.)

MAKE THE SMOKY EGGPLANT AND SPICY MISO SAUCE

3. Set a grilling rack on top of a stovetop burner and turn the heat on high. Place the eggplants directly on top and burn until the skins are completely charred through. Every inch of the skin should be completely blackened (if not, it will be very difficult to peel) and the flesh should be cooked, soft, and juicy.

4. Transfer the eggplants to a large bowl, cover with plastic wrap, and let sweat and cool for 1 hour. You'll see a puddle of smoky brown water at the bottom of the bowl; reserve 2 tablespoons and discard the rest. To remove the burned eggplant skin, I like to have a small stream of water running from the faucet as I peel it so that I can rinse my hands as I go. Don't worry if there are some tiny burned speckles left on the flesh. Roughly chop the eggplants and set them aside in the bowl with the smoky water.

5. Meanwhile, in a food processor, process the oil, sun-dried tomatoes, garlic, and shallots until finely minced (or you can do this by chopping if you prefer). Transfer the mixture to a medium saucepan, turn the heat to medium-high, and cook for 1 minute, until fragrant, stirring constantly. Add the miso paste, gochujang, cumin, and black pepper and *take the pan off the heat* while you mash the mixture together. Set the pan back on medium heat to cook for 1 minute, stirring constantly. Add the rice wine and cook for 30 seconds, until the alcohol evaporates. Add the stock, fish sauce, and brown sugar and sprinkle the unflavored gelatin over the surface. Cook and stir for about 2 minutes, until the gelatin has fully melted.

6. Stir the Pickled Chilies (how many? when in doubt, add a couple more) into the sauce, then pour the sauce over the chopped eggplants. Use two forks to mash the eggplant into the sauce. You'll have a bowl of red, slightly thick and oily awesomeness. I recommend letting the sauce sit for at least 1 hour before using. (You can make it ahead and refrigerate; just reheat before serving.)

TO FINISH

7. Bring a large pot of water to a boil. Meanwhile, on an oiled countertop, gently stretch a piece of dough out by pulling on both ends. It should stretch very easily, and don't worry about it being perfectly even. When you have a very long and thick strand, use the palms of your hands to press the dough out even thinner and wider, but be careful *not* to make it so thin that you can see through the dough. You should have a single, super-long noodle that's about 2 inches (5 cm) wide and 50 inches (127 cm) long. Gently lift the noodle and drop it into the boiling water. When the water comes back to a boil, cook for 40 to 50 seconds, until the whole noodle is floating on the water (during this time you can prep your next noodle). Remove the noodle with a slotted spoon, drain well, and set aside in a serving bowl. Repeat with the remaining noodle dough pieces.

8. Slather each noodle generously with smoky eggplant and spicy miso sauce and top with chile oil and finely diced scallions. Slurp immediately.

HANDKERCHIEFS WITH BURNED SCALLION PESTO

"Silk handkerchief," or in Italian, mandilli di seta, *is what sold me: paper-thin squares of pasta that drape, fold, and envelop a sauce as they slip effortlessly down the throat. I'd been seeking this specifically sensual texture in my pasta sheets for years, but every time I made them they'd come out more . . .* linen *than silk. Nothing wrong with linen, I guess—but it's not silk. I'd even tried using wonton wrappers as a replacement, but without the protein from the egg whites used in pasta, the wrappers didn't have enough texture and body for this use.*

Then I started putting tapioca flour in the pasta dough. It creates a slipperier mouthfeel, which, I don't know about you, is what I think "silk" is supposed to feel like. And one can truly understand the aptness of the "handkerchief" part when this slick, fabric-like pasta is twirled in a shiny, beautifully green sauce. Usually it's classic pesto—but my twist involves partly burned, partly fresh scallions and grated ginger, two god-sent soul mates, like tomato and basil, red dresses and pixie cuts, China and alcoholism.

MAKES 2 SERVINGS

SPECIAL EQUIPMENT: *hand-operated pasta machine or stand mixer with a pasta attachment*

HANDKERCHIEF PASTA

1½ cups (188 g) all-purpose flour, plus more for rolling out the dough

⅓ cup (40 g) tapioca flour (see page 6)

2 large eggs plus 1 egg yolk

¼ teaspoon fine sea salt, plus more for the pasta water

BURNED SCALLION PESTO

¼ cup (60 mL) extra-virgin olive oil, plus 2 tablespoons

6 ounces (170 g) green scallions, cut into 2-inch (5-cm) segments, white and green parts separated

2 anchovy fillets in olive oil

3 tablespoons pine nuts

1 cup (80 g) finely grated Parmigiano-Reggiano cheese, plus more for serving

2½ tablespoons grated ginger

1 tablespoon fish sauce

¼ teaspoon ground white pepper

⅛ teaspoon freshly ground black pepper, plus more for serving

A few drops white wine vinegar

MAKE THE HANDKERCHIEFS

1. In a large bowl, mix the flours, eggs, egg yolk, and salt with a large fork. When the mixture has come together with a crumbly texture, knead with your hands until a slightly dry ball of dough has formed. Transfer to the counter and knead vigorously for 5 minutes, until the dough is relatively smooth, not sticky, and has big cracks around its surface. Wrap the dough in plastic wrap and let it rest for 30 minutes.

2. Knead the dough *inside* the plastic wrap for 3 minutes. You'll notice that the dough has hydrated and become much softer and smoother to knead. Let it rest for 30 minutes more.

3. On a well-floured surface, divide the dough in half. Either with a hand-operated pasta machine or an attachment on your stand mixer, feed one portion of the dough through the widest setting (usually labeled no. 1). Fold one-third of the dough over itself and the other one-third over the top, like folding a letter, and feed it through the pasta machine again. Do this three or four times.

4. Pass the dough through the machine again but narrow the increments each time, until you get to no. 6 (if your pasta machine goes to no. 7, then do that). You should be able to see your hands through the thin pasta sheet. Cut the long pasta sheets into 4-inch (10-cm) squares and flour them well to keep separate.

5. Repeat with the other half of the dough, keeping the handkerchiefs well floured. If not using immediately, keep inside an airtight bag in the *freezer* until needed.

MAKE THE BURNED SCALLION PESTO

6. In a medium saucepan over medium heat, heat the ¼ cup olive oil. Add the white scallion segments and cook, stirring occasionally, until the scallions start to brown on the edges. Add the anchovies and cook until the scallions are deeply caramelized on all sides. Add the green scallion segments and cook until just slightly wilted, about 15 seconds. Set aside to cool completely, then transfer to the bowl of a food processor. Toast the pine nuts in a small skillet over medium heat until lightly browned, then add them to the food processor. Pulse the scallions and pine nuts until coarsely ground. Add the Parmigiano-Reggiano, ginger, the remaining 2 tablespoons olive oil, the fish sauce, white and black pepper, and vinegar. Run the processor until the mixture is smoothly pureed, then transfer it to a bowl. To prevent the pesto from oxidizing, lay a piece of plastic wrap directly onto its surface, making sure that there is no air in between. Set aside.

TO FINISH

7. Bring a large pot of water with a big pinch of salt to a boil. Drop the handkerchiefs into the water *one by one,* and cook for about 40 seconds, until al dente. With a large slotted spoon, drain the handkerchiefs well and transfer them to a large bowl. Add enough pesto to coat each handkerchief generously, then toss gently. Serve immediately with more grated Parmigiano-Reggiano and a dusting of black pepper.

3

MEET RICHARD

*Due to my general reluctance to say the word Beijing . . . I like to and often do call
Beijing by the nickname I chose for it—Richard, derived from a Proto-Germanic root
meaning "hard ruler." But, more important, Dick for short.*

2008. We all felt it. The shit actually hit the fan.

At the time, I had been romantically involved with New York for a blissful seven years. But my other love, Jason, my husband, was offered a job in Hong Kong in the critical month of August, the beginning of the Great Recession that would go on to alter the course of an entire generation. I didn't want to leave, but the job offer felt like a seat on a lifeboat that was slowly departing from the rapidly slanting decks of the *Titanic.* I admit, I panicked. Staying on the ship didn't exactly present itself as a smart life choice, especially when the captain of the ship said things like "They misunderestimated me." . . . So as devastated as I was, we jumped, and my newly made family— all four members and twelve legs (see chapter 6, "The Pups")—left New York in haste. I felt like Rose, but infinitely more capable of reason, and New York was Jack, though much taller and less

broke, as I watched our agonizing separation in a fabulously soundtracked slo-mo. It was heartbreaking, yet necessary.

At least, I told myself, Hong Kong is the Asian Jack, right?

But our relocation to Hong Kong turned out to be just a brief layover, only a year and a half, to be precise. I mean, in all honesty, it turned out I wasn't that into Hong Kong either. I'd already met the love of my life, New York. A rebound, even dressed in a glimmering skin-suit of Cantonese roast pork and tender shrimp wontons, just couldn't cut it.

Little did I know that my discontent was only just beginning. One day, we were sitting at our dining table on an otherwise pleasant afternoon when Jason got a peculiar look on his face, an alarming look that made me feel like perhaps he was about to tell me that he'd lost our dogs on the subway. But instead, he asked me whether I would consider moving again—and this time out of the "free world," way beyond the line of familiarity . . . to China.

I don't remember why I agreed to go, but it's certain that I didn't know what I was agreeing to. After all, I'd never set foot inside that country, which was undeniably an awkward part of my Taiwanese heritage. As a child growing up Taiwanese in the eighties, I was fed through both mother's milk and the stringently designed public education system a heavy dose of negative propaganda against "mainland China." How much of it was the truth? I had no idea. But the fact that they also said watching TV too closely would make us go blind made me cautiously optimistic.

Either way, within two months of our conversation, we uprooted ourselves again. Through the chaos and sound of jet engines outside our new apartment one afternoon, standing mildly disoriented next to the indifferent stacks of unpacked boxes, I looked out the window into a blanket of gray haze. I didn't know it at the time, but there I was, already a living tick stuck in the thick, filthy fur of a massive, hyper-autocratic beast.

Alas, Beijing.

It is generally ill-advised to go political if you want to sell cookbooks. But I don't care. There's no politically correct way to sugarcoat this. What's wrong with Beijing? Maybe nothing. What's wrong with me in Beijing? *Everything*. To ask why I was unhappy living in Beijing is like asking why one wouldn't want to indulge in a pile of hamburger meat swimming in a bowl of breakfast Cheerios. There's nothing wrong with hamburger meat, and there's certainly nothing wrong with Cheerios. But mashed together, they taste like shit.

Let me make one thing clear: Beijing itself isn't the problem. But unfortunately, China is an authoritarian country. And that means whatever compensating charisma Beijing—China's political center and command—shows in its ancient walls and forbidden palaces, statement skyscrapers and Olympic stadiums, technological innovations and even dangerously persuasive foods representing every region in China, for someone who actually lives there for a prolonged period of time, at the end of the day, all that charm makes little difference.

When I first arrived I was blissfully excited. Undeniably, a city cloaked in complicated ancient history, much of which is beautifully mysterious and some of which is evidently dark and savage, should be a pulsating magnet for anyone who is the least bit curious about the world at large, including me. Not to mention my adoration of the foods I found there, which obviously inspired many of the recipes in this book. I swear that I went to Beijing with my best effort at an open heart.

But ultimately, for lack of a better way to put it, *a dick is a dick*.

In fact, due to my general reluctance to say the word *Beijing* on a regular basis, I like to and often do call Beijing by the nickname I chose for it—Richard, derived from a Proto-Germanic root meaning "hard ruler." But, more important, *Dick* for short.

So, meet Richard.

First, a lot of people know that forcing people to live under censorship is kind of Richard's kink, but few living outside his borders have a sense of what that actually means. What is it to live under censorship? To look at the numbers, based on many analyses commissioned by different agencies, the score for China's availability of freedom of speech and press often places it in the bottom 5 percent of nations, similar to places like Syria, Iran, and Saudi Arabia on a list of 180 countries. And in terms of Internet freedom, it fares better than North Korea, but there the Internet is practically nonexistent.

But look, it's an entirely different thing to read a statistic than to actually live it—to personally bend to the rule that any narrow sliver of information that I can access, in any shape or form, including through a VPN (the virtual private network that bypasses the "Great Firewall" of China), I can do so because I'm *allowed* to.

Freedom of information—to give or to receive—became the other oxygen that I didn't know was vital until I lost it; until I was trapped inside a vacuum along with 1.3 billion others; until I realized I had to lower my voice in public when the conversation steered toward criticism of the government; until I had to watch what I said or did on the Internet because it could lead to serious repercussions regarding personal safety.

You are *allowed* to read. You are *allowed* to watch. You are *allowed* to speak. You are *allowed* to listen. Things I had taken as a birthright all of a sudden needed *allowing.* The only thing you could do with unchecked freedom was to *think,* as long as it was done in self-censored privacy, muted, in an ever-expanding loop of fury, shame, and self-loathing.

Permission, having to need it—*that's* my beef.

Second, air pollution. Yeah, Richard smells bad.

As a general rule, the World Health Organization has set the maximum safe level of PM2.5—the dangerous particulate matter in air pollution so small it can enter the bloodstream and lead to cardiovascular and respiratory illnesses—at 10 micrograms per cubic meter (μg/m3) on an annual mean. Richard's annual average of PM2.5 hovered around 110 to 135 from 2010 to 2016, the time we lived there. The WHO also set its daily maximum level at 25 μg/m3. Richard pushed that number well over 200 on 123 days in 2013 alone, a third of the year. Again, numbers, but what does it all mean in real life?

It means you smelled it—Richard's favorite cologne. A static, thickened, abrasive blanket of soot that reeked like the stinking rear end of a diesel pickup truck. If you're not too good at shutting down your feelings, you could sense it adhering to the helpless lining of your esophagus as you felt the slow leakage of your life expectancy.

This is why most times when you'd be flying into the city you couldn't see the land until the aircraft had descended laughably close to the ground. *Those weren't clouds.* This is why in most photographs, Richard drifts majestically, wrapped in a mysterious and dreamlike mist, suspiciously yellowish in coloring. *That wasn't fog either.* Most people keep umbrellas by their front door, but we kept a stack of 3M's industrial-grade respirators, "*curved low profile design, compatible with a variety of eyewear,*" as advertised, which we could only hope would slow the blackening of our lungs when we went down the street to buy a fucking bag of sugar.

Adults wear them. Children wear them. Even some lucky dogs with humans who care wear them. China's unofficial facial underpants.

How could anybody be cool with all this? I asked myself.

This brings me to the third, and perhaps the most stinging point. People—or at least too many people—didn't seem to mind Richard.

No, really—they don't mind that he's a dick, or worse, they don't even think that he's a dick. But what's that stuck in their mouth? Raise a reasonable speculation about Richard's masculinity at dinner and you'd be swarmed by an angry mob who are uniformly and almost comically defensive. *Don't talk about Dick! He might come on your face!* The right to vote?

A coercive piece of propaganda cooked up by American imperialism. Human rights? The hypocritical mentality of the West, which is incapable of accepting China's rise to power. Soon I realized that everything I felt strongly about on a basic level—like democracy, freedom of speech, freedom of the press, environmental and health concerns, pure statistical and logical facts, or fucking stone-cold mathematical science!—seemed to be fundamentally twisted, completely open for debate, or worst of all, *irrelevant* in other people's reality.

I was constantly ill at ease, among both locals and a significant batch of expats I interacted with. Why doesn't everybody care? Why isn't everybody mad? Was it because they were self-assured while I was emotionally confused? Was it because they were able to be somebody here while they were a nobody back home? Was it because their truth was more honest than mine? Was it hypocritical to stay? Was it ignorant to leave? Was I missing something? Who was right? Or was everybody wrong?

Yet I was still there, wasn't I? And what did that make me? I couldn't escape the constant self-loathing, the feeling that my presence there—whether directly or indirectly—justified or even emboldened Richard's douchiness. At some point, adapting to Beijing became more than a question of making compromises; I was in danger of losing my principles.

for A CROWD

Eating, generally speaking, is better as a social activity. Consciously or not, how we remember a meal is greatly influenced by who we shared the meal with, the ambiance, the sounds circling in the background, the energy of the conversations at the table. Good food can be remembered badly if shared with the wrong people. And vice versa.

Company is an ingredient in a meal.

LAKSA-FLAVORED PAELLA

My perception of paella has evolved greatly over the years. It started with the overly wet, tossed, and hence illegitimate versions my husband and I had in random restaurants in New York, and went to the flat and crispy, beautifully caramelized real deal we came across in its homeland, Spain. I'm not saying any of that puts me in a position of authority to say what I'm about to say, but the truth is that across my search, regrettably, I haven't met a paella that I would crave eating again.

Don't get me wrong—when done right, paella is a beautiful thing. The shallow disk of short-grain rice that has fully absorbed a meticulous layer of flavors, left undisturbed to be caramelized and crisped all around the bottom and edges, forming that quintessential burned crust of what they call **socarrat***? That part is practically majestic. But what leaves a pothole of dissatisfaction in my despicably greedy heart is that none of the paellas I've tried packed the initial punch of heavy-hitting flavors that one could be forgiven for expecting from its dramatic and promising entrance. All that glorious brownness, redness, and even blackness (if squid ink is involved) somehow come up a bit short on the flavor front.*

I'm not mad as I say this. I'm simply damaged. My taste buds have been irreparably ruined by the relentless madness of Southeast Asian flavors.

Take, for example, shrimp—the most common and widely used ingredient for flavoring paella. I mean, shrimp is shrimp, right? How can someone make shrimp **more shrimpy***? Well, Malaysians and Singaporeans can.*

If you haven't had a proper bowl of Katong laksa, the iconic Singaporean dish that originated in Malaysia that is rice noodles in curried coconut gravy, don't take my word for it. Book a flight, sit your ass down at a hawker center—a good one, obviously—and get a bowl. Then you'll bask in bafflement at how on earth a seemingly plain bowl of noodles could possibly cram in so much shrimpiness per square millimeter. Sure, you might see just a couple of shrimp in the bowl, or none at all—so where is all that flavor coming from?

Behold **dried shrimp***: the quintessential dope that injects its subject with a much-needed boost of shrimpiness. This deeper, funkier, and concentrated aroma, when combined with coconut milk and Thai curry pastes, is what will make paella sing here, once and for all.*

Unlike in the Semi-instant Laksa Mix on page 143, I'm taking a shortcut here to mimic the flavor of laksa without making the paste completely from scratch.

Oh, and don't for a second think that I've forgotten about the socarrat. I've made it double sided.

MAKES 4 TO 6 SERVINGS

SPECIAL EQUIPMENT: *14-inch (34-cm) paella pan (see Note, opposite); blowtorch (optional)*

SHRIMP PASTE

⅓ cup (40 g) dried shrimp (see page 6)

⅓ cup (80 mL) coconut milk

2 tablespoons coconut oil, melted

6 tablespoons (90 mL) water

1½ tablespoons Thai red curry paste

1 tablespoon Thai yellow curry paste

1 teaspoon curry powder

¾ teaspoon light brown sugar

½ teaspoon ground coriander

SHRIMP

8 jumbo-size (16/20 per pound/454 g) head-on shrimp

1 tablespoon fish sauce

Olive oil, for coating

PAELLA

2 tablespoons olive oil

½ yellow onion, finely minced

2 cups (400 g) short-grain rice, such as arborio (or I sometimes use sushi rice)

1¼ cups (300 mL) seafood or chicken stock, preferably unsalted or low-sodium

1 cup (240 mL) coconut milk

1 teaspoon paprika

¼ teaspoon freshly ground black pepper

Makrut Lime Leaf Oil, for brushing (page 13)

MAKE THE SHRIMP PASTE

1. In a blender, blend the dried shrimp, coconut milk, coconut oil, and water until smoothly pureed. Transfer to a small *nonstick* saucepan, along with the curry pastes, curry powder, sugar,

and coriander. Cook over medium heat, stirring frequently, until all the moisture has evaporated, then continue to toast the dried paste until it has turned a dark brown caramel color. The paste can be made a few days ahead of time and kept in the fridge until needed.

PREP THE SHRIMP

2. Thirty minutes before cooking, clean the shrimp under water. With scissors, cut away the small legs and thin shell along the abdomen area, exposing the meat (but do not remove the shell), then cut open the leg side of the head, splitting the tip of the head open so that you completely expose the inner wonder that is inside a shrimp's head. Then, with a small knife, score the meat so you can remove the vein. Place all the shrimp meat side up on a plate, then drizzle fish sauce evenly over the tops. Set aside in the fridge to marinate until needed.

COOK THE PAELLA

3. Preheat the top broiler on high. Coat the shrimp lightly and evenly with olive oil. Set aside.

4. Heat the oil in the paella pan over medium-high heat. Add the onion and cook, stirring often, until lightly browned. Add the rice and cook until the grains start to stick a little to the bottom of the pan. Add the stock, coconut milk, shrimp paste, paprika, and black pepper and stir to combine. Lower the heat to medium and cook, stirring often, until the rice has the consistency of a loose, creamy risotto, 10 to 15 minutes.

5. Shake the pan so the rice is redistributed evenly across it and cook, *repositioning the pan* over the stove to get more even heating if needed, until all the liquid has been completely absorbed by the rice (meaning you don't see any bubbling going on, just hear some sizzling on the edges of the pan) and the edges of the paella appear lightly crispy. Do not stir at this stage.

6. Turn off the heat and arrange the shrimp across the rice, meat side down. Pull the heads open as they rest on top so all the inner wonders can seep into the rice. Place the paella pan right underneath the broiler (I would say 1 to 2 inches for an electric oven or 2 to 3 inches/5 to 8 cm for a gas oven) and cook until the shrimp are slightly charred and cooked through, and the top of the paella is lightly toasted and crispy. If you can't get enough browning on the shrimp before the rice gets too burned, just apply more blister afterward with a blowtorch.

7. Brush a thin coating of Makrut Lime Leaf Oil all over the surface of the shrimp and rice. Serve immediately.

NOTE ON THE PAELLA PAN: *The correct thickness of the rice in a paella (about ½ inch/1.3 cm) is paramount, and this recipe is specifically meant for a 14-inch (34-cm) paella pan. If your pan is much smaller or larger than that, you need to adjust the quantity of the recipe accordingly.*

CRACKLING PORK BELLY

The idea is Cantonese roast pig, miniaturized. Sounds simple, but it really isn't. Different from most roasted whole hogs around the world, Cantonese roast pig has skin crackling that is blindingly golden, perforated, and evenly puffed with micro blisters and air bubbles throughout, almost like fried pork rinds. Learning to achieve this on a much smaller scale while keeping the meat moist and melty but not greasy has been a lifelong process of mistakes and enlightenment, dark ages and renaissance. As soon as I would think I had it nailed, I'd fail gloriously the next time.

In order to do this right, you need to be the kind of person who relishes a certain level of neurotic obsession, compulsive analness—the kind that isolates you socially but still gets you into parties because you'll bring this bad boy. Starting from the prepping of the pork skin down to babysitting it by the wee flame as you hover two inches above the skillet, nursing it intently, there almost has to be a state of mutual torment in order for it to be done right. But you'll do it all over again. Because you like the way it hurts. And if all that sounds too good to be true, then let's get into the specifics.

MAKES 8 APPETIZER SERVINGS OR 4 MAIN COURSE SERVINGS

SPECIAL EQUIPMENT: *spice grinder or food processor; wooden skewers*

2- to 2½-pound (900- to 1,200-g) slab skin-on pork belly (see Step 1)

2½ tablespoons fine sea salt

6 fresh bay leaves

½ star anise pod

Olive oil, for brushing

Canola oil, for frying

OPTIONAL FOR SERVING

Spicy mustard

Cooked rice

Orange Chile Sambal (page 23)

Fried Chile Verde Sauce (page 15)

Sweet Soy Sauce (page 26)

1. When it comes to buying pork belly, always choose a section that has multiple and even layerings of fat and meat; avoid those that come with a single thick layer of fat and a thick layer of lean meat. If you can't find that piece of pork belly of your dreams, don't settle. It's like getting married, okay?

2. Rinse the pork belly clean under cold water, pat it dry, and set it on a sheet pan that's not much larger than the pork. Grind the salt, bay leaves, and star anise in a spice grinder or food processor as finely as you can (you can tweak the ingredients of the salt rub to your liking but *do not* add any sugar or other sweetener because it will promote overbrowning later). Rub the salt mixture evenly on all sides of the pork belly, cover, and set aside on the counter to marinate for 1 hour.

3. Thirty minutes into marinating, preheat the oven to 265°F/130°C.

4. Rinse the pork belly clean of the marinade (tiny bits of bay leaves sticking is fine) and pat it dry. Brush that same sheet pan lightly with olive oil. Place the pork belly on it *skin side up,* cover the pork and pan tightly with aluminum foil, and roast for 2½ hours, until very soft but not falling apart.

5. You'll notice a considerable amount of fat and liquid in the pan; keep them there. Hold a handful of wooden skewers with all the sharp tips at the same level and start gently punching tiny holes all the way through the skin (not the meat). *Don't randomly jab at the skin.* Move systematically from one side to the other, from top to bottom, perforating the skin as densely and evenly as you can. The more little holes, the better the crackling will be. Keep the pork belly skin side up, then cover the pan tightly with plastic wrap. Place another sheet pan or a small chopping board on top and set a few cans on it to keep the pork belly flat, then transfer the setup to the fridge to chill for at least 4 hours but preferably overnight.

6. Forty minutes before serving, set the pork belly on a cutting board skin side down. Trim off any uneven edges on all four sides to obtain a straight-edged slab.

7. Now, take a minute to get familiar with the anatomy of your subject. You'll see that the skin is a translucent layer, distinctively different from the opaque white fat layer underneath. It's *very important* to know that you need to thoroughly blister this entire skin layer not just on the surface, not halfway, not 95 percent of the way, but *all the way through.* Failure to achieve that will result in crackling that is chewy and tough instead of crispy. How do you do this? *Slow and even heat.*

8. So, cut the slab of pork belly in half crosswise, because it's much easier to apply even heat across a smaller surface area. You can either cook the pork belly in two separate skillets or keep one portion refrigerated for next time (it will keep for just a few days). Place the pork belly skin side down in a large *nonstick* skillet with a layer of canola oil that's *as deep as the thickness of the skin,* and set it over low heat. Pork skin splatters, so keep the skillet 90 percent covered with a lid, and cook the belly for 20 to 30 minutes, depending on the thickness of the skin. It's really better to do this too slowly than too quickly. After 20 minutes, remove the lid and gently lift the pork belly up with a spatula to check on the skin. It should be blond at this point. Continue to cook for 5 to 10 minutes, until the skin layer is completely blistered and puffed and the sizzling/splattering sound subsides almost completely (which means all the moisture from the skin has been cooked off).

9. The crackling pork belly can be cut into 1-inch cubes and served with mustard as an appetizer or over rice with condiments such as Orange Chile Sambal, Fried Chile Verde Sauce, and Sweet Soy Sauce.

GRILLED BAO BURGER BUNS

More disk than bun, this perfect vessel for tender meats popularized in the United States by Xi'an Famous Foods shares the same culinary wisdom as an English muffin, double-sided crispiness on the outside with holey soft parts inside. But its flatness, by default, highlights the crispiness even more so. And its method is particularly ingenious where ovens are off-limits.

MAKES 6 LARGE OR 8 MEDIUM BUNS

SPECIAL EQUIPMENT: *stand mixer or handheld mixer with a dough hook*

2½ cups (342 g) bread flour, more as needed

3 tablespoons (45 g) heavy cream

2½ tablespoons (30 g) light brown sugar

1½ teaspoons (5 g) instant dry yeast

¼ teaspoon fine sea salt

⅔ cup (156 g) water

Vegetable oil, for grilling

1. In a bowl, using a stand mixer or handheld mixer with a dough hook attachment, combine the flour, cream, brown sugar, yeast, salt, and water. Mix until a shaggy dough forms, then knead on medium speed for 5 to 8 minutes, until very smooth and elastic. The dough should pull away completely from the bowl and should not be sticking to your hands.

2. Cover the bowl with plastic wrap and let the dough rise at room temperature until fully doubled, about 1 to 2 hours.

3. Transfer the dough to a lightly floured surface, punch the air out, and divide it into 6 equal portions for large burgers, as seen on page 170, or 8 portions for smaller burgers. Shape each portion into a ball, then roll it into a thick disk about 4 inches (10 cm) wide. Cover the disks with plastic wrap and let rise again for 45 minutes to 1 hour. They are ready when you can dent them with your fingertips and they do not spring back immediately.

4. Lightly coat a flat griddle or skillet with vegetable oil and set it over medium-low heat. When the griddle or skillet feels warm, place the dough disks on top, flipping once or twice, and toast until golden brown and crispy on both sides and cooked through in the middle. This should take about 9 minutes in total, so if your dough is browning too fast before the interior is cooked through, lower the heat. Let cool on a cooling rack until needed. These can be individually wrapped in plastic and kept frozen. Thaw and retoast before using.

CUMIN LAMB RIB BURGERS

Lamb may just be my favorite meat. The grassy gaminess, which is appalling to the less fortunate, is near and dear to my heart. I get deeply offended by some Asian restaurants that claim to have proudly rid their lamb of its signature lambiness—dumbfounded, really—because if I wanted beef, I'd order beef, huh?

This is a recipe that celebrates my love for gamy lamb by elevating it to an even higher standing with an unapologetic amount of its soul mate spice: cumin. Hand in hand, like twins in a womb, born to be in perfect unison. I serve them with smoky mashed eggplant fired up by Fried Chile Verde Sauce with a shrub of fresh mint, cilantro, and scallion lubed up in Greek yogurt tinged with Dijon mustard inside soft yet chewy Chinese-style bao that is granted the same respect and golden brown crispiness as an English muffin.

The oily roasting juice works its way through the nooks and crannies of the pulled meat down to the holes and chambers of the crispy bun, ending in the licking of your happy fingers, and finally, your coma of deep satiation.

MAKES 6 SANDWICHES/BAO

SPECIAL EQUIPMENT: *blowtorch; stand mixer or handheld mixer with a dough hook*

CUMIN LAMB RIBS

3 pounds (1.3 kg) lamb ribs (see Note on page 171)

Olive oil, for brushing

3 tablespoons fish sauce

5 tablespoons (84 g) Heinz yellow mustard

5 garlic cloves, grated

1 tablespoon grated ginger

1 teaspoon fine sea salt

SPICE CRUST

¼ cup (56 g) finely ground cumin (see Note on page 171)

2 tablespoons coarsely ground cumin (see Note on page 171)

2 teaspoons ground coriander

1½ tablespoons Sichuan or Korean chile flakes

1½ teaspoons ground Sichuan peppercorns

1 teaspoon ground white pepper

HERBY YOGURT

½ cup Greek yogurt

2 tablespoons finely chopped mint

2 tablespoons finely chopped cilantro

2 tablespoons finely chopped scallion

2 tablespoons Dijon mustard

2 garlic cloves, grated

1 teaspoon freshly ground black pepper

½ teaspoon fine sea salt

FOR SERVING

6 to 8 Grilled Bao Burger Buns (opposite)

2 cups (double serving) Smoky Daddy (page 297)

MAKE THE LAMB RIBS

1. Starting the night before or at least 8 hours before serving, wash the lamb ribs and pat them dry with a clean towel. Place them on a sheet pan set under the venting range hood and brush them with a very thin layer of olive oil. With the

range hood on, use a blowtorch to burn every square inch of the surface of the lamb ribs until deeply browned and caramelized. (I do this with cuts of meats that have uneven surfaces to give them that "seared" flavor before roasting.) Brush the fish sauce over the surface of the ribs as you continue to torch it, until all the fish sauce has dried and caramelized against the surface of the ribs, creating a salty "crust."

2. In a small bowl, mix the mustard, garlic, ginger, and salt. Rub the mixture thoroughly and evenly over every surface of the ribs. Place the ribs on a sheet pan, wrap with plastic, and marinate overnight (or for at least 3 hours) in the fridge.

3. Five hours before serving, in a small bowl, mix the finely and coarsely ground cumin, coriander, chile flakes, Sichuan peppercorns, and white pepper, then press the spice mixture over the whole surface of the ribs until it sticks. You want a thin, even crust all over. You may or may not use up the entire spice mixture. It's okay if you don't use it all.

4. Cover the sheet pan tightly with aluminum foil and roast in the oven for 4 to 5 hours, until the meat is extremely tender and the bones are completely loosened. *(This timing is based on lamb ribs. If you're using another cut, judge the doneness as appropriate for that cut.)*

TO SERVE

5. Meanwhile, prepare the Grilled Bao Burger Buns.

6. In a bowl, whisk the herby yogurt ingredients.

7. To serve, if you want the bone-in look on your burgers, cut the lamb ribs in between bones into sizes that fit the buns (the bones can be easily pulled away before you begin eating). If not, remove the bones, chop the meat into small chunks, and toss them in the roasting juices. *Reheat the buns on a hot skillet to crisp them up again* (you must do this; it makes a world of difference), then cut them open crosswise. Smear a good layer of Smoky Daddy on the insides of the buns and top with the lamb ribs. Drizzle with some of the roasting juices and douse with the herby yogurt. Serve immediately with lots of tissues. You'll need them.

NOTE ON LAMB: *Lamb ribs, aka lamb spare ribs or lamb riblets (not rack of lamb), are an economical and succulent cut of meat when available. They are very common in northern China and quite accessible online in the UK and the United States. When they're cooked properly, I love their fatty, sticky, extremely tender, and flavorful meat. If you cannot find lamb ribs where you live, you can certainly substitute lamb necks, leg of lamb, or any other cut that is good for roasting.*

NOTE ON CUMIN: *I like the texture and flavor of bits of broken cumin in my bite, but you can use all finely ground cumin if you don't have a spice grinder or a mortar and pestle.*

SICHUAN HOT CHICKEN

Somewhere around the summer of 2015 . . . or was it 2014 . . . anyhow, I noticed a minor turbulence in my Instagram feed, over and over, flashing me with this bright orangy-red thingy sitting on a piece of white bread they called Nashville hot chicken. Usually I let this kind of thing pass by as a blip in the ever-flowing hype of the Internet cosmos—you know, today it's this, tomorrow it's face-printed lattes.

But as I watched people gushing over Nashville hot chicken (fried chicken coated in spicy grease) while sitting halfway across the world in China (where they happen to be exceptional at making spicy grease), the blip started talking dirty to me. Sichuan/Nashville fusion? It sounds wrong. I mean, it can't be right. I want to say I'm sorry, but if I didn't do it someone else would, and sooner or later an abomination between the two worlds would be brought to your nearest Momofuku, ready to haunt your cardiologist.

Because make no mistake, this is the kind of guilty indulgence you'll feel like apologizing for. As if fried chicken alone isn't bad (awesome) enough, we need to drench it in a fiery, lip-tingling oil to make it worse (awesomer). So I say, you do whatever you need to do in the aftermath to feel better about yourself. Do that cleanse, go to church, whatever. . . . But right now, you're gonna sink the entire rim of your lower face into this crispy rouged monster, hear the sound of pleasure and pain crashing between your jaws, and grab a piece of that sweet, squishy pullman bread to mop up the blotches of mala paste around the corners of your mouth. Then you'll eat that, too.

Make it biweekly, at the most.

MAKES 4 SERVINGS

SPECIAL EQUIPMENT: *spice grinder*

CHICKEN AND MARINADE

8 mixed bone-in, skin-on chicken legs and thighs (or if you must, 6 bone-in, skin-on breasts)

2 large (25 g) green scallions

1 tablespoon grated ginger

¼ cup (80 g) Sichuan broad bean chile paste (doubanjiang; see page 8)

¼ cup (60 mL) soy sauce

1 tablespoon sake

1 tablespoon light brown sugar

2 teaspoons ground Sichuan peppercorns

1 teaspoon ground white pepper

½ teaspoon table salt

2 tablespoons water

MALA HOT PASTE

¼ cup (24 g) Sichuan or Korean chile flakes

2 tablespoons Sichuan peppercorns

1 tablespoon ground white pepper

1 teaspoon ground coriander

½ teaspoon ground cumin

⅛ teaspoon ground cinnamon

½ star anise pod

1 tablespoon toasted sesame oil

½ tablespoon soy sauce

1 teaspoon honey

1 teaspoon rice vinegar

5 garlic cloves, grated

¼ cup (60 mL) canola oil

5 tablespoons (70 g) unsalted butter

2 tablespoons chopped fresh cilantro

BREADING AND FRYING

1 cup (240 mL) buttermilk

1 large egg

1 cup (125 g) all-purpose flour

½ cup (40 g) potato starch or cornstarch (see page 6)

½ cup (53 g) rice flour (see page 6)

1 tablespoon baking powder

1 tablespoon each ground white and black pepper

2 teaspoons garlic powder

¼ teaspoon baking soda

1 teaspoon fine sea salt

Canola oil

FOR SERVING

Slices of squishy white bread (pullman or other loaf)

MARINATE THE CHICKEN

1. Place the chicken in a large bowl. In a blender, puree the scallions, ginger, Sichuan broad bean chile paste, soy sauce, sake, brown sugar, Sichuan peppercorns, white pepper, salt, and water until smooth, then pour the mixture over the chicken. Rub each piece to make sure it's evenly coated, then cover the bowl and marinate in the fridge for at least 6 hours or up to overnight, turning the chicken once halfway through.

MAKE THE MALA HOT PASTE

2. In a spice blender, blend the chile flakes, peppercorns, white pepper, coriander, cumin, cinnamon, and star anise until powderized. Set aside. Mix the sesame oil, soy sauce, honey, vinegar, and garlic in a small bowl and set aside. Heat the oil and butter in a small saucepan over medium-high heat for about 3 minutes, until brown bits start to form on the sides and bottom of the pan. Turn off the heat and add the powdered spice mixture. Stir and let cook for 1 minute, until the powder has darkened in color and smells fragrant. Add the sesame oil mixture and stir to combine evenly. Let sit for at least 1 hour (or you can make it the day before).

FRY THE CHICKEN

3. Remove the chicken from the marinade and rinse off any excess sticking to the skin and meat. Dab really dry with paper towels (this allows the buttermilk and breading to stick better) and set aside.

4. Prepare two bowls: In the first, whisk together the buttermilk and egg. In the second, whisk together the flour, potato starch, rice flour, baking powder, black and white peppers, garlic powder, baking soda, and salt. Drizzle about 1 tablespoon of the buttermilk mixture into the flour mixture and mix briefly with a fork; this will create tiny coagulations of breading that make a great crust.

5. Now wash your hands thoroughly. Working with one piece of chicken at a time, dip it into

the buttermilk mixture, turning and drenching several times until evenly coated, then drain slightly and transfer it to the flour mixture. Press the flour mixture lightly into the chicken, turning to coat it until you can't feel any sticky surfaces left. Tap the chicken to remove any excess flour, then set aside on a baking sheet. Rub off the coagulated breading sticking to your fingers and let it fall back into the flour mixture; this will create more crispy bits in the breading. Repeat to bread the rest of the chicken.

6. Let the chicken rest for 10 to 15 minutes before frying. This allows the breading to hydrate and creates a crispier crust.

7. Preheat the oven to 250°F/120°C.

8. Using a Dutch oven or other pot for frying that's at least 6 inches (15 cm) deep, pour canola oil in to a depth of 3 inches (8 cm) (this will prevent the oil from overflowing when you're frying). Heat the oil to 325°F/160°C, or until it bubbles up immediately around an inserted wooden chopstick. Without crowding the pot, in small batches, fry the chicken pieces until golden brown all around, 8 to 10 minutes for drumsticks and breasts and 10 to 12 minutes for thighs. Drain the chicken pieces well and transfer them to a sheet pan. Set the pan in the oven to keep the chicken warm while you fry the rest.

9. Reheat the mala hot paste over medium heat to loosen its consistency (the butter makes the paste thick as it cools and hard to spread). Mix in 1 tablespoon of the cilantro, then brush the hot paste over the fried chicken to coat it evenly. Sprinkle the chicken with the rest of the cilantro and serve with squishy white bread immediately.

CRACKLING-STUDDED PORK BELLY BURGER

In the institution that is Korean barbecue, there is a stand-alone branch called samgyeopsal-gui: *a dish of thick-cut pork belly served with lettuce, herbs, and condiments on the side. At first glance, you'll be excused for doubting the appeal of these unmarinated, utterly unseasoned, pale slabs of pork belly presented with what seems like a lack of care. But this is actually one of the rare culinary offerings—nigiri being another—in which the bareness is, in fact, keenly intentional and perfect.*

Seared and served immediately from the grill at the center of the table, there's something inexplicably magical about a simple piece of fat-laced pork belly that's properly rendered, caramelized, and crisped. Without distraction, we are immersed in a full assault of intense porky savoriness in every crunchy bit and greasy burst at the edges and juicy meatiness at the center. The flavor persists through layers of bold condiments, the deep aroma lasting even after swallowing. For today's oversaturated taste buds, it wakes up a primal, carnivorous part of our brain with a jolt of clarity.

I set out to create a burger that celebrates—elevates, even—this pure sensory pleasure.

First, I needed to create a pork patty, a pork belly patty. I not only wanted the patty to have crispy edges of pork fat, but I wanted it porkiness-studded, *like a diamond bracelet embedded with precious gems, but in pork form. How could I outdo crispy pork fat? Well, with* cured and aged *crispy pork fat. We're talking* guanciale cracklings . . . *Italian cured pork jowls cut and rendered into tiny, sparkling cubes of blistered and crunchy cracklings, fully encrusting this exceptional juicy patty—already made from pork belly, I should say again—with concentrated and explosive porkiness.*

A pure and explicit pork bomb.

Just as is done for samgyeopsal-gui, we underseason the patty to consolidate its porkiness, allowing the other flavor components to come in as separate layers: the toasted potato bun, the garlic aioli made entirely with toasted sesame oil, *and the shiso leaves marinated in spicy* ssamjang *(the sauce that is served with samgyeopsal-gui), cutting in on cue like actors in a well-orchestrated play. Even with such strong allies, King Pork still dominates in every bite. It'll leave you porked up and never wanting a beef burger again.*

MAKES 4 BURGERS

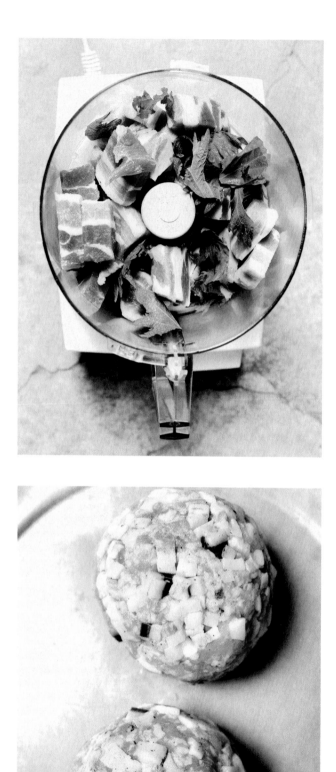

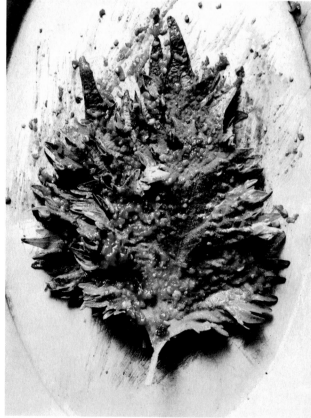

PORK BELLY PATTIES

1¾ pounds (800 g) skinless pork belly (see Note on page 180 before purchasing)

4 shiso or perilla leaves (see Note on page 180)

¼ teaspoon sea salt

⅓ pound (130 g) guanciale or fatty pancetta

TOASTED SESAME OIL AIOLI

1 large egg yolk

1 teaspoon Dijon mustard

¾ teaspoon freshly ground black pepper

⅓ teaspoon fine sea salt, plus more to adjust

¼ teaspoon honey

¼ cup toasted sesame oil, preferably Korean

SSAMJANG-MARINATED SHISO/PERILLA LEAVES

1 small shallot, grated

1 garlic clove, grated

½ teaspoon grated ginger

1 tablespoon gochujang (Korean chile paste)

2 teaspoons medium/yellow miso paste

2 teaspoons rice vinegar

½ teaspoon honey

24 to 28 shiso/perilla leaves

TO FINISH

3 tablespoons canola oil, for frying

4 potato buns

Unsalted butter, for toasting

MAKE THE PATTIES

1. Cut the pork belly into 1-inch (2.5-cm) chunks, scatter them on a sheet pan, and flash-freeze for 30 to 70 minutes, until just hardened. *Working in small batches (depending on the size of your food processor)*, combine the cubes and 4 shiso/perilla leaves in the processor and *pulse* until the mixture is ground but *not pureed.* You should still see tiny bits of fat throughout. Transfer to a bowl and repeat with the rest of the pork belly. When you have all the cubes ground, sprinkle the sea salt over the top and gently mix until even, but *do not overwork the mixture.* Divide it into 4 equal portions and shape them into large, tight meatballs.

2. If the guanciale or pancetta comes with skin, remove it. Cut the cured pork into slices about ⅛ inch (3 mm) thick, then cut the slices into strips the same width, then cut the strips into tiny dice. Divide the dice into 4 equal portions, then press each portion evenly onto the surface of each meatball. *Make sure you firmly press the dice into the meat, so the pieces are embedded into the surface of the patties.* Gently press and shape each ball into a thick patty that's slightly wider than the buns. You can prepare the patties up to 1 day ahead of time; wrap in plastic and keep chilled in the fridge until needed.

MAKE THE TOASTED SESAME AIOLI

3. In a heavy medium bowl that is placed on top of a wet towel to keep it from moving around, whisk the egg yolk, mustard, black pepper, salt, and honey until evenly combined. *Slowly drizzle in the sesame oil while whisking constantly,* which will form an emulsion and give you a light mayonnaise. Reseason with more sea salt if needed; it should taste prominently salty. You

can prepare this a few hours ahead of time. Keep the bowl wrapped in plastic and chilled in the fridge until needed.

MAKE THE SSAMJANG MARINADE

4. In a small bowl, whisk the shallot, garlic, ginger, gochujang, miso paste, vinegar, and honey. *Let the mixture sit for at least 1 hour* or up to several hours before using.

FRY THE PORK PATTIES

5. In a large *nonstick* skillet, heat the canola oil over medium heat, then add the pork patties, keeping 2 inches (5 cm) of space between them. If you're scared of splatter, wear a kitchen mitt. *Hold a large spoon and tilt the skillet to gather the hot oil toward one side, then continuously ladle the hot oil over the patties.* This creates beautiful caramelization on all sides of the patties and helps the cracklings crispen. As you go, more and more fat will be rendered from the patties and it's easier to perform this step. When one side is deeply caramelized and crispy, carefully flip the patties and repeat the process. When both sides are crispy, transfer to a plate and let rest for 5 minutes. If there's insufficient caramelization on any sides of the patties, finish them with a blowtorch.

TO FINISH

6. While the patties are resting, brush the ssamjang on both sides of 16 shiso/perilla leaves and lay them together to marinate for 5 minutes. Also, have ready 2 or 3 fresh shiso/perilla leaves for each burger. Slice the potato

buns in half crosswise and toast them in a pan or on a griddle with a little bit of unsalted butter until crispy on the edges.

7. Let the buns cool a little, then smear a generous amount of the aioli on *both sides of the bun*. To make one burger, lay a patty on a bottom bun and top with 4 marinated shiso/perilla leaves and 2 or 3 fresh leaves (I know this sounds like a lot, but trust me, they are BFFs), then close it off with the top bun. Serve immediately.

NOTE ON PORK BELLY: *The quality of the pork is quite important here, since the concentrated porkiness is the essence of the dish. The effort to source a good-quality (and hence flavorful) breed, I assure you, will be justified in the final result. You want the pork belly to be around 30 percent fat and 70 percent lean, so if your cut is fatter than this ratio, trim off the excess. You can just eyeball it. There's no need to get anal here. Be sure to weigh the pork belly after trimming.*

NOTE ON SHISO AND PERILLA LEAVES: *Shiso and perilla leaves (close relatives) come either entirely green or green on top and purple on the underside. I wish I could tell you what you can use to substitute for shiso/perilla leaves, but their unique fragrance is a match made in heaven with grilled pork, and there's no good alternative. They can be hard to find but are generally sold in Japanese or Korean grocery stores. But if you absolutely cannot find the leaves or they're too expensive where you live, then try fresh mint or tarragon—but in smaller amounts, as they are stronger-tasting herbs.*

GUIJIE LOBSTER BAKE

In Beijing there is a street near the northeast corner of the Second Ring Road that's infamously known as Guijie *(the street of round baskets). During the dark hours of the night, when the corrosive angst of living in this city bubbled almost over the edge, Jason would strap me on our electric scooter and brave the assault of toxic air along the way as we headed straight to this lantern-lit street for one (and only one) culinary refuge:* ma xiao. *The first word means "numb" and the second means "little." The two words together form the local nickname for a notorious late-night indulgence that is* mala xiaolongxia, *or numbing and spicy "baby lobster," aka crayfish.*

Potentially habit-forming is an understatement. It would be more appropriate to call it an addictive bloodbath.

Each voluptuous "baby lobster" is tumbled and braised in a chile oil–flooded sauce saturated with Sichuan spices and chile paste. Do not attempt to underestimate this dish by comparing it with Louisiana-style boiled crayfish; this is like confusing a sip of Bud Light with a keg of Flaming Lamborghini, a dangerous misstep punishable by having the pleasure and pain receptors in your brain whiplashed through every bug-crushing and head-sucking compulsion.

But you can't stop. No one can. And before your better judgment can pry itself out of your delirious consciousness, you find yourself mopping up every last drop of this lethal concoction with sponge-like noodles. The next day may not be pleasant, but you'll go back for more. And here's how I do more, with crayfish's daddy.

MAKES 4 SERVINGS

SHELLFISH MIXTURE
(3½ to 4 pounds/1.6 to 1.8 kg total; see Note on page 184)

5 mini (about ½ pound/220 g each), 3 small (about 13 ounces/360 g each), or 2 to 3 medium (about 1 pound/450 g each) lobsters (mine were mini)

½ pound (225 g/20 to 25 count) medium head-on, shell-on shrimp

1 pound (450 g) razor clams or baby geoducks

BROTH

1 stick (8 tablespoons/113 g) unsalted butter

10 garlic cloves, smashed

1 large or 2 small lemongrass stalks, smashed and cut into 1-inch (2.5-cm) segments

2 tablespoons to 1 small handful dried bird's eye chilies, depending on the heat level desired

2 tablespoons Old Bay seasoning

3 cups (720 mL) chicken stock, preferably unsalted or low-sodium, plus more as needed

½ cup plus 3 tablespoons (198 g) Mala Paste (page 20), plus more as needed

1½ teaspoons MSG (see Note on page 186)

1 large ear of corn, husked and cut into 4 chunks

FOR SERVING

4 portions thin wheat noodles of your choosing

Toasted sesame oil, to coat

Finely minced cilantro or scallions, for garnish

PREPARE THE SHELLFISH

1. Freeze the lobsters for 45 minutes to 1 hour to send them into a deep coma or hopefully death. With sharp kitchen scissors, remove the soft shell plates on their tails, exposing the meat, and cut open the bottom of their heads from between the legs all the way up to their eyes. Make a slit along the hard shell on the back (not the head). These cuts will allow the cooking liquid and flavors to seep in and makes them a lot easier to eat later on. Make the same cuts on the shrimp.

2. If you're using clams, soak them in salted water for at least 1 hour to make sure they have enough time to spit out all the sand in their guts and properly clean themselves. If you're using geoducks, remove the transparent membrane around the meat. Rinse well and set aside.

COOK THE SHELLFISH

3. In a wide, shallow Dutch oven or saucepan, heat the butter over medium-high heat. Add the garlic, lemongrass, and chilies and cook, stirring often, until the edges of the garlic start to brown. Add the Old Bay and cook for a few seconds, until fragrant. Add the stock, Mala Paste, MSG, and corn and lower the heat to medium. Stir to let the paste dissolve into the liquid, then cover the pan and let simmer for 5 minutes.

4. Arrange the lobsters and geoducks, if using, in the pan in a single layer, then cover the pan and cook 5 minutes for mini lobsters, 6 minutes for small lobsters, or 7 minutes for medium lobsters. If you're using razor clams or other non-shrimp shellfish, add them when the lobsters are 3 minutes from done. When the lobster time is up, scatter the shrimp evenly over the top, cover the pot, and cook for 2 minutes, until opaque and cooked through.

5. Give the pot a good stir, making sure all the shellfish are coated with the liquid. Taste and reseason with more Mala Paste if needed (or add more stock if it's too salty). Let sit for a few minutes to let the flavor soak in.

COOK THE NOODLES

6. Meanwhile, bring a large pot of water to boil and cook the noodles according to the package instructions. Rinse under cold water until completely cooled, then drain well and toss with toasted sesame oil to coat.

TO SERVE

7. Serve the shellfish and broth in large bowls and sprinkle the cilantro or scallions on top. Serve the noodles in bowls on the side. As you pillage through the lobsters, use a small spoon to scoop out all the rich lobster fat inside their heads and add it to the sauce. Drench the noodles in the broth and slurp with absolute conviction as you sweat.

NOTE ON THE SHELLFISH MIXTURE: *If you are fortunate enough to have access to crayfish—a*

highly seasonal privilege found in a select few places in the world—by all means go for it. If not, depending on your budget and availability, you can source a different mixture of shellfish that fits your needs. Go all out with all lobsters (but choose relatively small ones for this use) or more modestly with all shrimp or crayfish and clams.

If you use clams, it's important to note that different clams have different levels of brininess/ saltiness as well as different amounts of the juices they release, meaning you'll have to adjust the seasonings and the liquid level as you go. For example, baby geoducks are commonly found in Hong Kong. They're sweet and not salty and release a minimal amount of juice (razor clams are also in this category). Mussels are sweet and not salty but release a huge amount of juice. Steamer clams are salty and briny and release a good amount of very salty juice.

I would recommend using geoducks or razor clams because they won't affect the salt level of the recipe as much. But if you're using mussels or other types of clams, I would reduce the amount of chicken stock to 1½ cups first and reserve 2 tablespoons of Mala Paste, so you can adjust the liquid and seasoning at the end.

NOTE ON MSG: *MSG is a victim of modern food snobbery, the stigma against it is as stupid and baseless as a witch hunt. This seasoning is teeming in Doritos, Pringles, flavored potato chips, canned soups, instant noodles, KFC, and tons of other foods that people enjoy all the time without any type of "sensitivity," but somehow when it's in the context of a recipe it's all of a sudden given dirty looks. Yeah, too much of it makes you thirsty, just as salt does. Other than that, it's as "artificial" as the vitamins you take every morning. Omit it if you want, but consider doing so a meaningless sacrifice of pleasure and joy.*

LAMB AND CHEESE SLAB PIE
RUBBED WITH CUMIN-CHILE OIL

When beginning a cookbook, I'm guessing most writers, like myself, start by making a recipe list. A list of ideas that they stash away, one by one, like a child gleefully feeding her plastic piggy bank with oblivious optimism. Take caution there, my friends. Because those recipe ideas, whatever beautiful promises they may have whispered at the time they were conceived, are at least 30 percent likely to mature into throbbing failures, rendering their hopeful creator into a twitching mess on the kitchen floor. Hey, it's true, recipes really are like children.

However, against all odds, all three out of the three following recipes performed beautifully upon first trial. The one thing they have in common? Their use of an Asian-style hot water dough.

Unlike English-style hot water dough, which is flaky, pastry-like, and made with a considerable amount of lard or suet, the Asian style consists almost only of wheat flour and hot water, water at 130° to 140°F/55° to 60°C to be exact (and you have to be exact). This is the magic number that limits the formation of gluten to a precise amount that yields a soft yet chewy wonder. Not to mention that it's a dream to work with, because it rolls out obediently without attempting to retract and spring back. It's the same type of dough, with variations here and there, that is used for Taiwanese flaky scallion pancakes, Indian lachha paratha (layered flat bread), some dumplings, and, in this case, a wonderland of Chinese-style meat pies.

Within twelve months of moving to Beijing, I became eager to know how to make Chinese-style meat pies, soft yet slightly chewy, rolled thin, and pan-fried until crispy on the outside, meat juice rampant on the inside. One in particular, called **xianghe roubing**, had me at its massive hello. It is a flat, wide, oval-shaped meat pie stuffed with beef or lamb and cooked between two hot griddles, almost like a giant panini press. I couldn't say no to this stuff like misery couldn't say no to company. It was an endeavor that took me almost a decade to figure out and replicate . . . well, sort of.

Traditionally, almost all Chinese-style meat pies are cooked in hot press grills or in a skillet, which have their merits, but I wanted to introduce more crispiness to the crust by baking it in the dry heat of the oven. Then, instead of a pure lamb or beef filling seasoned with soy sauce, I took out 50 percent of that and replaced it with melty cheese seasoned with fish sauce. It's an incredible collaboration between different worlds of funk—with elements that you didn't even know could go happily together, creating a complex savoriness that is borderline narcotic for funk lovers. Then at the end, you give this pie an affectionate massage of fiery oil heavily scented with cumin and chilies.

MAKES 6 SERVINGS

SPECIAL EQUIPMENT: *stand mixer or handheld mixer with a dough hook*

PIE DOUGH *(I strongly recommend measuring by weight)*

3½ cups (438 g) all-purpose flour

2 teaspoons (8 g) light brown sugar

1¼ teaspoons fine sea salt

1 cup plus 1 tablespoon (267 g) hot water at 130° to 140°F/55° to 60°C

LAMB FILLING

1 tablespoon olive oil

10 small shallots, finely minced

4 garlic cloves, finely minced

2 teaspoons finely minced ginger

¼ teaspoon freshly ground black pepper

1 pound (455 g) ground lamb

1 tablespoon potato starch or cornstarch (see page 6)

1 tablespoon fish sauce

½ teaspoon ground white pepper

2 tablespoons chopped fresh mint, plus more to sprinkle

10 ounces (280 g) melty semisoft cheese, such as Gouda, finely diced

CUMIN-CHILE OIL

1½ tablespoons olive oil

2 teaspoons ground cumin

2 teaspoons chile flakes

1 teaspoon ground coriander

½ teaspoon ground Sichuan peppercorns

Olive oil, for coating pan and pie

MAKE THE DOUGH

1. In a bowl, using a stand mixer or handheld mixer with a dough hook attachment, combine the flour, brown sugar, and salt. Set aside.

2. Microwave about 1½ cups of water on high for 1 minute 20 seconds, which will bring it up to 130° to 140°F/55° to 60°C (but I highly recommend using a thermometer), then pour 1 cup plus 1 tablespoon (267 g) of the hot water over the flour mixture (I recommend doing this directly on top of the scale). Start mixing on low until the dough comes together, then turn to high speed and mix for 6 to 8 minutes, until the dough is extremely silky, soft, and smooth, like a baby's bottom. It should pull completely away from the bowl when running, but stick back when the machine stops. It should feel tacky but not overly sticky when you touch it with your hand. Adjust with more flour or water if needed to get it right.

3. Wrap the bowl and let rest for at least 1 to 2 hours before using. The dough can be prepared up to a day ahead, and kept wrapped and chilled in the fridge until needed.

MAKE THE LAMB FILLING

4. In a small skillet over medium heat, heat the olive oil. Add the shallots, garlic, ginger, and black pepper and cook, stirring often, until the shallots are very soft and translucent. Set aside to cool.

5. In a large bowl, combine the shallot mixture with the lamb, potato starch, fish sauce, and white pepper and mix until evenly combined. Add the mint and Gouda and mix until evenly incorporated. The filling can be made up to a day ahead and kept covered in the fridge.

MAKE THE CUMIN-CHILE OIL

6. In a small saucepan over medium-high heat, combine the olive oil, cumin, chile flakes, coriander, and Sichuan peppercorns. Cook until the chile flakes turn dark maroon in color, 2 to 3 minutes. Set aside. The oil can be made a day ahead and kept at room temperature.

MAKE AND BAKE THE PIE

7. One hour before serving, set a rack at the upper to mid level of the oven and preheat the oven to 500°F/260°C (with both top and bottom heat and fan on if available). Brush a thin coating of olive oil on a rimmed 16 × 12-inch (40 × 30-cm) sheet pan (for a thinner pie, use a sheet pan that is up to 30 percent bigger). Set aside.

8. Transfer the dough onto a well-floured surface and divide in half. Roll one portion out to about the thickness of a thin-crust pizza and in a shape that well covers the size of the sheet pan. Gently drape the dough over the pan, fitting it into the edges and corners so it completely fills the empty spaces. Scatter the filling over the dough in an even layer, pressing it down gently

without crushing the dough underneath until it's flat and leveled. Roll out the second portion of dough and drape it over the filling, then pinch the edges tightly together to seal. Use a small knife to cut the excess dough off right around the edges. *You don't want a margin of pie dough around the edges, like for pastry pies, so cut as close to the filling as you can without exposing it.*

9. Brush the top with a thin coating of olive oil, then use the knuckles of your fingers to make indentations all over the pie like it's a focaccia. These little divots are where the cumin-chile oil will settle. Crack a few turns of black pepper on the surface.

10. Place the sheet pan *directly on the very bottom of the oven* and bake for 15 minutes to crisp up the bottom. Then switch the oven to the top broiler on high and transfer the sheet pan to the upper to mid-level rack and bake for 6 to 8 minutes, until golden brown and crispy on top.

11. Let the pie rest for 5 minutes, then brush the cumin-chile oil generously all over the top. Sprinkle with chopped mint and serve immediately.

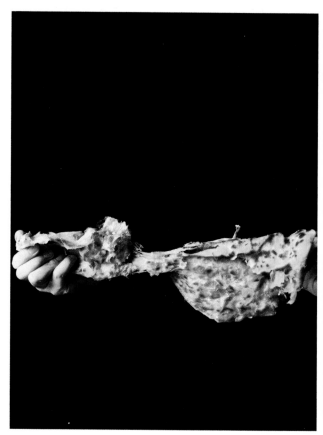

CHEWY LAYERED PARATHA

Here's another great use for and variation on Asian hot water dough. Some may know this type of layered flatbread as lachha paratha from India, or dabing from China, but here within my tender heart, it will always be known as my baby unicorn.

Behold, my culinary holy grail.

I'm not exaggerating. For as long as I've thought about food, I've been relentlessly after the secret of what makes this type of flatbread so incredibly crispy outside, with its wing-like lace, and so satisfyingly chewy and stringy inside, with its many completely separated, almost translucent layers. Many recipes out there produce a flatbread with one or the other quality, but I think that missing either of them renders it utterly trash. A few years ago, when I thought I'd gotten it right, I even published a recipe for flatbread on my blog. But in hindsight, it was close but not perfect.

What was missing? The hot water dough method.

My old recipe (which I called "layered roti") featured a dough that was too wet and too elastic, making it very hard to work with. And this is where the hot water dough method shines the brightest. It yields a dough that has a relatively low water content yet isn't tough. It removes some of the excess gluten, so it's a cinch to roll out yet still chewy at the end. And you can make small adjustments to it to adapt it for different applications. For example, because we're aiming for more chewiness in this dough, I'm switching out half of the all-purpose flour with bread flour. And because bread flour has a higher water absorbency than all-purpose, we need to add a tad bit more water than the previous recipe calls for. You see how it works?

To be frank, getting this recipe to exactly how I wanted it was already like, dude, my work here is done. *But just for the sake of a bonus, it is served with a tapenade-infused, savory whipped cream. I know.*

MAKES THREE 12-INCH PARATHAS

SPECIAL EQUIPMENT: *stand mixer or handheld mixer with dough hook and whisk attachments*

LAYERED PARATHA

(I strongly recommend measuring by weight)

1⅔ cups (227 g) bread flour

1¾ cups (219 g) all-purpose flour

2 teaspoons (8 g) light brown sugar

1¼ teaspoons (8 g) fine sea salt

1¼ cups (297 g) hot water at 130° to 140°F/55° to 60°C

6 tablespoons (78 g) canola oil

Olive oil, for cooking

TAPENADE WHIPPED CREAM

½ cup pitted green olives, drained well

2 anchovy fillets in oil, drained

Zest of ½ lemon

1 garlic clove, peeled

2 tablespoons Caramelized Onion Powder Paste (page 22)

1½ teaspoons capers, drained well

1 teaspoon Dijon mustard

¼ teaspoon freshly ground black pepper

½ cup heavy whipping cream

½ teaspoon fish sauce

FOR SERVING

My Ultimate Chile Oil (page 24; optional)

MAKE THE DOUGH

1. You must use a stand mixer or handheld mixer with a dough hook for this recipe to develop the kind of body this dough needs. If you don't have an electric mixer, I really wouldn't waste my time, unless you have the perseverance to knead a very sticky dough vigorously for 45 minutes to achieve the same result. In that case you have my full blessing.

2. In a bowl, using a stand mixer or handheld mixer with a dough hook, combine the bread and all-purpose flours, brown sugar, and salt. Microwave 1½ cups (355 g) of water on high for 1 minute 30 seconds to bring it up to 130° to 140°F/55° to 60°C (please measure with a thermometer to be sure), then add 1¼ cups (297 g—again, I urge you to measure by weight) to the flour mixture. Start kneading on low speed. When a dough has formed, turn to medium-high speed and knead for 10 to 13 minutes. The dough will appear to be wet and sticky at first, but in the end it should pull away completely from the sides and bottom of the bowl when the machine's running and stick right back when the machine stops. It should appear extremely smooth and shiny, sticky to the touch. Adjust with more warm water or flour to get it right if needed. Cover the bowl and let the dough rest at room temperature for at least 2 hours before using.

FORM THE PARATHA

3. Transfer the dough onto a well-floured surface and divide it into 3 equal portions. (Cooking portions this size will require a flat, nonstick 12-inch [30-cm] skillet; if yours is smaller, divide the dough into 4 portions instead.) Dusting with flour as needed to prevent

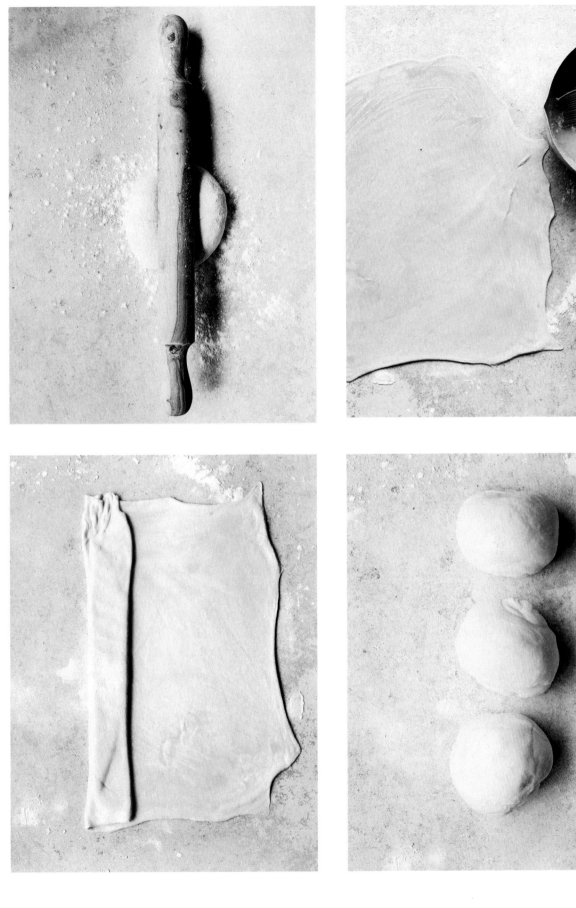

sticking, roll out one portion of the dough to a rough circle that's thin and 13 inches (33 cm) wide. The shape doesn't have to be perfect. Brush a generous layer of canola oil over the top, *extending all the way to the edges* (you'll need about 2 tablespoons for each portion of dough). Starting from one side, fold over the dough in 1½-inch (4-cm) increments, squeezing out any large air pockets as you go. When you have a long folded strip, fold it the other way in 1½-inch (4-cm) increments into a thick folded cube. Cover the ball with plastic wrap and repeat with the other dough portions. Let rest for 30 minutes.

MAKE THE TAPENADE WHIPPED CREAM

4. While the dough rests, in a food processor, combine the olives, anchovies, lemon zest, garlic, Caramelized Onion Powder Paste, capers, mustard, and black pepper. Pulse and run the machine until the mixture is finely ground, then set aside in a bowl.

5. With a stand mixer or handheld mixer with a whisk attachment, whip the heavy cream until soft peaks form. Fold the whipped cream and fish sauce into the olive mixture. Set aside.

ROLL AND COOK THE PARATHA

6. Dust one dough cube with flour. Set it between the palms of your hands, squeeze it, pause for a few seconds, and squeeze again to gently form it into a ball. Roll the ball out into a thin circle about 12 inches (30 cm) wide (or to the size of your skillet, as noted above). Heat a large, flat, nonstick 12-inch (30-cm) skillet over medium-high heat. Brush a thin coating of olive oil on the skillet, then transfer the dough sheet to the skillet. Brush the dough with olive oil. In a minute or so, the paratha will start to inflate with large air bubbles, puffing up almost like a pita bread. This is the sign that you did everything right. Now you can flip the paratha, back and forth a few times as needed, and cook until both sides are golden brown and crispy.

7. Serve immediately with the tapenade whipped cream, onto which you can drizzle My Ultimate Chile Oil for added heat.

GOOEY CHEESE SOUP DUMPLINGS ON A LACY CRUST

About a twenty-minute walk or five-minute electric scooter ride away from our apartment in Beijing, nestled around an unseemly corner on a narrow street that runs anonymously and parallel to a small city canal, there stands alone as a beacon a brightly lit two-story building that is one of Taiwan's successful restaurant franchises, Ding Tai Feng.

Ding Tai Feng is, of course, known for its world-famous soup dumplings, which are at least partially responsible if not crucial for soup dumplings' rapid rise and confirmed status in the international food scene. Whether the restaurant's location in Beijing was a random happy coincidence or evidence of the existence of a merciful higher power, I accepted this blessing with full gratitude and without reservation. Among the many scattered gastronomical refuges in this oppressive city, we probably visited Ding Tai Feng the most.

The restaurant is famous for a reason. The quality of soup dumplings at large is volatile at best, ranging from mediocre stumps of heavy dough and solid filling to transcendent hot juice pouches with fabric-thin wrappers and flooded centers. And the defining reason that Ding Tai Feng is a consistent representative of the platonic ideal soup dumpling lies in the engineering of its highly guarded secret dough.

Yes, a hot water dough.

Hot water dough allows the wrappers to be soft yet resilient, refined but not fragile; they will hold their fluid content with the maximum delicate sensitivity without breaking. Try using a normal dumpling wrapper, which is made with cold water, and you'll find your soup dumplings overly tough and stiff after steaming.

Since we now agree that hot water doughs are simple to make, I'm taking the liberty of including one more step in this recipe: adding flavors to the wrapping.

People don't typically worry about flavor when it comes to dumpling wrappers, which is why they can sometimes be pretty plain. Many modern adaptations start by adding coloring and whatnots to introduce more excitement, but for this one I want to go back to the simplest of human cravings: yeast. Soup dumpling wrappers must be unleavened, but that doesn't mean that we can't incorporate a small amount of cooked poolish (fermented bread starter) in the mix. The cooking kills the yeast, halting the fermentation process and preventing any rise, but still gives the dough a faintly bread-like aroma. Is it necessary? Naaaeeh . . . possibly not. But Ding Tai Feng certainly does it. So please indulge my finicky obsession with the important goal of a perfect soup dumpling dough.

When it comes to fillings, most of you already know that the soup inside soup dumplings is a result of mixing stock aspic (high in gelatin and thus solid at cool temperatures and liquid at high temperatures) into the ground meat, a technique that is ingenious and unsurpassable. But the downside of it is that it requires forging a highly gelatinous and concentrated stock, which takes hours if not days to be rendered, strained, and chilled. Therefore, I'm opting for the next best thing, a ready-made substance that is naturally solid at low temperature, but beautifully fluid in high heat: cheese.

More gooey than soupy, these dumplings are molten pockets of an assortment *of cheeses interspersed with ground pork and contained only by a thin, delicate cocoon of a wrapper. You can steam them, of course, but I took another liberty, awarding them with a shattering bottom layer of Parmigiano-Reggiano crust by cooking them in a skillet. Even if a rogue dumpling does take the path to eruption—the cardinal yet unavoidable sin of the soup dumpling religion—the accident joins the bottom crust and repents by transforming into crispy cheese. Sir, I rest my case.*

MAKES ABOUT 30 DUMPLINGS

SPECIAL EQUIPMENT: *stand mixer with a dough hook or handheld mixer with a dough hook; 1 wooden skewer*

DOUGH *(I strongly recommend measuring by weight)*

2 teaspoons (10 g) water

½ teaspoon (2 g) instant dry yeast

½ teaspoon (1 g) plus 1¾ cups plus 2 tablespoons (235 g) all-purpose flour, plus more as needed

½ teaspoon (3 g) fine sea salt

½ cup (115 g) hot water at 130°F/55°C

GOOEY CHEESE AND PORK FILLING

2 ounces (60 g) sliced prosciutto

½ pound (220 g) pork shoulder, cut into small chunks

1 shallot, peeled and roughly chopped

½ teaspoon grated ginger

1 teaspoon fish sauce

¼ teaspoon ground white pepper

⅛ teaspoon light brown sugar

3 tablespoons cold chicken stock

4 ounces (120 g) young (not aged) Gouda, cut into ¼-inch (0.5-cm) dice

½ cup (3.5 ounces/100 g) cream cheese

4 ounces (120 g) Brie, rind removed

FLOUR WATER

(per batch of 6 dumplings cooked in an 8-inch/20-cm skillet)

3 tablespoons water

1 tablespoon grated Parmigiano-Reggiano cheese

1½ teaspoons all-purpose flour

1 generous teaspoon olive oil

DIPPING SAUCE *(per batch of 6 dumplings)*

1 tablespoon balsamic vinegar

1 tablespoon finely grated ginger

MAKE THE DOUGH

1. In a small microwave-safe bowl, whisk the water, yeast, and the ½ teaspoon (1 g) flour. Cover the bowl and let it sit for 2 hours, until the mixture is very foamy and smells sour and fermented. Microwave on high in 5-second intervals, whisking twice in between, for a total of 15 seconds, until the mixture has thickened to a mayonnaise consistency.

2. In a bowl, using a stand mixer or handheld mixer with a dough hook, combine the yeast mixture, the 1¾ cups plus 2 tablespoons (235 g) flour, and salt. Microwave 1 cup (230 g) of water on high for about 1 minute to bring it to 130°F/55°C (measure it with a thermometer), then pour ½ cup (115 g) of the hot water evenly over the flour mixture.

3. Mix on low speed until a cohesive dough forms, then knead on high for 5 to 6 minutes,

until the dough is very elastic and smooth. The dough should completely pull away from the sides and bottom of the bowl while the machine is running. It should feel soft and tacky but shouldn't stick to your hands. If it feels too wet, knead in more flour to adjust. Wrap the bowl with plastic wrap and let rest for at least 2 hours.

MAKE THE GOOEY CHEESE AND PORK FILLING

4. In a food processor, grind the prosciutto into a paste. Add the pork shoulder, shallot, ginger, fish sauce, white pepper, and brown sugar and pulse until the pork is finely ground. Turn the food processor to run continuously, then use the feeding hole to pour in the chicken stock, 1 tablespoon at a time, until the mixture is smooth. Transfer the mixture to a large bowl and set aside.

5. No need to clean the processor. Add the Gouda, cream cheese, and Brie and run until evenly blended. Add the cheese mixture to the pork mixture and mix with a large spoon until evenly incorporated. Cover the bowl in plastic wrap and chill in the fridge for at least 2 hours.

MAKE THE DUMPLINGS
(SEE NOTE ON PAGE 202)

6. Break off and discard the pointy tip of a wooden skewer so it's about 4 inches (10 cm) long. Grab one-third of the dough (cover the rest) and tear off pieces that are about 1 tablespoon in volume. Toss them lightly in flour to prevent sticking.

7. Using your palm, press 1 piece of dough into a thick disk. Dust well with flour, then roll it into a thin wrapper about 3½ inches (9 cm) wide. It doesn't matter if it's perfectly round. Place a scant 1 tablespoon of the filling in the center and insert the wooden skewer gently into the center of the filling *without touching the bottom dough.* Bring the edges of the wrapper upward over the filling and wrap them in folds around the skewer. When the filling is fully enclosed, pinch the dough around the skewer with one hand, and twist and turn the dumpling with another to tighten the dumpling. Using two fingers, pinch against the skewer where the peak of the dumpling is and continue to twist the skewer until the excess dough breaks off from the dumpling. Finally, pull the skewer away. Set the dumpling on a sheet pan dusted with flour.

8. This easy technique leaves a hole at the peak of the dumpling where steam can escape during cooking, preventing eruption. If there's no steam hole after you pull out the skewer, poke a hole. Repeat making dumplings until you run out of filling and dough.

9. *You cannot keep the dumplings at room temperature or in the fridge for a prolonged period of time because the filling will sodden the wrapper, making it mushy.* So unless you're planning a restaurant-style production line (cooking the dumplings as fast as you're making them), I would highly suggest freezing them before use. Just wrap a full pan of dumplings in plastic wrap and freeze until hard. (You can keep them up to

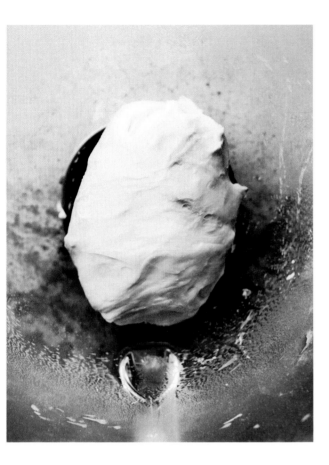

1 week in the freezer; they can be taken off the sheet pan and kept frozen in a plastic bag, but be sure to treat them very gently.)

TO FINISH

10. For a single batch of 6 dumplings at a time, I like to use an 8-inch (20-cm) *nonstick* skillet because I get more even heating that way. But depending on your situation, you can use a large *nonstick* skillet. If so, you should increase the amount of flour water accordingly. In a small cup whisk the water, Parmigiano-Reggiano, and flour in a small cup and set aside. Heat an 8-inch (20-cm) *nonstick* skillet over medium heat. Drizzle 1 generous teaspoon of olive oil into the pan, then arrange 6 dumplings in the pan. The dumplings should sizzle a bit when they hit the skillet. Pour the flour water into the skillet, then close the lid. Cook for about 7 minutes, until the bubbling sound of boiling water starts to subside. Remove the skillet from the heat and check to see if the crust in the pan is evenly browned. If not, reposition the skillet to brown the crust evenly.

11. Meanwhile, mix the balsamic vinegar and ginger to make the dipping sauce.

12. With a narrow spatula, loosen the bottom crust from the skillet, then slide the dumplings out of the skillet onto a plate. Serve immediately with the dipping sauce.

NOTE ON MAKING DUMPLINGS: *I don't mean to plug my blog here, but in the archive of ladyandpups.com under "Buffalo wing soup dumplings," there is a video showing how to shape and form the dumplings using the skewer trick. So watch it if the text alone does not do it for you.*

NAKED THAI DUCK SAUSAGE BUN

Thai sausage is a marvel on its own, to be commemorated for its audacity to not give a fuck and stick to its own path. It doesn't follow the general rules of sausage around the globe, which pursue the bounciness that is the emulsification of fat, protein, and liquid. Instead, Thai sausage forges a unique and direct passage toward deliciousness by adhering to a near half herbs—half meat ratio, creating a tribe of sausages that are almost fibrous in texture but drop a bomb of flavors, sensations, and delirious joy in your mouth. Some Thai sausages are even fermented and acidic.

Here we are making a cop-out version, neither fermented nor even encased—what I call a "naked" sausage. The appeal of this is, of course, the lack of need to deal with casings, both the acquiring of and the stuffing into, and also that these sausages are preshaped, precooked, and ready to be rocking and rolling in a searing skillet like golden caramelized tubes of glory.

You might be inclined to try swapping pork in place of the skin-on duck breasts, but the duck fat from the skin, both throughout the sausages and in the rendered bits that come in contact with the hot skillet, is what makes this sausage so moist, soft, and flavorful. So don't.

Here you might wonder, Without a casing, this might as well be a patty, no? *Okay, fine, go ahead.*

MAKES 4 XL SAUSAGES OR 6 HOT DOG-SIZE SAUSAGES

SPECIAL EQUIPMENT: *immersion blender, or stone mortar and pestle, or fine cheese grater like a Microplane*

NAKED THAI DUCK SAUSAGE

1 tablespoon Thai shrimp paste (see page 8)

5 lemongrass stalks, tender white parts only, finely diced

2½ inches (6.3 cm) of galangal (or if unavailable, ginger), finely diced (about 3 tablespoons)

1 tablespoon finely diced turmeric or 1 teaspoon ground turmeric

4 small shallots, peeled and roughly chopped

4 to 6 Pickled Chilies (page 25; see Note on page 206)

1 garlic clove, smashed

1 tablespoon fish sauce

1 tablespoon juice from Pickled Chilies (page 25)

1 pound (450 g, about 2 small) skin-on duck breasts

1½ tablespoons cornstarch

2 teaspoons Makrut Lime Leaf Oil (page 13)

½ teaspoon ground white pepper

½ teaspoon light brown sugar

GINGER MAYO

3 tablespoons mayonnaise

3 tablespoons Dijon mustard

3 tablespoons grated ginger

1 teaspoon Makrut Lime Leaf Oil (page 13)

TO ASSEMBLE

Olive oil, for cooking

Unsalted butter, for toasting

4 to 6 potato hot dog buns

1 large handful fresh mint leaves

Fried Chile Verde Sauce (page 15)

Lime wedges, for serving

Chile flakes, for serving

MAKE THE SAUSAGE

1. In a small skillet over medium heat, dry-toast the shrimp paste for 1 minute, scraping and turning with a spatula constantly, until it's slightly crumbly. In the tall cup that comes with your immersion blender, combine the toasted shrimp paste, lemongrass, galangal, turmeric, shallots, Pickled Chilies, garlic, fish sauce, and chile pickling juice. Use the immersion blender to blend until a fibrous paste has formed. (You can also use a traditional mortar and pestle to do this, but it will be a lot more time-consuming. If you don't have an immersion blender or a mortar and pestle, you can grate the lemongrass, galangal, and turmeric on a fine cheese grater and grate the shallots and garlic with a Microplane grater.)

2. If the duck breasts aren't already frozen, cut them into small chunks, then scatter them on a baking sheet and flash-freeze them for 30 minutes, until hardened (you won't be able to process the skin when it's soft, and the coldness improves the texture of the final result as well). If starting from frozen duck breasts, let them thaw just enough to cut them into chunks. Transfer the pieces of duck to a food processor and pulse until they are coarsely ground. Add the herb mixture, cornstarch, Makrut Lime Leaf Oil, white pepper, and brown sugar and run again until the mixture is finely ground. Transfer to a large bowl and divide into 4 portions for XL sausages or 6 portions for hot dog–size sausages.

3. Lay a large piece of plastic wrap on the counter and place a portion of the mixture in the middle. Fold the plastic wrap over the mixture as if you're closing a book, then hold down the seam side with one hand. With the other hand, use the straight edge of a pastry cutter to push and squeeze the mixture against the plastic wrap into a tightly packed tube (as seen in the left photo on page 206), then roll it inside the wrap until the wrap runs out. Hold the two ends of the wrapper in your hands, and roll the sausage on the counter until both wrapper ends are tightened into twists (as seen in the right photo on page 206). Wrap the sausage inside a piece of aluminum foil and again twist the ends to close (this keeps the plastic wrap from unraveling during cooking). Repeat to make the rest of the sausages.

4. Bring a large pot of water to boil. Add all the wrapped sausages and place a smaller lid over the top to keep the sausages submerged in water. Keeping the water at a simmer, cook for 8 minutes for the large sausages and 6 minutes for the small. Drain the sausages well but do not unwrap them.

5. Chill the sausages in a large bowl of iced water, or in the fridge for at least 4 hours, until completely cold. You can keep the wrapped sausages in the fridge for up to 3 days or up to 1 month in the freezer, but thaw them completely before using them.

MAKE THE GINGER MAYO

6. Whisk the mayonnaise, mustard, ginger, and Makrut Lime Leaf Oil until smooth. The ginger mayo may be made up to 2 days ahead and kept in an airtight container inside the fridge.

TO ASSEMBLE

7. Unwrap the sausages from the aluminum foil and plastic wrap. In a *nonstick* skillet over medium heat, add enough olive oil to generously coat the skillet. Cook the sausages until golden brown on all sides—and don't forget the tips as well.

8. Melt some butter in a large skillet over medium-high heat and toast the hot dog buns until crispy on the edges. Toss the mint leaves with a little Fried Chile Verde Sauce to coat them like a salad. Smear the insides of the buns generously with ginger mayo. Arrange a thin lining of mint salad in each bun and place a sausage in the middle. Serve with lime wedges and extra chile flakes (or Pickled Chilies) for heat.

NOTE ON CHILIES: *I like to use my pickled chilies to add a dose of acidity to the mixture, but you can simply use chile flakes instead, or your favorite brand of pickled chilies.*

ITALIAN MEATBALLS IN TAIWANESE ROUZAO SAUCE

America has hamburgers. Japan has sushi. Italy has pasta. As shallow and generalizing as it is, in terms of a culinary ambassador that serves almost as a symbol of national identity, what does my homeland, Taiwan, have? If somebody says Taiwanese beef noodle soup one more time, I'm going to cry over my boba tea.

Rouzao, man. Rouzao is the shit.

Rou means "meat" and zao, believe it or not, means "parched." Two words that might not seem to make sense together, but in Taiwan they represent a sticky, gelatinous meat sauce made with pork belly and fried shallots. How is rouzao more monumental to Taiwanese cuisine than, say, the more commonly recognized beef noodle soup? Because Taiwanese foods will still stand with or without beef noodle soup, but if you pull rouzao out of the equation, the entire ecosystem will collapse into a sad pile of confused rubble. Why? Because rouzao is in everything. It's on rice, it's in noodles, it's used to season blanched vegetables—hell, it's even added to cakes! Think Italian cooking without tomatoes. Think Mexican cooking without corn. Think The Notebook without Ryan Gosling.

I'm utterly incapable of being impartial about rouzao—and specifically rouzao fan, which is rouzao on rice, aka lurou fan. You hover a bowl of that stuff in front of my face and I'm hardwired to react, salivate, and secrete adrenaline, a response so ingrained in my being that I can't tell if it's nature or nurture. Which is why I'm including a recipe in this book as a social experiment. Tell me—it's not just me, right?

But look, I know how hard it can be to convince people to cook something they're unfamiliar with. Therefore, I'm deploying one of my tactics for incentivizing anyone to make anything . . . and that is to turn it into meatball form.

Okay, Taiwanese people who are about to skewer me on a spike, settle down, because I'm not even done with my treason yet. To push my sacrilegious sedition even further, it's an Italian-style meatball pumped with intensified porkiness from coarsely ground guanciale and a banknote of Parmigiano cheese for complexity. Flavorwise, it still embodies all the mesmerizing seduction of a traditional rouzao, the essence of which comes from fried shallots, and this recipe has a ton, and I mean a ton. But instead of a pot of ambiguous brownness, it now parades in the form of melty meatballs that collapse under the slightest pressure of a spoon, surrounded by the disintegrated fried shallots in a gravy of soy sauce and molasses and aroma-infused lard, as it all rampages through every nook and cranny of a bowl of hot, steamed sushi rice. And to cut through all the heavy-hitting richness, it's accompanied by a few sweet and tangy tea-soaked prunes.

If you still want to nail me to a cross, well, let me finish eating this first.

MAKES 21 MEATBALLS, TO SERVE 6 OR 7

TEA-SOAKED PRUNES

1 cup (240 mL) water

1½ tablespoons light brown sugar

1 teaspoon loose black tea or 1 black tea bag
(I prefer Assam)

1 star anise

2 whole cloves

1 small cinnamon stick

1 teaspoon sea salt

30 whole pitted prunes

MEATBALLS

3 ounces (90 g) guanciale or fatty pancetta, cut
into small chunks

2 pounds (900 g) ground pork

½ cup (25 g) panko breadcrumbs

Heaping ¼ cup (40 g) grated Parmigiano-
Reggiano cheese

2 large shallots, grated

1½ tablespoons potato starch or cornstarch (see
page 6)

1 tablespoon dark soy sauce

¾ teaspoon light brown sugar

BRAISING LIQUID

½ cup (120 mL) soy sauce

3 tablespoons (45 mL) Chinese rice wine or sake

2 tablespoons molasses

2½ cups (600 mL) water

1½ cups (75 g) Dry Fried Shallots (page 17; see
Note on page 210)

2 tablespoons fish sauce

1 tablespoon plain powdered gelatin (see Note
on page 210)

1 teaspoon ground white pepper

¼ teaspoon five-spice powder

¼ teaspoon ground cinnamon

FOR SERVING

Steamed short-grain white rice

MAKE THE TEA-SOAKED PRUNES

1. In a small saucepan, combine the water,
brown sugar, tea, star anise, cloves, cinnamon
stick, and sea salt. Bring to a simmer over
medium heat and cook for 5 minutes. Add the
prunes and simmer for 5 minutes more. Turn
off the heat and chill in the fridge for at least
2 hours before using but preferably overnight.
(The prunes can be made up to 2 weeks ahead of
time. They get even better.)

MAKE THE MEATBALLS

2. In a food processor, pulse the guanciale until
it is in small bitty pieces but *not ground*. Transfer
to a large bowl and add the pork, panko, cheese,
shallots, potato starch, soy sauce, and brown
sugar. Mix until evenly incorporated, then divide
the mixture into 3 equal parts. Divide each part
into 7 small meatballs. Toss each meatball back
and forth in your hands to make sure it's *firmly
packed*. Set aside.

MAKE THE STEW

3. Preheat the oven to 320°F/155°C.

4. In a large *nonstick* skillet over medium-
high heat, brown the meatballs until deeply
caramelized all around. (There's no need to
add oil because the meatballs themselves will
produce enough fat.) Add the soy sauce, rice
wine, and molasses and cook, swirling the

meatballs in the liquid, until the meatballs are glazed and the liquid is slightly thickened.

5. Transfer everything to a large clay pot (or any pot that has good heat-retaining properties, like a cast-iron pot or Dutch oven). Gently mix in the water, fried shallots, fish sauce, gelatin, white pepper, five-spice powder, and cinnamon and bring the mixture to a simmer over medium-high heat.

6. You want to reduce the amount of moisture lost in the oven as much as possible, so if the lid of your pot has a steam hole, *place a piece of parchment paper on top of the pot*. Cover with the lid, transfer the pot to the oven, and bake for 2 hours, until the meatballs break at the slightest pressure. (You can also cook the meatballs over low heat on the stove, but you'll have to come back frequently to scrape the bottom to prevent burning, so I prefer the oven.)

7. This part of the recipe can be made up to 3 days ahead of time (in fact, I encourage it). Reheat slowly over low heat before serving.

8. By the way, you'll notice a thick layer of fat floating on the surface of the dish. I really urge you *not* to skim off the fat, or at least to keep most of it, because this is supposed to be a rich dish. The flavor-packed lard is a key factor in giving the rice an almost voluptuous body and texture.

TO SERVE

9. Ladle the meatballs and the sauce over steamed short-grain rice. Serve with the tea-soaked prunes.

NOTE ON FRIED SHALLOTS: *You cannot make rouzao without fried shallots. Nope. Can't do. You can use a little effort to make your own (see page 17), or use store-bought if available (usually found in Chinese or Southeast Asian supermarkets). Believe me, they're worth it.*

NOTE ON GELATIN: *Traditionally this dish is made with skin-on pork belly that is cut into very small pieces. The skin gives the sauce that sticky richness, which is crucial to the proper success of this recipe. So since the meatballs do not contain skin, we add unflavored gelatin to make up for it.*

THAI LAAP-STYLE PASSION FRUIT—SHRIMP CEVICHE

There's a general ambivalence toward passion fruit that troubles me. As an acidic fruit, its intense fragrance, pervasive and peerless, it is somehow outgunned by minor-league citruses such as lemon and lime on the world stage. In Mandarin the name for passion fruit is "hundred fragrance fruit," and how fitting, as the exquisite makeup of its aroma cannot be described by a single idea.

Then, as an antioxidant-rich superfood, it is somehow tucked behind the grossly overrated pomegranate, which is equally seedy if not more so, if you're factoring that in, but more important, boring-tasting in comparison.

This neglect is strange. And what a shame: a top-tier fruit, left utterly alone in greatness.

I say this with a sincere agenda to repent. Because I, too, have only recently begun to notice and appreciate passion fruit's versatile and transformative quality in orchestrating flavors, both in sweet and savory dishes. Its vibrantly yellow and wildly perfumey flesh makes a great case for dishes that call for intensity as well as refreshment. And in this recipe, it is a matchmaker, even a bridge between three dishes: Thai laap, a meat-based salad flourishing with Southeast Asian herbs like lemongrass, galangal, mint, and cilantro; goong che nam pa, a Thai raw shrimp appetizer, a carpaccio if you will, that is deluged with a fiery, sour, and garlicky fish sauce dressing that will blow your head off; and last, ceviche, seafood "cooked" by acidity instead of heat and tossed with various aromatics and herbs as a cooling summery delight.

The merging of these three dishes is logical and smooth, a teeming festival of fragrances, flavors, and textures, with the contrasting crunch of broken passion fruit seeds and toasted cornflakes. At the end, I opened the last passion fruit I had on hand and ate it by the spoonful, squinting at the pleasure of its piercing sourness up front and the wondrously permeating aroma that follows. Makes me wonder if maybe you don't even need this recipe. Just eat a passion fruit, man.

MAKES 6 APPETIZER SERVINGS

SPECIAL EQUIPMENT: *immersion blender (preferred); mortar and pestle or rolling pin*

SHRIMP MARINADE

12 ounces (340 g) small (51 to 60 count) fresh raw peeled shrimp (see Note on page 213)

½ cup (120 mL) freshly squeezed lemon juice

2 passion fruits

4 garlic cloves, peeled

2 teaspoons grated peeled galangal (or if unavailable, ginger)

2 tablespoons fish sauce, plus more to adjust

½ teaspoon light brown sugar

¼ teaspoon ground white pepper

TOASTED CORNFLAKES

¼ cup cornflakes

2 lemongrass stalks, tender white parts only

2 shallots, thinly shaved or sliced

5 or 6 makrut lime leaves, lightly bruised with a knife to release their fragrance

4 or 5 Pickled Chilies (page 25), finely chopped

3 tablespoons roughly chopped fresh mint

3 tablespoons roughly chopped fresh cilantro

3 tablespoons finely diced scallions

1 teaspoon Makrut Lime Leaf Oil (page 13)

MARINATE THE SHRIMP

1. With a small knife, make a deep slit along the back of each shrimp without cutting through, butterflying it, if you will. Remove the vein, if any. Place the cleaned shrimp in a bowl as you work. Drain the bowl well, then add the lemon juice. Press a piece of plastic wrap on the shrimp to keep them submerged. Marinate in the fridge for 25 to 30 minutes; this will "cook" the shrimp in the lemon juice by 50 percent, leaving them half cooked and half raw.

2. While the shrimp are marinating, cut the passion fruits in half and scoop out all the seeds and juices into a blender or the tall cup that comes with your immersion blender. Add the garlic, galangal, fish sauce, brown sugar, and white pepper and blend until the passion fruit seeds are little black specks. Drain off all the lemon juice from the shrimp, then add the passion fruit mixture. Marinate again for 10 minutes.

MAKE THE TOASTED CORNFLAKES

3. Pound the cornflakes in a mortar and pestle until finely crushed (or crush them with a rolling pin). Toast them in a dry skillet over medium-low heat, stirring or swirling the skillet frequently, until evenly browned. Set aside.

TO FINISH

4. Slice the tender white parts of the lemongrass as thinly as humanly possible, then transfer them to a large bowl. Add the shallots, makrut lime leaves, pickled chilies, mint, cilantro, and scallions. Add the shrimp and all the passion fruit liquid, then toss until combined. Season with more fish sauce if needed. Transfer to a serving plate, then drizzle Makrut Lime Leaf Oil evenly on top and sprinkle with toasted cornflakes. Serve immediately.

NOTE ON SHRIMP: *Use small shrimp for this recipe because medium and large ones can be too chewy. If you are not comfortable eating or are unable to source fresh raw shrimp, you can skip the first step. Marinate the shrimp with a bit of fish sauce, then cook them in a skillet until opaque and cooked through. Cool, then proceed with the next step.*

PIZZA

Pizza has the potential to be Italy's ramen, a democratic arena
of creativity, progressivism, and tolerance, if only the Italians
could just chill the fuck out about it. Is it really pizza?
Who says so, and who cares? Neither the tomato itself nor
baking stuff on top of a fermented dough was an original
Italian idea, and if the Italians from a few hundred years
ago were dumb enough to give a shit about that, then
there wouldn't even be such a thing as pizza today.
All the dishes we eat today were fusion at some point in
history. And to say that this progression should stop and freeze
at an arbitrary point for the sake of national pride is both
dangerous and dumb-sounding.

TOM YUM MARGHERITA PIZZA

This profoundly fragrant tomato sauce, inspired by tom yum, the spicy and sour soup from Thailand, makes for a sultry version of the classic pizza margherita. Southeast Asian herbs like lemongrass, galangal, and makrut lime leaves integrate so incredibly well with tomatoes that I imagine if a large influx of migrants from Thailand were ever to settle in Italy (or vice versa), this pairing would be inevitable.

If you don't already have a jar of homemade shrimp and chile coconut oil on hand, there are many shrimp- or dried shrimp—based chile sauces that you can find in Asian supermarkets and use as a substitute. I can't say that every single one of them will be marvelous, but I also can't imagine why they wouldn't be.

MAKES TWO 12-INCH (30-CM) PIZZAS

SPECIAL EQUIPMENT: *pizza stone, large flat cast-iron griddle (what I typically use), or heavy pizza pan; pizza peel*

PIZZA DOUGH

1 recipe Pizza Dough (page 40)

Flour, for dusting the surface

Cornmeal, for dusting the pizza peel (optional)

TOM YUM TOMATO SAUCE

Two 14-ounce (400-g) cans peeled plum tomatoes

3 (2 ounces/58 g) lemongrass stalks, finely sliced

3 small shallots, peeled

2 makrut lime leaves, with the central stem removed

2½ tablespoons finely chopped galangal (or substitute 3 tablespoons chopped ginger)

2 tablespoons freshly squeezed lime juice

1 tablespoon light brown sugar

2 teaspoons fish sauce, plus more as desired

2 tablespoons extra-virgin olive oil

1 teaspoon Thai shrimp paste (see page 8)

½ teaspoon freshly ground black pepper

TOPPING

2 balls (4.5 ounces/125 g each) fresh mozzarella cheese

Pickled Chilies (page 25), finely diced

3 garlic cloves, thinly sliced

Shrimp and chile coconut oil (see page 258) or other Thai shrimp chile paste/oil

1 teaspoon Makrut Lime Leaf Oil (page 13)

1 tablespoon extra-virgin olive oil

Fresh Thai basil or mint leaves

1. Prepare the pizza dough 1 day ahead of time and refrigerate it until you need it.

MAKE THE TOM YUM TOMATO SAUCE

2. In a blender, combine the plum tomatoes and their juices, lemongrass, shallots, makrut lime leaves, galangal, lime juice, brown sugar, and fish sauce. Blend for a couple of minutes, until extremely smooth.

3. In a large saucepan over medium heat, combine the olive oil, Thai shrimp paste, and

black pepper. Cook, stirring with a wooden spoon, until the paste has disintegrated into the oil and has slightly browned. Add the tomato mixture, mix well, and partially cover the pot with a lid. Turn the heat to medium-low and simmer until the liquid has reduced by two-thirds into a thick tomato sauce. Season with more fish sauce if desired. This sauce can be made a couple of days ahead of time and kept in the fridge until needed.

BAKE THE PIZZA

4. Over the years, I've come to the conclusion that this is the best way to produce restaurant-style pizza in a home oven. Forty minutes before serving, set a baking rack 2 to 3 inches (5 to 8 cm) below the broiler. Preheat the empty oven to 500°F/260°C. After the oven is preheated, turn the top broiler on high.

5. While the oven is preheating, transfer one ball of the pizza dough to a well-floured surface and dust with more flour on top to prevent sticking. Use the knuckles on your fingers to gently and slowly dent the dough, pushing and spreading it from the center outward until it's about 13 inches (33 cm) wide (it will shrink a bit during cooking). Think of it as if you're pushing the air bubbles outward and concentrating them on the outer rim of the pizza. If you're like me

and like a pizza with a really puffed, bubbled, and chewy rim, then leave the rim slightly thicker than the rest of the dough. If the dough is resisting and springing back too much, just let it rest for another 5 to 10 minutes and continue.

6. Arrange the dough into a disk on a pizza peel dusted with flour or cornmeal. Spread a layer of tom yum tomato sauce over the dough, leaving a thin margin of bare dough on the edge. Break the mozzarella into small chunks and spread them evenly over the sauce, then sprinkle finely diced pickled chilies (I use about 2 or 3 per pizza) and thinly sliced garlic (about 1½ garlic cloves per pizza) evenly on top.

7. Heat a pizza stone, large flat cast-iron griddle (what I typically use), or heavy pizza pan on the burner over high heat, *until it starts to smoke slightly*. Gently slide the pizza onto the hot stone/griddle/pan and transfer the hot stone/griddle/pan onto the baking rack below the broiler. Bake until the pizza is puffed, golden, and charred in some spots, about 8 minutes, watching carefully.

8. While the pizza is in the oven, mix the Makrut Lime Leaf Oil and olive oil. Set aside.

9. Prep and bake the second pizza.

TO SERVE

10. Drizzle 1 to 2 tablespoons shrimp and chile coconut oil (or other chile paste/oil) on each pizza, followed by 2 teaspoons of the Makrut Lime Leaf Oil mixture for fragrance. Top with torn Thai basil or mint leaves, if using, and serve immediately.

PIZZA TONNATO WITH CHINESE PANCETTA

I lied. There's no tuna, or tonnato *in Italian, here. I don't actually eat tuna, for the same reason that I believe we, as a sentient species, should at least strive to be marginally more civilized than locusts and not eat another species to total extinction. So please, try.*

But the reason I'm calling this pizza tonnato—other than that it sounds nice—is that it's entirely inspired by an Italian dish called vitello tonnato, *featuring a mayonnaise-like sauce made with canned tuna that goes* majestically *with meat. And since I don't do tuna, I've swapped in canned mackerel, smoothly pureed into a creamy sauce highlighted by capers, mustard, shallots, and ginger. I know, I know, at a glance, none of this sounds promising. Mayonnaise made with canned mackerel? On pizza? And with what, Chinese pancetta?*

You can walk away, like I care. I mean, this pizza is so good that it's very self-assured. But before you go: lap yuk *is Chinese-style cured pork belly common in the south of China and Hong Kong and easily found in Chinatowns or Asian groceries anywhere else. Why not use Italian pancetta? Lap yuk is cured in sugar, soy sauce, and rice wine, then hung to dry, giving it a much sweeter flavor profile and a prominent fragrance of rice wine. Believe it or not, it works more marvelously than pancetta in this recipe, emanating a deeply porky aroma and a stronger presence against the also assertive mackerel sauce. But that's not all. Here the lap yuk is sliced paper-thin and reprocessed, pressed in layers of chile flakes and dried oregano.*

And in case I need to remind you, this type of fish-based sauce goes majestically *with meat. Especially, yes, pork, and even more especially,* pork fat.

So here's what you're getting: When the oven heat hits, the sweet fat of the lap yuk sizzles and fries the chile flakes, then descends as a stream of spicy pork fat with an almost cinnamony aroma. The mackerel sauce collapses and the lap yuk crisps, as the crust holds what is a mildly fishy (in the best sense, think tuna sandwich) and garlicky wet bed crinkled with sweet, spicy, rendered pork bits. Walk away, like I care.

MAKES TWO 12-INCH (30-CM) PIZZAS

SPECIAL EQUIPMENT: *pizza stone, large flat cast-iron griddle (what I typically use), or heavy pizza pan; pizza peel*

PIZZA DOUGH

1 recipe Pizza Dough (page 40)

Flour, for dusting the surface

Cornmeal, for dusting the pizza peel (optional)

CHINESE PANCETTA/LAP YUK

1.4 pounds (100 g) Chinese lap yuk/Chinese cured pork belly (see Note on page 222)

3 tablespoons chile flakes

1½ tablespoons dried oregano

MACKEREL MAYONNAISE

Two 0.9-ounce (125-g) cans mackerel in olive oil (I use Waitrose sustainable)

Extra-virgin olive oil, as needed

¼ cup (60 g) store-bought mayonnaise

1 large egg yolk

1 tablespoon Dijon mustard

2 teaspoons rice vinegar

½ teaspoon ground white pepper

¼ cup (60 mL) heavy cream

2 small shallots, peeled

1½ tablespoons capers, drained

2 teaspoons grated ginger

1 teaspoon fish sauce

TOPPING

3 garlic cloves, thinly spliced

Freshly ground black pepper

Extra-virgin olive oil

Grated Parmigiano-Reggiano cheese

1. Prepare the pizza dough 1 day ahead of time and refrigerate it until you need it.

MAKE THE CHINESE PANCETTA

2. With a sharp knife, remove the skin from the lap yuk, then slice it lengthwise like strips of bacon but *as thinly as humanly possible* (if using guanciale, ask the butcher to slice it thinly like prosciutto for you). Mix the chile flakes and dried oregano, then scatter a thin and even layer on a large piece of parchment paper. Place a single layer of sliced lap yuk on top, then sprinkle another layer of chile flakes and oregano on the lap yuk, then top with another layer of lap yuk, and so on and so forth. Cover with another piece of parchment paper, fold it like you're packaging deli meat, and let it cure in the fridge for at least 1 day or up to 1 week, until needed.

MAKE THE MACKEREL MAYONNAISE

3. Drain the olive oil from both cans into a measuring cup (set the drained mackerels aside). You should have about ¼ cup of oil, but if not, make up the difference with extra-virgin olive oil.

4. In a blender, combine the mayonnaise, egg yolk, mustard, rice vinegar, and white pepper. With the machine running, slowly drizzle in the ¼ cup oil through the feeding hole. You should have a loose mayonnaise in the blender. Scrape the sides and bottom, then add the reserved mackerels, cream, shallots, capers, ginger, and fish sauce. Blend until smoothly pureed. You can make the sauce a day ahead and keep it in an airtight jar in the fridge.

5. Forty minutes before serving, set a baking rack 2 to 3 inches (5 to 8 cm) below the broiler. Preheat the empty oven to 500°F/260°C. After the oven is preheated, turn the top broiler on high.

6. While the oven is preheating, transfer one ball of the pizza dough to a well-floured surface and dust with more flour on top to prevent sticking. Use the knuckles on your fingers to gently and slowly dent the dough, pushing and spreading it from the center outward until it's about 13 inches (33 cm) wide (it will shrink a bit during cooking). Think of it as if you're pushing the air bubbles outward and concentrating them on the outer rim of the pizza. If you're like me and like a pizza with a really puffed, bubbled, and chewy rim, then leave the rim slightly thicker than the rest of the dough. If the dough is resisting and springing back too much, just let it rest for another 5 to 10 minutes and continue.

7. Arrange the dough into a disk on a pizza peel dusted with flour or cornmeal. Spread a layer of mackerel mayonnaise on top, as you would with tomato sauce, leaving a thin margin on the edge. Twirl and drape 4 or 5 slices of lap yuk over the mayo and sprinkle thinly sliced garlic evenly all over (about 1½ cloves per pizza). Crack a few turns of freshly ground black pepper over the pizza as well.

8. Heat a pizza stone, large flat cast-iron griddle (what I typically use), or heavy pizza pan on the burner over high heat, *until it starts to smoke slightly*. Gently slide the pizza onto the hot stone/griddle/pan and transfer the hot stone/griddle/pan onto the baking rack below the broiler. Bake until the pizza is puffed, golden, and charred in some spots, about 8 minutes, watching carefully.

9. Prep and bake the second pizza.

TO SERVE

10. Drizzle the pizzas generously with extra-virgin olive oil and shower with grated Parmigiano-Reggiano cheese. Serve immediately.

NOTE ON LAP YUK: *Lap yuk (Chinese cured pork belly) can be easily found in Chinese supermarkets and Chinatowns, usually hung with Chinese sausages. When buying lap yuk, choose one that has at least 50 percent distributed fat. If you cannot find lap yuk, try to find guanciale (cured pork jowl).*

BASTARDIZED HAINAN CHICKEN RICE

*Don't expect this to be like anything from your favorite Hainan chicken joint. One of the national prides of Singapore, Hainan chicken's integrity and authenticity are highly regarded and scrutinized, which is why I'm declaring yet again that this thing I'm making is **not** that. This is my bastard version, vile and misbegotten, and yet, for me, it delivers far more complexity and sustenance than one of more legitimate blood.*

It's my Jon Snow of chicken rice.

*You could say that with its charred skin, it doesn't even look like Hainan chicken, and the cooking method departs from the traditional stovetop poaching to a more precisely controllable slow-baked technique that yields unbelievably supple, silky, and juicy flesh. The bones will and should remain a shade of pink, which, if you haven't been properly informed, is the highly precise and intended doneness of this dish. But make no mistake about it—a person who keeps babbling solely about the chicken in chicken rice is someone who doesn't know chicken rice. It's not rice chicken. It's chicken **rice**. The rice is the point.*

Incredibly fragrant, glossed with chicken fat, and founded on the precious poaching broth, an elixir of pureed Southeast Asian herbs and rendered chicken juice, this green-hued rice exhales an aroma so haunting that it should be labeled as hazardous around people with carb-dependency issues. The equally important condiments are a hybrid of the classic ginger oil with sweet soy sauce and a more robust, forceful chile sambal made with fried shallots.

Note that the entire recipe can be prepared several hours ahead of time. Only the rice needs to be kept warm.

MAKES 4 LARGE OR 6 SMALL SERVINGS

SPECIAL EQUIPMENT: *blowtorch; immersion blender (preferred)*

CHICKEN

½ teaspoon plus 1½ teaspoons fine sea salt

1 small (around 2.6 pounds/1.2 kg) free-range chicken (weight without head or feet)

4 cups (1 L) chicken stock, plus more as needed

5 garlic cloves, smashed

3 lemongrass stalks, roughly cut

3 small shallots, peeled

3 makrut lime leaves

3 tablespoons roughly chopped galangal (or use ginger, but it won't be the same)

3 pandan leaves (see Note on page 229), roughly chopped, plus 1 whole leaf

¼ teaspoon ground white pepper

Canola oil or any flavorless vegetable oil

3½ cups (700 g) short-grain white rice

Two 2-inch (5-cm) slices of ginger

CONDIMENTS (ALL CAN BE MADE AHEAD)

Ginger Sauce (page 229)

Chile Sambal with Fried Shallots (page 229)
Sweet Soy Sauce (page 26)
Orange Chile Sambal (page 23; optional)
Fried Chile Verde Sauce (page 15; optional)

MAKE THE CHICKEN

1. Rub the ½ teaspoon of salt evenly over the skin of the chicken and let the chicken sit for 10 minutes on a large sheet pan. Use a toothpick to sew together the skin around the neck opening above the breasts (this protects the breast meat, which dries out easily). Set the sheet pan on the stove underneath the range hood and turn the vent fan on. With a blowtorch held a few inches away from the chicken, slowly render and brown the chicken skin all over. Be patient with this step, because you want the skin to be evenly caramelized (it won't be crispy) but not overly burned. To torch the entire chicken should take 10-plus minutes. Set aside. (This step is really for people with a phobia of white chicken skin. If you do not suffer from such a condition, you can omit this step. Instead, pour 4 cups [1 L] of boiling water evenly over the chicken skin and cavity, then rinse again under cold water.)

2. Preheat the oven to 300°F/150°C, with the fan off.

3. In a blender, blend the stock, garlic, lemongrass, shallots, makrut lime leaves, galangal, chopped pandan leaves, the remaining 1½ teaspoons sea salt, and the white pepper until coarsely pureed. Transfer to a pot or Dutch oven that is *just large enough to fit the entire chicken inside,* then bring the liquid to a simmer and cook for 5 minutes. Add the chicken (*reserve any chicken fat left on the sheet pan in a small bowl for cooking the rice*) and ladle the stock mixture over the chicken a few times.

4. Transfer the pot to the oven, uncovered. Roast the chicken for 60 to 65 minutes, *flipping it over every 15 minutes or so,* until the internal temperature of the inner thigh reads 173°F/78°C.

5. Drain the chicken, reserving the broth, and transfer it to a sheet pan. Use a pastry brush to gently brush away any herbs that are sticking on the skin, then wrap the chicken all around with plastic wrap. Submerge it into an ice bath until cooled completely (this stops the cooking and turns the internal juice into aspic, which is a signature trait of Hainan chicken), about 1 hour. Unwrap the chicken and brush a thin coating of canola oil all over it, then leave at room temperature *uncovered* until needed. You can prepare the chicken up to several hours ahead of time.

COOK THE RICE

6. Strain the chicken cooking broth through a fine sieve, pressing on the solids with a wooden spoon to extract as much liquid as possible; discard the solids. *Skim off the surface fat and add it to the reserved chicken fat from torching the chicken.*

7. Place the rice in a large sieve and rinse/wash under running water until the water runs clear. Wipe the original pot clean with a paper towel, then add the chicken fat and heat over medium-high heat. Add the ginger and cook until fragrant, then add the rice and cook, stirring constantly, for a few minutes, until it starts to stick to the pot. Add 3½ cups of the strained broth (if there's not enough, add more chicken stock to make 3½ cups) and the remaining whole pandan leaf and mix evenly.

8. If you have a large enough rice cooker, you can use it to cook the rice according to the manufacturer's instructions. If not, cover the pot with the lid and turn the heat down to *medium-low to low* (on a scale from 1 to 10, I would say about a 3). Cook for 35 minutes, *undisturbed,* then turn off the heat and let sit for 5 minutes. Open the lid and give it a stir (it's expected to have little burned crispy bits on the bottom, but leave them there), close the lid, and let sit for another 5 minutes.

TO SERVE

9. Serve the rice hot with the chicken at room temperature. You can choose to remove or keep the bones (many food stalls serve it boneless), but either way, cut the chicken in small pieces and serve with the condiments.

NOTE ON PANDAN LEAF: *Pandan leaf is a long, narrow, blade-like leaf that is widely used in Southeast Asian cooking—imperative even, if you ask me. It has a unique aroma that is hard to substitute with anything else. Try to find it in your Asian grocery stores or Chinatown, and when you do, buy a bunch and freeze them and you'll have enough for a long time to come.*

GINGER SAUCE

Ginger sauce is a classic, mandatory condiment that is served with Hainan chicken rice. Something as tested and time-honored as this isn't really asking for my opinion, but I have a feeling that it won't object to my adding fish sauce for complexity and a touch of Makrut Lime Leaf Oil for fragrance.

MAKES ½ CUP

SPECIAL EQUIPMENT: *immersion blender (preferred)*

6 tablespoons (90 g) peeled and roughly chopped ginger

¼ cup canola oil

1 tablespoon fish sauce

¾ teaspoon fine sea salt

½ teaspoon Makrut Lime Leaf Oil (page 13)

In a blender or using an immersion blender (my preference), blend the ginger, oil, fish sauce, and salt until smooth. In a small saucepan over medium heat, cook the mixture for about 5 minutes, stirring constantly, until the oil is completely separated from the chopped ginger. Stir in the Makrut Lime Leaf Oil. Let sit for at least 2 hours before using. Can be made a day ahead and kept at room temperature.

CHILE SAMBAL WITH FRIED SHALLOTS

This chile sauce classically has nothing to do with Hainan chicken rice. Absolutely nothing. And it came to me as a little knob of nothing on top of the roasted pig over rice (babi buling) we had in Bali. That was, until I put it in my mouth and decided that it should be the pope of a new religion in which meat is worshipped over rice. It, too, guarantees revelation.

MAKES ½ CUP

3 red jalapeños or 2 long red cayenne chilies, finely chopped

2 tablespoons canola oil

½ teaspoon rice vinegar

1 teaspoon fish sauce

¼ cup (56 g) Dry Fried Shallots (page 17)

In a small saucepan, combine the red jalapeños or red cayenne chilies, oil, vinegar, and fish sauce. Cook over low heat for about 10 minutes, stirring constantly, until the chilies are very soft. Stir in the Dry Fried Shallots and let sit for at least 2 hours before using. Can be made a day ahead and kept at room temperature.

KORI-MEX BIBIMBAP WITH MINCED BEEF MOLE

Bibimbap: *a Korean dish of rice crisped inside a hot stone bowl, then tossed with an almost equal amount of various and separately prepared vegetables, a little bit of meat, and a dollop of chile paste for seasoning.*

Mole: *a Mexican paradox that is a sauce made with a seemingly endless number of ingredients, many of which— dark and unsweetened chocolate, for example—strike a sense of wonder. And allegedly it's the shit.*

Tex-Mex: *America's version of Mexican food from the southwest United States in which, as long as there's avocado, shredded Cheddar, and sour cream, it's "Mexican."*

Taco rice: *Japanese Tex-Mex—a Japanese version of America's version of Mexican food from Texas.*

This: *All of the above.*

MAKES 4 TO 6 SERVINGS

MINCED BEEF MOLE

1 pound (450 g) ground beef

1 tablespoon potato starch or cornstarch (see page 6)

1 tablespoon soy sauce

1 medium yellow onion, cut into blender-friendly chunks

10 garlic cloves, peeled and smashed

Leaves from 2 fresh thyme sprigs

¾ cup (95 g) raisins

3 tablespoons unsalted butter

½ cup (160 g) gochujang (Korean chile paste)

3 tablespoons smooth peanut butter

2 tablespoons tomato paste

2 tablespoons Mexican chile powder

2 tablespoons smoked paprika

2 teaspoons dark brown sugar

1 teaspoon ground cinnamon

¾ teaspoon ground cumin

½ teaspoon ground cloves

½ teaspoon ground allspice

½ teaspoon freshly ground black pepper

1½ cups (360 mL) chicken stock

2 teaspoons soy sauce

1.2 ounces (35 g) dark unsweetened chocolate, chopped

TOMATO SALSA

2 medium tomatoes

2 small shallots

1 teaspoon freshly squeezed lemon juice

½ teaspoon fine sea salt

½ teaspoon fish sauce

1 small handful fresh cilantro, roughly chopped

⅛ teaspoon freshly ground black pepper

⅛ teaspoon ground cumin

OTHER SUGGESTED TOPPINGS

Egg yolk

Sliced or diced avocado

Chopped kimchi

Shredded Cheddar cheese

Sour cream

Chopped scallions

BANCHAN (SMALL DISHES)

Cucumber Banchan (page 234)

Bean Sprout Banchan (page 234)

Caramelized Mushroom Banchan (page 235)

TO ASSEMBLE

Toasted sesame oil

6 cups (865 g) steamed short-grain white rice

MAKE THE MINCED BEEF MOLE

1. In a large bowl, combine the ground beef, potato starch or cornstarch, and soy sauce. Mix until even and set aside.

2. In a blender or with an immersion blender, blend the onion, garlic, thyme, and ¼ cup (31 g) of the raisins until smoothly pureed. Set aside.

3. In a large sauté pan or Dutch oven over medium-high heat, melt the butter. Add the ground beef mixture and cook, using a wooden spoon to break it up into small pieces, until browned all over. Use a slotted spoon to transfer the beef onto a plate, then add the onion puree to the pan. Turn the heat down to medium-low and cook, stirring frequently, until the mixture has turned dark in color and caramelized and lost about half its volume.

4. Add the gochujang, peanut butter, tomato paste, chile powder, smoked paprika, brown sugar, cinnamon, cumin, cloves, allspice, and black pepper. Mix until smooth and cook for 4 to 5 minutes, stirring frequently, until the paste starts to caramelize on the bottom and sides of the pot. Return the beef to the pot and add the remaining ½ cup (62 g) raisins, the stock, and the soy sauce. Bring the mixture to a simmer and cook, stirring occasionally, for about 10 minutes, until slightly thickened. Add the chocolate and cook for 15 minutes, until the mixture has thickened into a ragu-like sauce.

5. Let the sauce sit for at least 6 hours at room temperature, or you can make it several days ahead (recommended) and keep it in the fridge until needed. Reheat over low heat before using.

MAKE THE TOMATO SALSA

6. Cut the tomatoes and shallots into fine dice, then place them in a fine sieve set over a large bowl. Mix in the lemon juice and salt and let sweat for 10 minutes. Use a wooden spoon to press on the tomatoes and shallots to squeeze out any excess juice, discard the juice, and place the tomatoes and shallots in a medium bowl. Toss with the fish sauce, cilantro, black pepper, and cumin. Set aside until needed.

CRISP THE RICE

7. For each serving, heat a small cast-iron skillet over high heat until it starts to smoke. Brush the bottom and sides generously with toasted

sesame oil, then spread a layer of steamed short-grain rice about 1½ inches (4 cm) deep. Continue to cook for a couple of minutes, until the bottom of the rice starts to get a little crispy.

TO SERVE

8. Top each serving of rice with the tomato salsa, all the suggested toppings, banchan, and a generous ladle of minced beef mole. Stir everything together and serve immediately.

CUCUMBER BANCHAN

Banchan are those tiny, complimentary side dishes they serve in Korean restaurants when you only order a soup and keep asking for refills. Think of cucumber and bean sprout banchan (see below) as hybrids between pickles and salads. They are there not only to check the vegetable-consumption box as we chow down on chocolate over carbs, but also to serve as crucial textural elements in bibimbap. Crunchy, nutty, and refreshing, they keep the dish from getting tiresome.

MAKES 2 PACKED CUPS

6 baby cucumbers (about 28 ounces/800 g), thinly sliced

2 teaspoons fine sea salt

2 teaspoons toasted sesame oil

1 teaspoon toasted sesame seeds (see page 100)

½ teaspoon fish sauce, plus more as desired

1 garlic clove, grated

¼ teaspoon freshly ground black pepper

In a large bowl, gently toss together the cucumber slices and salt. Let sweat for 5 minutes, then massage the cucumbers with your hands to completely collapse and wilt them. Fill the bowl with fresh water to wash off the salty water, then squeeze the cucumbers as dry as you can. Set the cucumbers in a medium bowl. Toss with the sesame oil, sesame seeds, fish sauce (taste and adjust), garlic, and black pepper. Set aside until needed.

BEAN SPROUT BANCHAN

MAKES 2 PACKED CUPS

1 pound (450 g) bean sprouts

2 teaspoons fine sea salt

1 tablespoon toasted sesame oil

2 garlic cloves, grated

1 teaspoon chile flakes

½ teaspoon fish sauce, plus more as desired

¼ teaspoon freshly ground black pepper

1 teaspoon toasted sesame seeds (see page 100)

1. In a large bowl, gently toss the bean sprouts and salt. Let sweat for 5 minutes, then massage the sprouts with your hands to completely collapse and wilt them. Fill the bowl with fresh water to wash off the salty water, then squeeze the sprouts as dry as you can.

2. In a large skillet, heat the sesame oil over medium-high heat. Add the sprouts, garlic, chile

flakes, fish sauce, and black pepper and cook for 2 minutes. Taste and adjust with more fish sauce if desired. Toss in the sesame seeds, then set aside until needed.

CARAMELIZED MUSHROOM BANCHAN

There is often a mushroom banchan at the table in Korean restaurants. But they suck as often as they show up. The mushrooms are typically watery, slimy, and bland, while they could be caramelized, concentrated, and awesome. We're doing the latter.

MAKES 3 CUPS

4 tablespoons olive oil

12 ounces (350 g) shiitake mushrooms, washed and thinly sliced

2 teaspoons toasted sesame oil

1 garlic clove, grated

1 tablespoon soy sauce

½ teaspoon toasted sesame seeds (see page 100)

Heat a large wide skillet over high heat, then add 2 tablespoons of the olive oil. Spread half of the mushrooms in a single layer, then cook them *undisturbed* for about 2 minutes, until the first sides are deeply caramelized. Toss and turn and cook for 3 minutes or so, until the mushrooms are deeply browned on all sides, shriveled, and have lost about two-thirds of their volume. Transfer to a plate and repeat with the remaining olive oil and mushrooms. When the second batch of mushrooms is finished, return the first batch to the pan, along with the sesame oil, garlic, and soy sauce. Stir to combine. Cook until the moisture from the soy sauce has completely evaporated. Toss in the sesame seeds, then set aside until needed.

CRISPY WHOLE-FRIED SANDSTORM CHICKEN

A sandstorm is a very different animal from coal-related air pollution. The first, a natural phenomenon, is mostly annoying but otherwise unlikely to cause severe health problems unless you do something really stupid during the storm. It's characterized by a dark, murky, almost orange overtone that makes everything look as if you're wearing yellow-tinted sunglasses. The latter, on the other hand, is a byproduct of burning coal that veils the affected region with a diffuse gray to opaque white smoke made up of particles small enough to enter your bloodstream, which can lead to cardiovascular illnesses or, of course, lung cancer. The two might be mistaken for one another in, say, a photo, but they are easily distinguishable by people with intimate experiences of both.

Not to brag, but here you're looking at one of those people.

But the word **sandstorm** *also has happier associations for me. I'm talking about an utterly overlooked culinary delight that the Cantonese call sandstorm chicken (okay, technically it's called "wind dust chicken," but let's be poetic about it). A whole chicken is marinated, then deep-fried until the skin is incredibly crispy, then served underneath a sand dune of fried garlic. It is literally and figuratively a force of nature.*

Here I've adapted it to be more home kitchen—friendly with a technique of shallow-frying, and the skin is padded with a coating of potato starch that fries into a craggy, jagged suit of crispiness. Then instead of pure fried garlic, which can be a bit monotonous, I mixed in almost an equal amount of grated Parmigiano-Reggiano cheese, plus dustings of Sichuan peppercorns.

Typically, this dish is cut to small pieces before serving, but I say, if one has fried a whole chicken, one has earned the primal pleasure of tearing it limb from limb, with fat running rampant and acting as an adhesive for the pungent, savory, salivatingly delicious "sand." You'll find there aren't a lot of things in life that are this satisfying to weather through.

MAKES 4 SERVINGS

SPECIAL EQUIPMENT: *large, nonstick wok or deep skillet (4 inches/10 cm deep)*

CHICKEN

1 small (2.3- to 3-pound/1.2-kg max) free-range chicken (weight without head or feet)

1 tablespoon Shaoxing wine

1 tablespoon fish sauce

1 tablespoon dried galangal powder or ground ginger (see Note on page 239)

1 teaspoon ground white pepper

½ teaspoon sea salt

Potato starch (see page 6), for coating

Canola oil, for frying

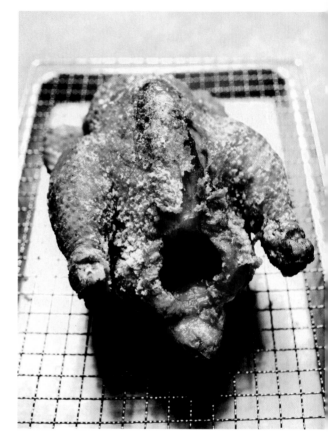

SAND

½ cup Fried Garlic Powder (page 27; reserve the frying oil)

1 small handful dried bird's eye chilies

⅓ cup (26 g) grated Parmigiano-Reggiano cheese

½ teaspoon ground Sichuan peppercorns

¼ teaspoon freshly ground black pepper

⅛ teaspoon sea salt

MARINATE THE CHICKEN

1. Clean the chicken inside and out, then pat it dry and set it aside on a sheet pan.

2. In a small bowl, whisk the wine, fish sauce, galangal powder, white pepper, and sea salt. Rub the mixture evenly over the chicken, including

the cavity, then cover with plastic wrap. If you can, marinate the chicken overnight in the fridge. If not, marinate for at least 2 hours before frying.

FRY THE CHICKEN

3. Rub the marinade over the chicken again so the skin is moist and damp. Gently press the potato starch all over until you have a thin but tight coating all around. Use a toothpick to sew the skin together at the neck flap (this keeps the breasts protected and juicy). Tuck the wing tips underneath themselves.

4. Find a large, nonstick wok or deep skillet (4 inches/10 cm deep) that will fit the chicken but leave enough room on the sides for you to use a ladle to baste the chicken with hot oil. Add

to the pot the oil that was used to make Fried Garlic Powder, then add more canola oil until it reaches a depth of 2 inches (5 cm). Heat over high heat; when the oil bubbles up immediately around an inserted wooden chopstick, turn the heat down to medium.

5. Carefully lower the chicken into the oil, *breast side up first*. Tilt the wok or pot if you have to, to gather some oil on the side, then use a ladle to slowly baste the parts of the chicken that are not submerged in hot oil. Do this slowly and gently so you don't flush away the potato starch coating on the skin. You'll notice the coating starts to form crinkling and shaggy crispy bits on the skin. When the bottom side has turned golden brown, *insert one tip of large tongs into the cavity of the chicken, lift, and turn it 90 degrees so that one leg side is now facing down*. Keep basting the chicken with hot oil, including inside the cavity. When the second side is golden brown, turn it again so the remaining leg side is facing down. Continue basting and turning a few times if needed, until the entire surface is deep golden brown and the internal temperature of the inner thigh is 173°F/78°C. Drain any excess oil from the cavity, then let the chicken rest *breast side up* on a cooling rack for 5 minutes.

MAKE THE SAND

6. While the chicken is resting, leave 1 tablespoon of the frying oil in the wok or pot and cook the dried chilies over medium heat until they turn dark red in color. Turn off the heat and add the Fried Garlic Powder, Parmigiano-Reggiano, Sichuan peppercorns, black pepper, and sea salt. Mix evenly and immediately transfer onto the chicken on a serving plate (don't let the garlic powder stay in the hot wok for too long or it'll burn).

7. Pillage right in with your bare hands.

NOTE ON GALANGAL POWDER: *Galangal powder is a classic, ingenious pairing with chicken in southern Chinese cuisine. In appearance it looks just like ground ginger, but it's not, just as galangal is not ginger. It's more fragrant and complex. Nowadays you can easily find it online if not in Chinese supermarkets.*

FRENCH QUENELLES
(FISH DUMPLINGS) GONE MAD

I don't know if you know this, but the best extinguishers for the painful sensation caused by spicy foods are sugar, milk, and cream. I don't remember who told me this, but time and time again this advice has successfully released me from seemingly eternal agony.

So, an idea came to mind.

During my dog years in Beijing, the closest thing to an emotional consolation had to be the immediate access to Sichuan cuisine, one of mankind's most glorious, second-to-none cultural riches that—whether a physical location or not—should be recognized by UNESCO as a World Heritage Site. I mean, if a meatpacking factory in Uruguay can be a World Heritage Site, then spicy town should be at least as qualified. Among Sichuan cuisine's surprisingly diverse offerings, there is one that everyone must order regardless of one's bowel capacity to handle such awesomeness, and that is a dish called water boiling fish.

Sounds very Jenny Craig, but there's nothing "watery" about it.

In fact, I often wondered if the word water *is just a euphemism for the earth-scorching, mind-meltingly hot and numbing* chile oil *that floods the entire tub of sliced catfish and comes to the table still roiling in unsettling aggression. Like, you know, how people say "rest" instead of "die"—which in this case makes a very apt comparison.*

I love this thing. I'm in love *with this thing. I love it so much that I even created it at home—something that nobody should be doing, like cooking your own meth—and published it on my blog after we left Beijing. Well, consider this version its 2.0.*

*Can a timeless classic be improved? In rare cases, I daresay yes. Why not merge the tongue-melting, skull-numbing Sichuan classic with the unapologetically heavy-creamed artery bomb that is Lyon's iconic dish—*quenelles*? Basically, they're soft and fluffy fish mousse dumplings that are swaddled in an exceedingly rich and cream-based sauce, which, if you've been paying attention, is where things get interesting.*

Can fire and water coincide in a single existence? Culinarily speaking, yes, they can, in an aggressively spicy concoction that comes with a built-in antidote. The light and mildly sweet mousse dumplings work sublimely as buoyant vessels that deliver a complex mixture of flavor that is spiced, numbing, savory, intensely aromatic, and burning, but smoothed over by an undertone of sweet, heavy cream. Bite by bite, inch by inch, a continuous mingling of sensory escalations and reconciliations.

MAKES 6 SERVINGS

QUENELLES (FISH DUMPLINGS)

⅔ pound (300 g) skinless fillets of pike or catfish (see Note on page 244)

½ cup (121 g) heavy cream

1 large egg

2 teaspoons potato starch or cornstarch (see page 6)

1 teaspoon fish sauce

¼ teaspoon ground white pepper

6 ounces (170 g) peeled and deveined tiger shrimp (see Note on page 244)

CREAMED SICHUAN BOILING SAUCE

2 tablespoons canola oil

2 tablespoons Sichuan broad bean chile paste (doubanjiang; see page 8)

5 garlic cloves, finely chopped

2 teaspoons finely chopped ginger

2 scallions, diced

2 tablespoons Shaoxing wine or sherry

1 cup chicken stock (or fish or shrimp stock)

¾ cup (180 mL) heavy cream

1 tablespoon soy sauce

1 tablespoon juice from Pickled Chilies (page 25), or other chile pickling juice that's acidic

1 tablespoon mushroom powder (see page 9)

2 teaspoons ground Sichuan peppercorns

1 teaspoon strawberry jam, or whatever jam you have on hand

¼ teaspoon ground cumin

¼ teaspoon freshly ground black pepper

1 teaspoon Dijon mustard

MALA POURING OIL

⅓ cup (80 mL) canola oil (see Note on page 244)

1 large handful whole dried bird's eye chilies

7 garlic cloves, smashed and peeled

5 Pickled Chilies (page 25) or pickled jalapeños

2½ tablespoons whole Sichuan peppercorns (see Note on page 244)

1 tablespoon chile flakes

½ teaspoon freshly ground black pepper

FOR SERVING

Fresh cilantro leaves, for garnish

Steamed white rice

MAKE THE QUENELLE DOUGH

1. If you're using frozen fish fillets, make sure you weigh them *after they are defrosted, cleaned, and patted dry.* Cut the fillets into small chunks and transfer them to a food processor. Pulse/run the machine until the fish is finely pureed and bouncy. Scrape the sides, then add the cream, egg, potato starch, fish sauce, and white pepper and pulse/run again for about 1 minute, until the mixture resembles springy mousse. Add the shrimp cut into bite-size chunks, then pulse a few times just until incorporated.

2. Transfer the mixture to a large bowl and cover with plastic wrap. You can make this the night before and keep it in the fridge until needed.

MAKE THE CREAMED SICHUAN BOILING SAUCE

3. In a small saucepan over medium-high heat, combine the canola oil and Sichuan broad bean chile paste and cook, stirring, until fragrant, about 1 minute. Add the garlic, ginger, and scallions and cook, stirring, for another minute, until fragrant. Add the wine, stir, and cook until the liquid has mostly evaporated, then add the stock, cream, soy sauce, chile pickling juice,

mushroom powder, Sichuan peppercorns, jam, cumin, and black pepper (but not the mustard!) and stir to combine. Keep the mixture at a gentle simmer, stirring occasionally, for 10 minutes, until slightly reduced.

4. Strain the sauce through a fine sieve, pressing on the solids to extract as much liquid as humanly possible, then discard the solids. You can prepare the sauce the night before and keep it covered in the fridge until needed.

COOK THE QUENELLES

5. Twenty minutes before serving, bring a pot of water with a hefty pinch of salt to a boil (as if you're cooking pasta). Dip a large, elongated ladle into the hot water, then scoop about ½ cup of the quenelle dough, as if you're scooping ice cream. Gently scrape the mixture into the boiling water with another spoon (a rough football shape is the goal), then repeat until the mixture is used up. You should have about 5 or 6 large quenelles. Let the quenelles cook on one side for 2 minutes, then gently turn them and cook for 2 minutes more. They should fully float and swell up to the surface of the water.

6. Transfer the Sichuan boiling sauce to a sauté pan that *will fit all the quenelles in a single layer* and bring it to an active simmer over medium heat. With a slotted spoon, drain the quenelles well and transfer them into the sauce. With the sauce at an active simmer, cook the quenelles for 5 minutes, basting them frequently with the sauce. Gently and evenly whisk in the Dijon mustard, then turn off the heat and set aside.

MAKE THE MALA POURING OIL

7. In a small saucepan, combine the canola oil, dried chilies, garlic, and Pickled Chilies and start heating the mixture over *medium-high* heat. Stirring constantly, cook until the garlic starts to brown slightly, then add the Sichuan peppercorns, chile flakes, and black pepper. *Turn the heat up to high* and cook until the chile flakes start to turn dark red.

TO SERVE

8. Pour the hot oil evenly over the quenelles, which should make sizzling sounds as the oil hits their surface. Garnish with torn cilantro leaves and serve with a large spoon to scoop into the cloud-like quenelles like parfaits. Serve with the sauce over steamed rice.

NOTE ON PIKE OR CATFISH: *Traditionally quenelles are done with pike, but here I use catfish, which is cheap, easy to find, and yields a great result.*

NOTE ON SHRIMP: *You can also use scallops or crayfish if available.*

NOTE ON CANOLA OIL: *I know ⅓ cup of oil sounds like a lot, but trust me, this is already considered "moderate" compared to the real Sichuan boiling fish, which is literally submerged in a bloodbath of chile oil.*

NOTE ON SICHUAN PEPPERCORNS: *If you don't like biting into whole Sichuan peppercorns, which can stun beginners, you can substitute ground, but add it in the last 10 seconds of cooking the oil.*

MALA SMOKED MEAT WITH TAHINI MUSTARD

You can be excused for not understanding why the world needs smoked meat, or pastrami, as another form, if you have not been to Schwartz's in Montreal. Note that this is coming from someone who's lived in New York, the international stronghold of pastrami worshippers, thanks to the infamous Katz's Deli, which practically put pastrami on the map. Thus it's an almost treasonous declaration, but in my humble opinion, if Katz's were Yoda—and you think that it couldn't possibly go higher than that—then Schwartz's . . . Schwartz's is the fucking Force itself.

Over the years, with knowledge passed down from masters like Michael Ruhlman, I have developed a method to harness the Force without using any large smokers or special equipment, a "faux smoked meat" recipe that I published on my blog in 2014. That should've been enough. I should've stopped there. But come on, everyone knows how that story goes.

Slowly, a creeping darkness stirred from within my heart—seductive, burning, powerful, and inevitable—polluting my mind with a sacrilegious craving, drawing my will toward a disturbing yet irresistible version of the respected classic. Even though it would be condemned as against the teaching of my masters, the Dark Side, it called me.

My friends, meet the Darth Vader of smoked meat. A colossal hunk of short rib section, with its much superior distribution of fat and texture over brisket, encased in a thick spice-suit of mind-bending Sichuan peppercorns, chile flakes, and Sichuan broad bean chile paste (doubanjiang). Still mildly smoky, still tingling with coriander and mustard seeds, it is in some ways like the Chosen One but unquestionably more potent, intoxicating, and complicated, and therefore far more interesting. I serve it with a nutty Japanese tahini mustard and sauerkraut, over rice.

May the Force be with you.

MAKES 8 TO 10 SERVINGS

NOTE ON TIMING: *The meat cures for 3 or 4 days and then bakes for 12 hours. You do not need to attend the meat during baking, which is why I like to start the baking process at around 11 P.M. and finish at 11 A.M. the next day, but you can plan it according to your own schedule. Because there's a steaming process that reheats the smoked meat before serving, you can technically bake it up to 3 days ahead of time. But I do find that it is at its most succulent prime on the first day, so I would recommend making it on the day of serving.*

SPECIAL EQUIPMENT: *spice grinder; large pot; steamer or steamer rack*

SHORT RIBS AND BRINE

4- to 5-pound (2- to 2.5-kg) single hunk of boneless short ribs (see Note on page 248)

2 quarts (2 L) water

6.6 ounces (185 g) kosher salt (please measure by weight because each brand varies)

¼ cup (40 g) smoked sea salt

1 cup (189 g) light brown sugar

⅓ cup (70 g) dark brown sugar

2 tablespoons pink curing salt (see Note on page 248)

1 tablespoon pickling spice

7 garlic cloves, smashed

Three 3-inch (8-cm) slices (20 g) ginger

2 quarts (2 L) ice water

SPICE CRUST

¼ cup plus 2 tablespoons (23 g) Sichuan peppercorns

¼ cup (36 g) Korean chile flakes for medium spiciness, use more or less as desired

¼ cup (32 g) black peppercorns

¼ cup (16 g) coriander seeds

¼ cup (41 g) mustard seeds

2 tablespoons white peppercorns

2 teaspoons ground cumin

1 black cardamom pod

2 tablespoons smoked paprika

3 tablespoons yellow mustard

2 tablespoons Sichuan broad bean chile paste (doubanjiang; see page 9)

1 teaspoon dark brown sugar

½ teaspoon liquid smoke

1 garlic clove, grated

TAHINI MUSTARD SAUCE

¼ cup plus 2 tablespoons (90 mL) whole milk

¼ cup (64 g) Japanese or Chinese tahini (see Note on page 248)

3 tablespoons Dijon mustard

2½ tablespoons Garlic Confit Sauce (page 14)

3 tablespoons light brown sugar

1 tablespoon plus 1 teaspoon soy sauce

2 teaspoons toasted sesame oil

¼ cup finely chopped cilantro

¼ cup finely chopped scallions

FOR SERVING

Sauerkraut, store-bought or homemade

Slices of rye bread or steamed rice

CURE THE MEAT

1. Start 4 or 5 days ahead of time. Find a large pot that will fit the whole hunk of short ribs. Make sure it has a lid, and clear out a space in the fridge where the whole pot can fit. Set the pot on the stove and add the water, kosher salt, smoked sea salt, light and dark brown sugars, pink curing salt, pickling spice, garlic, and ginger. Bring to a simmer over high heat, whisking occasionally until all the salt has dissolved, then add the iced water to cool down the brine. When the brine has cooled to *room temperature,* sink the meat into the brine until *completely submerged.* Cover with a lid and set it in the fridge to brine for at least 3 or preferably 4 days.

COOK THE MEAT

2. Preheat the oven to 220°F/105°C. Remove the meat from the brine, rinse it clean under water, pat it dry, and set it aside on a large tray.

3. In a large skillet, combine the Sichuan peppercorns, chile flakes, black peppercorns, coriander seeds, mustard seeds, white peppercorns, ground cumin, and cardamom. Cook over medium heat, stirring constantly, until the spices start to pop and smell fragrant. Pick out the black cardamom first and transfer it to a spice grinder. Grind until the cardamom is coarsely ground, then add the remaining spices and pulse until everything's coarsely but evenly ground. Stir in the smoked paprika and set aside.

4. In a small bowl, whisk the mustard, Sichuan broad bean chile paste, brown sugar, liquid smoke, and garlic. Rub the mixture all over the meat, coating it evenly. Press the spice mixture into the meat until the entire surface is tightly and evenly coated. (You may have extra spices left; use the mixture on roast meats or in stews or stir-fries.)

5. Wrap the meat in double layers of aluminum foil and place it on a baking rack. Cut a few slits in the bottom of the foil to let excess fat and liquid drain, then place the baking rack on the middle rack and a sheet pan on the bottom rack to catch the drippings. Bake for 12 hours, unattended.

STEAM THE MEAT

6. You may be wondering why the steaming is necessary. Well, first, smoked meat is traditionally smoked, then steamed, and I find that the steaming process further softens and moistens the meat, finishing it with a specific aroma when the spices are clouted by hot mist. It just isn't quite smoked meat without the steam. About 1 hour before serving, remove the aluminum foil from the smoked meat (and remove the bones if there are any; see the Note on short ribs) and place the meat in a large steamer (or you can place a steamer rack in a large pot with water underneath). Cover and steam over medium-high heat for 45 minutes.

MAKE THE TAHINI-MUSTARD SAUCE

7. In a medium bowl, whisk the milk, tahini, mustard, Garlic Confit Sauce, brown sugar, soy sauce, sesame oil, cilantro, and scallions into a creamy sauce.

TO SERVE

8. You can enjoy the smoked meat either in sandwich form or over rice, in a weird Jewish-meets-Chinese type of marriage. For a sandwich, spread a generous layer of the tahini-mustard sauce on both slices of rye bread. Add a hunk of sauerkraut and a high stack of sliced Sichuan mala smoked meat. Cut and serve. To serve with rice, just put everything on top of each other and dig in.

NOTE ON SHORT RIBS: *I prefer boneless short ribs for pastrami/smoked meat over brisket for its even fat distribution and also because it is much easier to source.*

NOTE ON PINK CURING SALT: *Pink curing salt, also called DQ curing salt or Prague powder #1 or Insta cure #1, is a specific type of salt used for food preservation to prevent bacteria and fungus growth, and also is what gives the smoked meat its dark red coloring. It can be found easily online.*

NOTE ON TAHINI: *Japanese or Chinese tahini/ white sesame paste is darker and more nutty and robust than Middle Eastern tahini. If you cannot find Japanese or Chinese tahini, you can substitute a Middle Eastern variety, but expect a milder flavor.*

4

THE BREAKUP

For me it was a matter of survival, of staying sane. I cooked like a self-loathing desert ostrich burying her head under an endless terrain of sand.

My relationship with Richard went by in a heavy daze. My mind was crawling with questions, but my body retreated into detachment. Many nights I had the urge to scream at him, but instead I sat silently on my bed, in frozen acquiescence. Each morning I opened the curtains to a smoky sky and saw his face, then simply closed them again. We started to fight a lot. There were often, on my end at least, tears of extreme disappointment, from hurts that we couldn't and didn't want to take back. The relationship between Richard and me grew cold, stagnant, yet there was turbulence underneath.

I became less willing to go outside. Even when I made an effort to do so, more often than not I returned home mute, in a wordless smolder. On a sweltering summer day in which both the air and the soot inside emulsified like a cream soup in a blender, I found myself once again trapped in a cab and cornered into agreement on the touchy politics between Taiwan and China, something I considered emotionally equivalent to a verbal rape.

Richard just stood quietly, watched.

Had he ever loved me? I wobbled home, pinned by emotional splinters, while on TV some travel-show host was grazing on *cacio e pepe* in the mockingly beautiful city of Rome, seemingly in another universe. In eerie silence, I floated into the kitchen . . . and came out two hours later with my very first, handmade fresh *tonnarelli* (think fat spaghetti).

That . . . that was the beginning of my breakup with Richard.

For the record, the pasta didn't taste like salvation, but more like rubbery tubes with an extra smack of mockery. It sucked. But that moment was the turning point in our toxic relationship. Despite how silly it may sound, measuring my level of mental stability by how I feel about making fresh pasta at any given moment is an accurate, scientific, and time-honored tradition.

Many years ago back in New York, I tried making fresh ravioli for the first time, and it failed in the same unmistakable fashion, so I, as any other healthy, internally fulfilled human being would, simply stopped trying. However, this time, as I looked around at the emptiness where I stood, with Richard smiling creepily on the right . . . I turned left.

I started to cook more. Not just more frequently, but more obsessively, desperately, like a leech on open flesh. A new recipe could fail once, fail twice, fail compulsively to no apparent end—it didn't matter. I took it as good pain. I took it as refuge. I would rather fixate on something else—*anything* else—than the constant inner antagonism I was living with. I dove deep into books on pasta making; plowed through a dozen adjustments with variations on flour, yolk, egg white, and water ratios; was cooped up for several weeks of voluntary confinement before eventually emerging again, dangling a handful of *tonnarelli* that I was finally happy with. And after that, I jumped right back in for the next escape.

Cooking had been a hobby, but slowly it became a drug, then an addiction. I'm not saying it was healthy, or that I was proud, or that any of this was a proactive or even justifiable outcome of my violent contempt for my surroundings. I could have gotten a job. I could have become an activist. Since I stayed, I could have fought. If I'd wanted I could have picked up and left. But I didn't. I just cooked.

Early in my addiction I snorted recipes that took hours, but before long I started shooting up cooking projects that took days. I began to make breads, with microorganisms that farted gasses in my kitchen, and together we joked about what it's like to have big holes in our hearts. I even started to bake pastries, reconciling with an activity that had sent me into a deep state of worthlessness via a few muffin-making sessions in my college years, episodes that are best forgotten entirely. I began to try my hand at charcuterie, which gave a high that often stretched on for weeks, if not months, plus a delicious withdrawal that tasted like summer in a French château. Fortunately or not, it is extremely easy—too easy—to buy cooking ingredients online and have them delivered to your doorstep in China, and because of that, I could go on fussing with recipes for days on end without ever leaving the apartment.

Sometimes I forgot how long I stayed inside. Sometimes I lied about having gone out.

And that can't mean anything good. I'm sure even alcoholics draw a line somewhere, perhaps at having vodka delivered biweekly. But for me it was a matter of survival, of staying sane. I cooked like a self-loathing desert ostrich burying her head under an endless terrain of sand, and before long, this method of survival began to taste like delicious noodles in intense broth and flaky buns that crumbled in denial.

Looking back, I'm not sure if how I dealt with my situation was shameful or glorious. It felt passive at times, but also empowering. It didn't shrink Richard, but I grew bigger in size. Two years into it, in 2012, sunk deep in my mental exile next to a stack of recipes growing restless at my passivity, I finally did the unspeakable.

I started a food blog.

for SNACKING

Breaking foods into meal categories is like profiling people by their race; it's wrong and proves inaccurate. Breakfast, lunch, or dinner, who says so, and who gives a shit? Eat whatever you want at whenever time of the day. Having said that, it is equally inefficient to run a long list of recipes without any sort of guiding principles, so it might be helpful to know that what separates the recipes in this chapter, "For Snacking," from the last chapter, "For a Crowd," is really just the portion size.

Big portions for crowds. Small portions for snacks.

SALIVA CHICKEN MEATBALLS

This is a playful adaptation of a very popular appetizer seen in almost every Sichuan restaurant in China, and perhaps in the United States, too.

As Chinese culture has a quirky sense of humor when it comes to naming food (such as "rolling donkey in dusts," "wok helmet," and "dog biting pig," to name a few), this dish is known as "saliva chicken." Not only will it make you salivate upon first look, but the combination of soft poached chicken sitting in a spicy and numbing puddle of sesame sauce and chile oil is dangerously addictive.

There's a yakitori joint down the hill from where we live in Hong Kong, and they add chopped chicken knuckles (the soft cartilage between the bones of drumsticks and thighs) to their minced chicken sticks. That combination is perfect for this dish, and instantly kicks the meatballs to another level of contrasting textures and flavors. If you can't find chicken knuckles, just omit them—the meatballs will still be delicious.

MAKES 4 APPETIZER SERVINGS

SPECIAL EQUIPMENT: *takoyaki pan (optional)*

MEATBALLS

1 pound (450 g) boneless skin-on chicken thighs

¼ pound (105 g) chicken knuckles/cartilage (if unavailable, omit)

1½ tablespoons grated ginger

1½ tablespoons sake

2½ teaspoons toasted sesame oil

2 teaspoons fish sauce

1¼ teaspoons ground white pepper

Canola oil, for shaping the meatballs

SESAME SAUCE

½ cup (127 g) tahini

3 garlic cloves, smashed

1½ tablespoons soy sauce

1 tablespoon toasted sesame oil

2 teaspoons balsamic vinegar

½ teaspoon sugar

½ cup crushed ice, plus more if needed

2 tablespoons finely chopped cilantro or scallions

TO FINISH

My Ultimate Chile Oil (page 24)

Finely ground Sichuan peppercorns, for dusting

MAKE THE MEATBALLS

1. Keep 50 percent of the skin on the chicken thighs (discard the rest or use it to make schmaltz for another recipe), then cut the thighs into small chunks. Scatter on a sheet pan and flash-freeze for 1 hour, until hardened. Meanwhile, season the chicken knuckles, if using, with a little bit of salt and pepper, then cook in a skillet over medium-high heat until evenly browned on all sides. Finely mince them until they resemble coarse breadcrumbs, then set aside in a large bowl.

2. Transfer the frozen chicken chunks to a food processor and pulse several times (you might have to scrape the bottom a few times) until coarsely ground. Add the ginger, sake, sesame oil, fish sauce, and white pepper and run the processor until the mixture is even and smoothly ground. Transfer to the bowl with the chicken knuckles and mix everything together evenly.

3. Rub your hands with a bit of oil, then shape the mixture into 15 small meatballs. My tool for cooking the roundest and most evenly browned meatballs is—a takoyaki pan (the specially designed pan with large holes that makes takoyaki, Japanese octopus balls)! I place each meatball into each hole on the takoyaki pan, brushed with a bit of oil, then I cook them over medium heat, turning each meatball frequently with a wooden skewer, until evenly dark brown and cooked through, about 10 minutes. If you don't have a takoyaki pan, you can do this in a skillet, or bake the meatballs on a sheet pan under the broiler for 12 to 14 minutes.

MAKE THE SESAME SAUCE

4. In either a blender or a food processor, combine the tahini, garlic, soy sauce, sesame oil, vinegar, sugar, and ¼ cup of crushed ice. Blend until the mixture is smooth, then add 2 more tablespoons of the crushed ice at a time and continue to blend for 30 seconds, adding ice until the sauce is the texture of loose mayonnaise. Set aside (or refrigerate for up to 3 days). Just before using, mix in the cilantro or scallions.

TO FINISH

5. Generously douse the meatballs with sesame sauce, then smother again with My Ultimate Chile Oil. Dust with finely ground Sichuan peppercorns.

WONTONS WITH SHRIMP AND CHILE
COCONUT OIL AND HERBED YOGURT

Dear coconut oil,

Bro, I don't know if you've heard, but pretty much anywhere outside of Southeast Asia, until recently, you've been mostly associated with butt creams and fantasy vegan baking contests. I know, how fucking rude. You could have been known as the flavor booster that you are, rubbing shoulders with toasted sesame oil and truffle butter, or the grassiest extra-virgin olive oil inside gourmet food stores, but instead, the vegans got to you first.

And you, shrimp wontons, what's your problem, and why are you so afraid of flavor? Have you ever tried to swim outside of your pool of lovely yet boring soup, with those Cantonese noodles that might as well be dental floss, and for once, get out of your comfort zone? Don't tell me that I don't know what it's like to be put in a box. I had to knock down firewalls just to watch Stephen Colbert and eat a dozen doughnuts to get through the emotional pain of walking from my room to my mailbox, so what's your excuse?

Here, meet coconut oil. He's kind of new here and trying to make something of himself, too. I think you guys will really hit it off. Afterward we can all start a group chat and talk about our pathetic lives.

MAKES 35 TO 40 WONTONS, TO SERVE 7 OR 8

SHRIMP WONTONS

1½ pounds (650 g) small to medium (41 to 50 count) shell-on, head-on tiger shrimp

¼ pound (130 g) fatty ground pork, really cold

1 large egg white, whipped until foamy

1 teaspoon grated ginger

1 teaspoon potato starch (see page 6)

¾ teaspoon toasted sesame oil

½ teaspoon fine sea salt

¼ teaspoon ground white pepper

35 to 40 Cantonese-style wonton wrappers

Flour, for the sheet pan

SHRIMP AND CHILE COCONUT OIL

Shrimp heads and shells, from above

8 makrut lime leaves

1 small (22 g) lemongrass stalk, roughly chopped

1 tablespoon chopped peeled ginger

1 tablespoon Korean chile flakes

¼ teaspoon fine sea salt

¼ teaspoon ground paprika

⅛ teaspoon freshly ground black pepper

½ cup (120 mL) coconut oil

½ cup (120 mL) canola oil

1 tablespoon water

TOMATO AND ORANGE SALSA

5 anchovy fillets in olive oil, drained

17 or 18 (5 ounces/140 g) cherry tomatoes

½ small navel orange (1.7 ounces/40 g), segmented

1 small shallot, peeled

1 garlic clove, peeled

1 teaspoon finely minced ginger

1 or 2 Pickled Chilies (page 25)
1 tablespoon freshly squeezed lemon juice
2 teaspoons fish sauce

FOR SERVING
Plain yogurt
Finely chopped chives and cilantro
Freshly ground black pepper

MAKE THE SHRIMP WONTONS

1. Peel the heads and shells from the shrimp and reserve. Devein the shrimp, then cut them into small pieces and set them aside on a bed of ice cubes. In a food processor, combine the ground pork (I usually use half-thawed ground pork from the freezer, or you can flash-freeze it for 30 minutes to 1 hour) and 1 tablespoon of the whipped egg white (reserve the rest). Run the machine until the pork and egg white are whipped into a thick, bouncy paste, 30 to 40 seconds. Add half of the shrimp, the ginger, potato starch, sesame oil, salt, and white pepper and process again continuously until the mixture is smooth and bouncy. Add the remaining shrimp and pulse a few times, just until they are incorporated into the paste but still remain in chunks.

2. Place about 2 teaspoons of filling in the center of a wonton wrapper. *Do not* try to overstuff the wontons. It speaks to a character flaw if you cannot appreciate a perfectly balanced wonton—both in the ratio of dough to filling and in its form: it says that you have

an empty hole in your heart the size of an overstuffed wonton. So don't. Now, dab whipped egg white around the filling, then bring the edges of the wrapper upward together and pinch gently for a few seconds to close. I don't really follow any folding rules when it comes to wontons because I quite like the curving, organic shapes, which should look like eggs the moment they're dropped into boiling water. Repeat to fill and form the rest of the wontons. Place the wontons on a lightly floured sheet pan, then freeze until hard. You can now transfer them gently into an airtight bag and keep frozen until needed (they should be good for at least 3 months in the freezer).

MAKE THE SHRIMP AND CHILE COCONUT OIL

3. Place all the shrimp heads and shells in a food processor with the makrut lime leaves, lemongrass, ginger, chile flakes, salt, paprika, and black pepper. Run the machine until everything's finely chopped. Transfer the mixture to a medium *nonstick* saucepan and add the coconut and canola oils. Cook over medium heat, stirring frequently, until the shells and chile flakes are starting to brown and the mixture becomes foamy, 7 to 10 minutes. Turn off the heat and stir in the 1 tablespoon of water, which will help release any flavors sticking to the solids. Let cool completely, then strain the mixture through a sieve, pressing on the solids to extract as much liquid as you can. Discard the solids. The oil can

be made beforehand and kept in an airtight container in the fridge for up to 3 weeks (or freeze to keep it longer). Warm it through just before serving.

MAKE THE TOMATO AND ORANGE SALSA

4. Cook the anchovies in a small skillet over medium-high heat until slightly browned and nutty, then transfer to a blender with the rest of the ingredients. Blend on high until completely and smoothly pureed. Can be made up to 3 days ahead and stored in the fridge in an airtight container.

TO FINISH

5. Bring a pot of water to a boil, then gently drop in the wontons and cook until they float to the surface, about 3 to 4 minutes for fresh and 5 minutes for frozen. Drain well and transfer to a bowl. Add a generous amount of tomato-orange salsa and an equal amount of plain yogurt, then drench the bowl with shrimp and chile coconut oil. Sprinkle with chopped chives and cilantro and a dusting of black pepper.

KOREAN-STYLE BEEF TARTARE

A French tartare de boeuf *and a Korean* yukhoe *walked into a bar. Instead of fighting over their wild differences, they chatted flirtatiously about the innocent yet filthy pleasure of Shin Ramyun gilded in melted American cheese, and made a baby while at it . . .*

There's no punch line here. Just a foolish hope for world peace.

MAKES 2 SERVINGS

2 egg yolks

0.4 pound (180 g) beef eye of round

1½ tablespoons finely minced shallot

1½ tablespoons finely minced capers

1½ tablespoons finely chopped chives

2½ teaspoons gochujang (Korean chile paste)

1½ teaspoons Dijon mustard

1 teaspoon toasted sesame oil

½ teaspoon soy sauce

¼ teaspoon honey

⅛ teaspoon freshly ground black pepper

Sharp white Cheddar, for grating

Slices of country bread, toasted, for serving

1. If you can, the day before serving, break 1 egg yolk inside a small cup, then place it inside the fridge *uncovered.* This will thicken the egg yolk. But if you can't prep ahead, a regular yolk is fine.

2. Flash-freeze the beef for 30 minutes, until hardened but not frozen. Cut the beef into ⅛-inch (3-mm) slices, then into ⅛-inch (3-mm) strips, then into ⅛-inch (3-mm) cubes. Place in a large bowl with the thickened egg yolk, shallot, capers, chives, gochujang, mustard, sesame oil, soy sauce, honey, and black pepper. Mix well and plate on a shared serving dish in a small mound. Shave a generous amount of sharp white Cheddar on top, then top with another egg yolk. Serve immediately with toasted bread.

SPICY CHICKPEA POPPERS

My husband has been for years—like fifteen years—asking me why don't I make southern fried black-eyed peas, a twitch that he can't seem to shake ever since he saw Alton Brown doing it on TV. Girls, if I have a piece of marital advice, it's to never, and I mean never, be everything that your husband wants you to be. But once in a while, just randomly and carelessly, come up with something that screams you but at the same time lets him know you care, sort of, just a little bit.

MAKES 4 SNACK SERVINGS

SPECIAL EQUIPMENT: *spice grinder*

SPICE MIX

2 teaspoons ground Sichuan peppercorns

2 teaspoons chile flakes

½ teaspoon ground white pepper

½ teaspoon ground coriander

½ teaspoon ground kombu

¼ teaspoon ground cumin

¼ teaspoon five-spice powder

¼ teaspoon light brown sugar

¼ teaspoon sea salt, plus more as needed

CRISPY CHICKPEAS

Canola oil, for frying

One 15-ounce (425 g) can chickpeas, drained and peeled

1½ tablespoons buttermilk

1 tablespoon plus ¼ cup (31 g) all-purpose flour

2 teaspoons garlic powder

½ teaspoon baking soda

½ teaspoon ground white pepper

¼ teaspoon fine sea salt

A good handful fresh Thai basil leaves

TO FINISH

1 garlic clove, grated

2 teaspoons Garlic Confit Sauce (page 14)

1. Even though some of the spices are already ground, we will process them a second time to get a finer powder that will stick well to the chickpeas. In a spice grinder, grind the spice mix ingredients to a fine powder. Set aside.

2. In a deep frying pan or Dutch oven, pour enough oil to reach a depth of 2 inches (5 cm). Heat over medium-high until the oil bubbles up immediately around an inserted wooden chopstick.

3. Meanwhile in a large bowl, toss the chickpeas with the buttermilk and the 1 tablespoon of flour until they are evenly coated in this light batter. In a separate large bowl, mix the remaining ¼ cup (31 g) flour, the garlic powder, baking soda, white pepper, and salt. Add the coated chickpeas to the flour mixture and toss until you have a slightly wet but crumbly mixture. It may look like the chickpeas are kind of sticking together, but it's okay.

4. In a large bowl, mix the garlic and Garlic Confit Sauce. Set aside.

5. Now, *in several small batches as needed,* add the breaded chickpeas to the hot oil and start breaking them apart with a chopstick. It's okay if they are in small clumps of 2 to 4 chickpeas. Fry for a couple of minutes, until the chickpeas are golden brown all around. Transfer with a slotted spoon to the bowl with the garlic sauce and repeat to fry the rest of the chickpeas.

6. Add the basil leaves to the frying oil and *immediately cover the pot with a lid, leaving a small slit for the steam to escape.* When the popping sound has subsided, remove the lid and fry the basil until crispy. Transfer with a slotted spoon to the bowl with the chickpeas.

7. Toss the chickpeas to coat them evenly with the garlic mixture, then add the spice mixture and toss until evenly coated. Season with more salt if needed. Serve immediately.

KOREAN PORK BELLY TACOS WITH PEAR ON STICKY RICE TORTILLAS

There are two types of people out there: people who prefer flour tortillas and people who prefer corn tortillas. I prefer neither. And that makes me an alien.

Look, I'm sure it's because I haven't actually been to Mexico. I'm sure that once I do, I'll be Team Flour or Team Corn, or hey, maybe even Team Both. But until that happens, I am Team Sticky Rice Tortilla.

I guess you can say they're Korean tortillas: chewy, sticky rice tortillas topped with garlicky and caramelized pork belly, freshened up with a gochujang salsa and burned scallion salad teeming with toasted sesame oil. Fatty, salty, sweet, sour, and herby. Serve them with wedges of lime—I guess that's kind of Mexican, too.

MAKES 4 SNACK SERVINGS

SPECIAL EQUIPMENT: *blowtorch*

GOCHUJANG SALSA CHILE SAUCE

10 cherry tomatoes (3 ounces/85 g)

2 small shallots, peeled

1 garlic clove, peeled

3 tablespoons gochujang (Korean chile paste)

1 tablespoon Orange Chile Sambal (page 23)

1½ teaspoons freshly squeezed lemon juice

½ teaspoon honey

PORK BELLY AND MARINADE

⅔ pound (300 g) skinless pork belly (or boneless beef short ribs, if preferred)

½ small Fuji apple (2.5 ounces/70 g), peeled and cored

¼ medium yellow onion, peeled

3 garlic cloves, peeled

1 small shallot, peeled

3 tablespoons soy sauce

1 tablespoon toasted sesame oil

½ teaspoon honey

⅛ teaspoon freshly ground black pepper

⅛ teaspoon orange zest

Canola oil, for the pan

STICKY RICE TORTILLAS

¾ cup (90 g) sticky rice flour (see page 6)

¼ cup (30 g) spelt or rye flour

¼ cup plus 1 tablespoon (75 g) water

2 tablespoons (28 g) unsalted butter

½ teaspoon light brown sugar

¼ teaspoon table salt

BURNED SCALLION SALAD

1 jumbo scallion, white parts only (or the equivalent amount of regular scallions, 4 to 5 scallions)

1 small handful thinly shredded lettuce

1 tablespoon toasted sesame oil

1 teaspoon toasted sesame seeds (see page 100)

Pinch of Korean chile flakes

Few turns of freshly ground black pepper

FOR SERVING

1 sweet, crisp pear

MAKE THE GOCHUJANG SALSA CHILE SAUCE

1. Blend the sauce ingredients in a blender into a slightly chunky sauce. Let sit for at least 2 hours before using, or make it up to 3 days ahead and keep in the fridge until needed.

MAKE THE PORK BELLY

2. Cut the pork belly (or short ribs) into slices about ⅓-inch (1-cm) thick and place them in a bowl. Blend the rest of the ingredients except the canola oil in a blender until smoothly pureed, then pour the marinade over the pork, coating it evenly. Cover and marinate in the fridge for at least 1 hour or up to 6 hours.

3. Heat a large, flat *nonstick* skillet over medium-high heat and coat thinly with canola oil. Scrape off any excess marinade on the surface of the meat (because it will burn easily), then arrange the pieces in the skillet *without crowding*. Do not move the meat until the first side is deeply caramelized; turn and repeat with the other side. Let rest on a plate for 5 minutes, then chop it into small pieces.

MAKE THE STICKY RICE TORTILLAS

4. Knead all the ingredients in a large bowl until even and smooth. The surface of the dough should be smooth and crack-less. If it seems dry, knead in another teaspoon of water. Then divide the dough into 8 equal-size balls.

5. Heat a large, flat skillet over high heat until very hot. Place one ball in between two pieces of parchment, then press a flat-bottomed plate on top as hard as you can to flatten the ball into a thin tortilla. Toast the tortilla in the skillet until one side is evenly covered in browned spots, then flip and toast the other side until browned and slightly puffed up. Repeat to make the rest. You can keep the tortillas stacked and loosely covered with plastic wrap to keep warm. They may stick to each other a little, but you shouldn't have a problem peeling them away. If you make the tortillas more than 1 hour before serving, they will toughen up slightly; warm them back up in a hot skillet.

MAKE THE BURNED SCALLION SALAD

6. With a sharp knife, cut the jumbo scallion into short but super-thin shreds (julienne cut). I have a tool that does this, but if you don't, or don't have the exquisite knife skills to pull this off, you can simply cut it into very small dice. Soak the cut scallion in ice water for 1 minute, then drain and squeeze dry. Scatter onto a sheet pan in a thin but uneven layer, then char the surface with a blowtorch until the edges are slightly burned. This process takes the aggressiveness off the raw scallions, adding a smoky, burned flavor but still maintaining the crunch. Toss the charred scallions with the rest of the salad ingredients. Set aside.

PREP THE PEAR

7. Use a fruit peeler to remove the skin from the pear, then keep "peeling" it into thin slices.

TO SERVE

8. To make each taco, combine the pork, chile sauce, and scallion salad on a sticky rice tortilla and top with 1 or 2 slices of pear. Serve immediately.

OPA RICE BALL

After Dumpling, our Maltese, passed away, we went on a short getaway to Seoul hoping for a distraction from our overwhelming sadness. We wandered like a pair of crippled zombies through the numbing daze of human tidal waves on city streets flaring with neon lights, staring expressionlessly into a flux of sounds, colors, tastes, and disorientations. It isn't easy to remember much from a place where you went to forget, and I made no attempt to do so. But one thing did come back with me; after two years of filtering and settling, it still hovered at the back of my mind like an attentive friend.

This giant spicy rice ball.

Perhaps it was its remarkable body mass that made an impression. Perhaps it was the sharp yet fluently seasoned meat filling colliding with the sticky and mildly sweet sushi rice. Or perhaps it was the unsuspected crunch scattered throughout. I don't know. But it stuck. And if something is still sticking even after two years, one has to make it permanent.

MAKES 8 BALLS

SPICY BEEF FILLING

½ pound (220 g) 75 percent lean ground beef

2 garlic cloves, grated

1½ teaspoons grated ginger

1 tablespoon soy sauce, plus 1 teaspoon for cooking

1 teaspoon toasted sesame oil, plus 1 teaspoon for cooking

1 teaspoon honey

1 teaspoon cornstarch

⅛ teaspoon freshly ground black pepper

¼ cup (60 g) mayonnaise

2½ tablespoons (50 g) gochujang (Korean chile paste)

½ teaspoon yellow mustard

⅓ cup finely diced scallions

RICE BALLS

8 cups steamed sushi rice, at room temperature

1 cup (40 g) crispy rice cereal

2 teaspoons toasted sesame oil

¼ teaspoon fine sea salt

Six 8 × 11-inch sheets Korean toasted seaweed (see Note on page 271)

MAKE THE SPICY BEEF FILLING

1. In a bowl, combine the beef, garlic, ginger, the 1 tablespoon soy sauce, the 1 teaspoon sesame oil, the honey, cornstarch, and black pepper. Mix until evenly combined.

2. Heat a *nonstick* skillet over medium-high heat. Add the remaining 1 teaspoon sesame oil

to coat the bottom, then add the beef mixture. Using a wooden spoon to break up the beef, cook until the meat is evenly browned and broken up. Add the remaining 1 teaspoon soy sauce and mix evenly, cooking until the soy sauce starts to caramelize around the beef bits. Transfer to a bowl, then chill in the fridge for around 20 minutes, until *cooled completely*.

3. Add the mayonnaise, gochujang, mustard, and scallions and mix evenly.

MAKE THE RICE BALLS

4. To make a rice ball, lay a large piece of plastic wrap on the counter and place 1 cup of

the sushi rice in the middle. With a slightly wet hand, press the rice down into a compact, round disk. Spread about 2 heaping tablespoons of the beef filling in the middle, then bring the edges of the plastic wrap upward to slowly close the whole thing into a ball surrounding the filling. Cup your hands around the rice ball to tighten it as compactly as you can, then twist the plastic wrap until it tightly secures the rice ball in shape. Repeat to make 7 more rice balls. Set aside.

5. In a large skillet, mix the crispy rice cereal, sesame oil, and salt until each grain is coated evenly. Cook over medium-high heat, stirring frequently, until the cereal starts to turn darker

in color. Set aside on a large plate to cool completely.

6. Tear the seaweed sheets into small pieces and place them in a food processor. Run the machine until the seaweed is ground to tiny flakes. Set aside on a large plate.

7. Unwrap a rice ball, then roll it in the cereal until it covers about 30 percent of the surface. Roll it next in the ground seaweed, using your hands to press the seaweed into the ball and cover the whole surface.

8. You can prepare the rice balls a few hours ahead of time, but only coat the ones you're going to eat right before serving so the crispy rice stays, well, crispy.

NOTE ON SEAWEED: *Korean-style toasted seaweed is seasoned with sesame oil and salt. If you can't find it, you can use nori, Japanese toasted seaweed for making sushi (make sure it's unflavored). But if you do, add 2 teaspoons toasted sesame oil and ¼ teaspoon fine sea salt to the food processor.*

BAKED CORN RICE CRACKERS

This recipe for rice crackers is tweaked from Japanese senbei, *their traditional puffed rice crackers, with added sweetness and flavors from cornmeal, spices, and herbs. It is my alternative to fried tortilla chips, which are incompatible with my wish to fit back into 95 percent of my wardrobe. When fully dried and puffed in the oven, the cracker is extremely crispy and sturdy, wonderful for scooping up perfectly made guacamole.*

MAKES 4 SERVINGS

¼ cup (50 g) cooked short-grain rice or jasmine rice, at room temperature

½ cup (80 g) sticky rice flour (see page 6)

¼ cup plus 3 tablespoons (50 g) fine-ground cornmeal

2 teaspoons light brown sugar

2 teaspoons baking powder

½ teaspoon sea salt

½ teaspoon ground coriander

⅛ teaspoon ground cumin

¼ cup plus 1 tablespoon (75 g) water

2 tablespoons (28 g) canola oil

1 small handful fresh mint leaves, finely chopped

1 egg white, lightly beaten

1. Set an oven rack on the middle level and preheat the oven to 400°F/200°C, preferably with the fan on.

2. Make sure the rice is at room temperature; if it's at all warm it will prematurely activate the baking powder. Place the rice in a food processor and run the machine until it turns into a sticky paste. Add the sticky rice flour, cornmeal, brown sugar, baking powder, salt, coriander, cumin, water, and canola oil. Pulse a few times, then thoroughly scrape the sides and bottom of the bowl and run until the mixture comes together into a sticky ball, within 1 minute. If it doesn't (this depends on the wetness of the rice), add 1 teaspoon more water and run again. Add the mint leaves and pulse until evenly incorporated.

3. Prepare two sheets of parchment paper at 16 × 12 inches (40 cm × 30 cm). Place the dough between the two sheets and slowly roll it out into a thin sheet slightly thicker than a tortilla (it should not extend past the edges of the parchment). Peel the top parchment away, then place the dough (still on the bottom parchment) on a baking rack (not a sheet pan) and bake on the middle rack for 10 minutes. Lift the cracker and baking rack out of the oven and gently remove the bottom parchment (the dough should be dry enough for you to do so). Brush a thin layer of egg white on top of the cracker, then return it to the oven.

4. *Lower the temperature to 325°F/160°C,* and bake for 15 to 18 minutes, until the cracker is thoroughly dried. Let cool completely on a cooling rack, then shatter it into pieces.

5. Serve the crackers the same day with Thai Guacamole.

THAI GUACAMOLE

The number of self-proclaimed "best" guacamole recipes out there probably equals the number of people making it, which means it's about three, tops. I mean, this dish is constantly insulted as being easy, basic, almost downgraded to a social entitlement. A béarnaise is for the elitist, but a mean guac is the people's dip. Sure, it's easy to whip up a blob of loose and browning goo to go with tortilla chips from a bag and call it a guac party. But a good guac—one that holds up its tippy form with a creamy but firm consistency, that is relatively cool in temperature, not lukewarm, that is thoughtfully seasoned while remaining fiercely green—is not, I declare, mindless.

This recipe is how I like my guac, injected with a heavier aroma from garlic confit, and with a deep breeze of Southeast Asian fragrance using Makrut Lime Leaf Oil. I use fish sauce whenever I can to replace salt, but in this case, I want to reduce the moisture level for a firmer texture. So, sea salt. If you can't be bothered to make the garlic confit in the name of a humble guacamole, then at least promise me this, that you'll try the lime leaf oil. It makes a difference.

MAKES 4 SERVINGS

2 Pickled Chilies (page 25) or pickled jalapeños, finely chopped, plus some to sprinkle on top

1 teaspoon Garlic Confit Sauce (page 14)

2 teaspoons Makrut Lime Leaf Oil (page 13), plus more to drizzle

2 small shallots, finely minced

3 medium cold avocados, pitted, peeled, and diced

1 tablespoon freshly squeezed lime juice

½ teaspoon fine sea salt, more or less, to taste

⅛ teaspoon ground cumin

⅛ teaspoon freshly ground black pepper

½ handful each cilantro leaves, fresh mint, and finely chopped scallions

Extra-virgin olive oil, for drizzling (optional)

Baked Corn Rice Crackers (page 272) or tortilla chips, for serving (optional)

1. In a large bowl, mix the Pickled Chilies (or jalapeños), Garlic Confit Sauce, Makrut Lime Leaf Oil, and shallots. Add the avocado and pour the lime juice evenly over the top, then sprinkle the sea salt, cumin, black pepper, and most of the herbs on top. Mash with a large fork to your preferred consistency (I like it slightly chunky) and transfer to a serving bowl.

2. Sprinkle on a little more chopped Pickled Chilies and the remaining herbs, then drizzle with a bit more lime leaf oil. I like to drizzle a bit of extra-virgin olive oil on top as well to make it pretty and shiny, but that's up to you. Serve with corn rice crackers or tortilla chips, if you'd like.

CHICKEN FLOSS AND HERB SANDWICH

Nothing about this sounds right. Chicken floss? *Leftover shredded chicken, lightly breaded and fried until the life-giving moisture has departed from each shriveled strand, crunchy and condensed, then stuffed into a freaking sandwich? As if that doesn't sound like a saliva-sucking sponge. As if concentrated chickenness inside crispy strings lubricated by a moist, refreshing, and deeply savory herb salad dressed in pureed fried green chilies and Dijon mustard would ever sound remotely enticing. Don't make this. It doesn't make sense.*

MAKES 1 SERVING

CHICKEN FLOSS

¼ cup (31 g) all-purpose flour

¼ cup (30 g) potato starch (see page 6)

1½ teaspoons fine sea salt

½ teaspoon freshly ground black pepper

½ teaspoon ground white pepper

¼ teaspoon ground cumin

1 packed cup thinly shredded leftover roast chicken, skin included

Canola oil, for frying

1 handful herbs and aromatics (such as basil, mint, tarragon, parsley, cilantro, and diced scallions)

1½ tablespoons Fried Chile Verde Sauce (page 15)

2 teaspoons Garlic Confit Sauce (page 14)

1 teaspoon Dijon mustard

½ teaspoon grated shallot

Small splash of extra-virgin olive oil

TO FINISH

1 slice crusty bread

Mayonnaise, for the bread

MAKE THE CHICKEN FLOSS

1. In a large bowl, whisk the all-purpose flour, potato starch, salt, peppers, and cumin. Toss the shredded chicken in the mixture until evenly coated, then set the chicken in a fine-mesh sieve and shake off any excess coating. Set aside.

2. Add 1 inch (2.5 cm) of canola oil to a deep frying pan. Heat over high heat until the oil bubbles up immediately around a wooden chopstick. Add the chicken *in a single layer* (do it in two batches if need be) and fry until the chicken floss is golden brown and crispy. Drain well on a paper towel.

MAKE THE HERB SAUCE

3. Hand-tear the mixed herbs into large pieces and toss in a medium bowl with the Fried Chile Verde Sauce, Garlic Confit Sauce, mustard, shallot, and a small splash of olive oil.

MAKE THE SANDWICH

4. Cut the bread in half, and spread one side with mayonnaise. Top with half the herb salad and lots of chicken floss, then the rest of the herb salad. Mayo the other piece of bread and top off the sandwich.

VIETNAMESE-STYLE CHOPPED LIVER TOAST

I'm not trying to bad-mouth banh mi. I'm sure there's a really good one somewhere, hidden inside the tender foliage of the Vietnam jungle, shielded, protected from the dangerous exposure that is this cynical, cynical world. That's all cool, because it explains why I've never had a great one.

When I think of banh mi, I think **bready,** *and that's not a good word when it brings to mind an airy, lofty French baguette with a small, unbalanced ration of pickled root vegetables, a thin smear of liver pâté, and a wisp of Vietnamese bologna.* **Disproportionate** *is perhaps another word to describe it, or* **stingy,** *without sugarcoating. Look, I completely understand it as a product of an underprivileged society under colonial rule, but I'm just saying that when I fancy a banh mi, I don't technically have to honor its history. Which brings us to an open-face option.*

This chopped liver rips off April Bloomfield's recipe, but it's reincarnated with that Vietnamese dazzle, the salivating funk of fish sauce, the warm prolonging blend of spices, the creamy emulsification with lemongrass-blended chicken oil—schmaltz, if you will—and at last, it all makes inexplicable sense on top of crusty French baguette and the sweetly brightening pickled radishes. Serve with lots of fresh herbs, the eternal Vietnamese wisdom. With that, I have no contest.

MAKES 5 TOASTS

SPECIAL EQUIPMENT: *immersion blender; spice grinder; truffle shaver or mandoline*

LEMONGRASS CHICKEN OIL *(see Note on page 281)*

¼ pound (100 g) solid chicken fat and/or skin, cut into small dice

2 stalks (30 g) lemongrass, white parts only

QUICK PICKLED RADISH

2 tablespoons white vinegar

2 tablespoons water

1 tablespoon sugar

½ teaspoon fine sea salt

¼ teaspoon lemon zest

1 watermelon radish or green radish (or any preferred radish)

VIETNAMESE-STYLE CHOPPED LIVER

½ pound (215 g) chicken livers

1 tablespoon olive oil

3 tablespoons plus 2 teaspoons finely minced shallots

1½ teaspoons grated ginger

1 garlic clove, grated

2 tablespoons cognac

2 tablespoons Chinese rice wine

2 teaspoons fish sauce, plus more as needed

½ teaspoon red wine vinegar

⅛ teaspoon pho spice (see page 135)

1½ tablespoons lemongrass chicken oil (see above)

1 teaspoon Dijon mustard

⅛ teaspoon ground white pepper

⅛ teaspoon freshly ground black pepper

5 diagonal baguette slices, toasted

Chopped fresh mint leaves or cilantro, for serving

MAKE THE LEMONGRASS CHICKEN OIL

1. In a small *nonstick* saucepan, cook the chicken fat (and/or skin) over medium heat. Meanwhile, smash the lemongrass stalks until flattened, then roughly chop them. When all the oil has been rendered from the fat or skin and you have tiny crispy bits floating around in the oil, add the lemongrass. Cook for 15 seconds more, then turn off the heat. Let cool, then transfer everything into the tall cup that comes with your immersion blender and blend for 1 to 2 minutes, or as long as it takes to get close to a smooth puree.

MAKE THE QUICK PICKLED RADISH

2. In a medium bowl, whisk the vinegar, water, sugar, salt, and lemon zest until the sugar and salt are dissolved. Peel the radish, then slice it with a truffle shaver or mandoline until you have about 40 thin slices. Submerge the sliced radish in the liquid and soak for at least 20 minutes before using. The radish pickles can be made up to 4 hours ahead.

MAKE THE CHOPPED LIVER

3. Clean the chicken livers under running water to get rid of any blood clumps and whatnots. If the two lobes of chicken liver came connected, separate them with scissors. Soak the livers in ice water inside the fridge for at least 2 hours and up to overnight; the livers will become slightly pale in color. Dab them completely dry with a paper towel.

4. In a large *nonstick* skillet over high heat, heat the olive oil until it starts to smoke. Add the livers, gently spacing them apart from each other (wear a mitt when you do this because chicken livers love to splatter), then partially cover the skillet to avoid splattering. Cook for 1 minute *undisturbed.* Turn the livers *once,* and cook for another 1 minute. *They should be deeply caramelized on the outside but still lightly pink on the inside.* Transfer to a dish and set aside.

5. Add the 3 tablespoons of minced shallots and cook until slightly softened, about 30 seconds, then add the ginger and garlic and cook just until fragrant. Add the cognac, wine, fish sauce, vinegar, and pho spice and cook until the liquid is reduced to about 3 tablespoons. Return the livers to the skillet,

and cook for a few seconds, until the liquid is reduced to about 2 tablespoons.

6. Transfer the livers and pan liquid to a large bowl and add the lemongrass chicken oil, the remaining 2 teaspoons minced shallot, the mustard, and the white and black peppers. Use a large fork or spoon to mash the livers and combine until the mixture is chunky but creamy. Season with more fish sauce if desired.

TO SERVE

7. Serve the chopped livers right away on a sliced toasted baguette, with plenty of pickled radish and topped with chopped fresh mint or cilantro.

NOTE ON LEMONGRASS CHICKEN OIL: *The amount of lemongrass chicken oil in the recipe is determined by the minimal amount that's required to be blended properly with an immersion blender. This amount would be too little to be worked properly inside a regular blender. If you have only a regular blender, you'll have to double the recipe at least. The oil can be kept in an airtight jar in the fridge for up to 2 weeks. It adds great flavor to roasted vegetables or as the base of tomato sauces.*

FRIED RAZOR CLAMS WITH THAI TARTAR SAUCE

I will always have the fondest associations with fried oysters. The slow strolls through the incandescent magic that was the West Village in the spring, the endearing sight of the lovely Pearl Oyster Bar snugged on Cornelia Street, flickering in dappled light, the foolish indulgence and reckless oblivion of youth when there was nothing but anticipation, nothing but possibility, nothing else but New York City.

I am, of course, far from all of that these days, and these are obviously not Pearl's fried oysters. Life shifts. We adapt. We move on. It may not be the way we would like it to be. But hopefully the journey is—and perhaps this is enough—delicious.

MAKES 4 SNACK-SIZE SERVINGS

THAI TARTAR SAUCE

¼ cup plus 2 tablespoons (90 g) mayonnaise

2 tablespoons thick Greek yogurt

1 small handful Thai basil leaves

1½ small shallots, peeled and cut into rough chunks

6 cornichons, cut into rough chunks

1 tablespoon chopped cilantro leaves

1 tablespoon grated ginger

2 teaspoons Makrut Lime Leaf Oil (page 13)

1 teaspoon fish sauce

½ teaspoon lime zest

½ teaspoon freshly squeezed lime juice

⅛ teaspoon freshly ground black pepper

FRIED RAZOR CLAMS

Canola oil, for frying

⅓ cup (56 g) potato starch (see page 6)

⅓ cup (40 g) fine cornmeal

½ teaspoon fine sea salt

½ teaspoon ground white pepper

½ teaspoon baking powder

½ pound (220 g) shucked razor clam meat, from about eight or nine 5-inch (13-cm) razor clams (see Note on page 284)

FOR SERVING

Ground white pepper

Lime wedges

Thai basil leaves

MAKE THE THAI TARTAR SAUCE

1.   The Makrut Lime Leaf Oil is the key flavor in this sauce, so please do not skip it. Put all the tartar sauce ingredients in a food processor and pulse until everything is finely chopped. This can be made up to 1 day ahead of time and kept in an airtight container in the fridge. Stir again before serving.

MAKE THE FRIED RAZOR CLAMS

2.   Add canola oil to a deep frying pan to a depth of at least 1½ inches (4 cm), then heat over medium-high heat to 330°F/165°C, or until

the oil bubbles immediately around an inserted wooden chopstick.

3. In a large bowl, whisk the potato starch, cornmeal, salt, white pepper, and baking powder. Swirl and coat the meat in its own liquor, then transfer into the breading mixture. Toss and squeeze with your hand to apply an even and thorough coating all around the clams.

4. Carefully drop the coated clams into the frying oil. *Do not crowd the pan.* The clams should have enough room to swim around. Now, frying clams *do* splatter, so wear a mitt and operate with tongs to move the clams in the hot oil. While one batch of clams fries, coat the next batch. When the clams are medium golden brown, drain well and transfer them to a rack to drain. Repeat to make the rest of the clams.

TO SERVE

5. While hot, dust the clams with more white pepper and serve immediately with a wedge of lime, more fresh Thai basil leaves, and some Thai tartar sauce. Just a friendly reminder that this would make an awesome fried clam roll in a butter-toasted potato bun.

NOTE ON RAZOR CLAMS: *Why razor clams? Aside from the fact that they're super meaty and sweet, the shells come already opened and the meat is easy to remove. But if you're an expert at shucking clams, by all means use littleneck clams, or whatever you have available around you. Oysters? Oh yeah.*

BLACK HUMMUS

If there was ever a food equivalent of a lesser sibling, forever living under the shadow of its more popular and wildly successful brother, sulking in its own underappreciated beauty in a random corner of the pantry next to a half-used bag of tapioca pearls . . . for sure, it would be black sesame seeds. It's unjust, it really is. While the world is busy marveling at all forms of its brother, the white sesame seed—sprinkled, pureed, or pressed into oils—we forget that black sesame seeds can do the very same things, all of them, and perhaps even better in some cases.

Like any good hummus, this version, made with black beans and black sesame paste, is creamy, silky, and wrap-around-your-tongue smooth. But it's also bolder in its black-suited sleekness, more intentional, stating its desire to impress with every dollop of aromatic, spicy, nutty complexity. Serve it with my faux-sourdough pita breads, or really just about any carbs you can throw its way (I even eat it with rice sometimes), and it's a satisfying snack or appetizer that never disappoints.

A trick that I do with many hummus, sesame paste, or even sausage recipes is that instead of using ice water, I blend ice cubes directly into the mixture to form a smooth emulsion. It keeps the content cold while slowly releasing its liquid, which is exactly what a successful emulsion likes! Just make sure that you run the processor long enough for the ice cubes to melt completely, which is essential for a super-silky hummus texture anyway.

MAKES 4 SERVINGS

BLACK BEAN AND BLACK SESAME HUMMUS

One 15-ounce can (425 g) black beans, drained (295 grams after draining)

2 garlic cloves, peeled

7½ tablespoons (113 g) black sesame paste (easily found online)

2 tablespoons (30 mL) freshly squeezed lemon juice

½ teaspoon fine sea salt, plus more for seasoning

¾ teaspoon cayenne

½ teaspooon brown sugar

3 to 6 ice cubes

TOPPING

2 tablespoons extra-virgin olive oil

1 tablespoon toasted sesame oil

½ teaspoon ground cumin

½ teaspoon chile flakes, plus more for sprinkling

¼ cup drained canned chickpeas

FOR SERVING

1 tablespoon toasted white sesame seeds (see page 100)

2 tablespoons finely minced cilantro

Pita bread or crusty bread

MAKE THE BLACK HUMMUS

1. Place the black beans and garlic in a food processor and pulse and scrape the sides and bottom a few times, until the mixture is finely chopped. Add the sesame paste, lemon juice, salt, cayenne, and brown sugar. Run

the processor, scraping the sides and bottom several times in between, until the mixture is as smoothly pureed as humanly possible. Add the ice cubes one at a time and run the processor until each ice cube has completely melted/ emulsified with the hummus. Stop adding ice once you've reached your desired consistency. Season with more sea salt if desired.

2. The color of the black hummus when it's just finished will look, well, not quite black, but more like an unappetizing concrete gray. Just let it sit for 30 minutes and the color will darken.

MAKE THE TOPPING

3. In a small skillet, combine the olive oil, sesame oil, cumin, and chile flakes and cook over medium-high heat for 1 minute, until fragrant. Add the chickpeas and cook for 30 seconds to warm them through.

TO SERVE

4. Spoon the chickpeas and spiced oil over the black hummus. Mix together the toasted sesame seeds and minced cilantro with an extra pinch of chile flakes and sprinkle all over the top. Serve with pitas or crusty bread.

MAPO TOFUMMUS

Tofu is bland. Don't let its supporters, including me, tell you otherwise. Flying solo, it carries a subtle but offbeat taste that comes from soy milk, which, depending on whether you grew up accustomed to it or not, could be either a very good or a very bad thing. Having said that, I love tofu, perhaps in the truest sense because I wholly embrace it for what it is, but, more important, what it isn't. Tofu is not about taste. Tofu is a texture thing.

Hard, medium, silken like panna cotta—think of tofu as a mere vessel, an empty field of impending dreams. It's like Mars, if you will, in that any exciting thing about it has to be outsourced, like Matt Damon. This will open up a whole window of promise.

Tofummus, for example, is what happens when you turn the least popular end of the spectrum of tofu, the firm variety, into a silken, creamy, luscious bed of hummus–like substance that begs for company. In this case, its soul mate, if you know what I'm talking about.

This is mapo tofu, the quintessential icon of Sichuan cuisine, one of its most successful exports across the world, numbing with Sichuan peppercorns and fiery with fermented chile bean paste, turned into a dip (an overdue development, if you ask me). The tongue–stinging, bloodred chile oil and deeply savory pork bits are immediately cooled down by the silky smooth touch of the pureed tofu, a most delicious reconciliation for the taste buds. And if you're feeling kinky, make it a threesome with chewy scallion and garlic naan.

MAKES 4 APPETIZER SERVINGS

MAPO SAUCE

3 ounces (90 g) ground pork or beef

1 teaspoon plus 1 tablespoon toasted sesame oil

½ teaspoon potato starch or cornstarch (see page 6)

3 tablespoons canola oil

1 tablespoon Sichuan broad bean chile paste (doubanjiang; see page 8)

1 teaspoon mushroom powder (see page 9)

½ teaspoon finely minced fermented black beans, or 1 teaspoon of the darkest miso you can find

½ to ¾ teaspoon Korean chile flakes

2 garlic cloves, grated

2 teaspoons grated ginger

1 teaspoon ground Sichuan peppercorns, plus more for dusting

⅛ teaspoon ground cumin

2 tablespoons Shaoxing wine or sherry

¼ cup chicken stock

1½ teaspoons apricot jam

¼ teaspoon ground white pepper

5 drops rice vinegar

TOFUMMUS

1 pound (450 g) firm tofu

2 tablespoons Garlic Confit Sauce (page 14)

1½ teaspoons toasted sesame oil

⅓ teaspoon fine sea salt

Finely diced scallions
Helldust (page 28; optional)
Chewy Scallion and Garlic Naan (page 291)

MAKE THE MAPO SAUCE

1. In a small bowl, mix the ground pork (or beef) with the 1 teaspoon sesame oil and the potato starch (or cornstarch) until smooth. In a small saucepan, heat the canola oil and the remaining 1 tablespoon sesame oil over medium-high heat. Add the ground meat, breaking it up as finely as you can with a wooden spoon, and cook until evenly browned. Add the Sichuan broad bean chile paste, mushroom powder, fermented black beans or dark miso, and chile flakes and cook, stirring often, for 1 to 2 minutes, until the chile flakes have turned dark maroon in color. Add the garlic, ginger, Sichuan peppercorns, and cumin and cook until just fragrant, about 1 minute. Add the wine, scraping any caramelization that is sticking to the sides and bottom of the pan, and cook until the alcohol has evaporated. Add the stock, jam, white pepper, and vinegar, turn the heat to low, and simmer until the liquid has reduced by half and is slightly thickened. The mapo sauce can be made a couple of days ahead of time. Reheat until warm before serving.

MAKE THE TOFUMMUS

2. Tofu is made from boiled soy milk, which makes it technically "cooked." But if you're not a fan of the taste of soy, boiling the tofu again will make it taste more well rounded (although this may also make the puree slightly grittier). If you decide to boil it, cut the tofu into chunks the size of large marshmallows and cook them in boiling water for 5 minutes. Drain well and let cool and continue draining on a clean towel in the fridge, then transfer to a food processor. If you're not boiling it, simply pat the tofu dry with a clean towel and place it in a food processor. Run the processor for 1 to 2 minutes, until the tofu is smoothly pureed. Add the Garlic Confit Sauce, sesame oil, and salt and run again until incorporated. The tofummus should still be quite dull in flavor at this point.

TO SERVE

3. Serve the tofummus covered in warmed mapo sauce, topped with finely diced scallions and dustings of more ground Sichuan peppercorns. To add more heat, sprinkle with Helldust. Serve with Chewy Scallion and Garlic Naan.

CHEWY SCALLION AND GARLIC NAAN

People may be looking for a lot of things in a naan: the char, the bubbles, the butter, the garlic. And they are all correct. But if you ask me, there's one element that surpasses all of the above in defining what a great naan should be, and that is **chewiness**. *In this recipe, tapioca flour, an unconventional aid, is added to the dough to bring a tender chew to the overall body. Once that's taken care of, the rest is easy.*

MAKES 4 PIECES OF NAAN

SPECIAL EQUIPMENT: *stand mixer with a dough hook; blowtorch*

1 cup (130 g) bread flour, plus more as needed

¼ cup (30 g) tapioca flour (see page 6)

1 teaspoon light brown sugar

1 teaspoon instant dry yeast

¾ teaspoon roasted barley tea powder (see page 9)

½ teaspoon fine sea salt

2 tablespoons (28 g) Greek yogurt

⅓ cup (80 g) plus 3 teaspoons water

2 tablespoons finely chopped scallions

4 tablespoons (½ stick/56 g) unsalted butter, melted, plus more as needed

1 garlic clove, finely minced

⅛ teaspoon freshly ground black pepper

MIX THE DOUGH

1. In the bowl of a stand mixer with the dough hook attachment, combine the bread flour, tapioca flour, sugar, yeast, roasted barley tea powder, salt, Greek yogurt, and the ⅓ cup of water. Mix on low speed until a cohesive dough has formed, then knead for another 3 minutes, until smooth and elastic. Turn to medium-high speed, then add 1 teaspoon more water and knead until fully incorporated. Repeat with two more additions of 1 teaspoon water. *I have found that adding water* after *the dough has developed a considerable amount of gluten greatly improves the dough's overall elasticity and texture.*

2. Continue to knead on medium-high speed for another 10 to 15 minutes. In the end, the dough should be extremely smooth and elastic; it will pull completely away from the bowl as the machine is running but be just sticky enough to leave an opaque film on the bowl's side. When the machine stops, it will immediately stick back

to the bowl. Adjust with more flour or water accordingly. At last, add the scallions and knead until fully incorporated.

LET THE DOUGH RISE

3. Cover the bowl and let the dough rise until fully doubled, 45 minutes to 1 hour. Transfer the dough to a lightly floured surface and fold it over itself a few times. Divide the dough into 4 equal portions and shape each into a round ball. Cover the balls loosely with plastic wrap and let rise again until they have expanded by about 80 percent more, 30 to 45 minutes.

4. Meanwhile, prepare the melted butter in one bowl, and in another, mix the minced garlic and freshly ground black pepper. Set aside.

5. Set a rack 3 inches (8 cm) below the broiler and preheat the top broiler on high.

SHAPE THE NAAN

6. Lightly oil the counter with the melted butter and place a dough ball on top, then butter the top surface of the dough ball liberally. Use the thick part of your palm to spread the dough out in a circular motion, like wiping a window. If you feel that there is friction between the dough and your hand, apply more butter. You may feel that the dough is springing back, but it's okay; take your time to spread it out until you have a disk about the thickness of a thin-crust pizza. Mix the rest of the melted butter (at least 2 tablespoons) with the garlic mixture and set aside until needed.

COOK THE NAAN

7. Preheat the broiler on high and heat a large cast-iron skillet over high heat until slightly smoking. *Gently* peel the dough from the counter and lay it in the skillet, then transfer the pan right below the broiler. Bake until the air bubbles on the dough are *lightly* blistered and browned. *Do not* bake until the entire naan is browned because it will be tough and crispy instead of chewy.

8. Home ovens usually aren't hot enough to char the air bubbles before the dough gets overcooked, so apply more char to the naan with a blowtorch afterward. Brush the surface lightly with garlic butter.

9. Reheat the skillet and repeat with the rest of the dough balls.

CREPE X WITH BLACK MUSTARD SEEDS

There's a relatively fancy Yunnan restaurant in Beijing under the name Hua Ma Tiantang (Flower, Horse, Paradise). The last time I visited was possibly five years ago, and if after five years I'm still mumbling about a crepe I ate there, we can all agree that an investigation is warranted.

You don't have to have tried Yunnan cuisine to be intrigued. You simply have to know about its blessed geographic positioning as a Chinese province nestled in between Sichuan, Vietnam, Myanmar, and Thailand. It's almost unfair, culinarily speaking. If Yunnan cuisine were a movie, it would be produced by Steven Spielberg, directed by J. J. Abrams, and starring Tom Hanks and the whole Kardashian family. Its greatness is inevitable by affiliation alone.

Take this crepe, for example.

It is unlike any other crepe I have ever tasted, chewier than the French variety but soft and elastic, ruthlessly speckled with nutty pops of black mustard seeds throughout and a compounded fragrance of mixed herbs that arises above the sum of its parts. Taken as a whole, it doesn't taste simply like a mixture of flour, mustard seeds, scallion, mint, and cilantro, but **beyond.** *It's a superior anomaly—neither Chinese nor Southeast Asian, neither here nor there, but a transcendent mutation. It's Crepe X.*

Enjoy these crepes on their own, as they are enough. But if insecurity hits, serve them with a spicy, sweet, and tangy roasted tomato chutney.

MAKES 3 SMALL CREPES

SPICY ROASTED TOMATO CHUTNEY

1½ cups (220 g) cherry tomatoes, halved

¼ cup (60 mL) juice from Pickled Chilies (page 25)

5 or 6 Pickled Chilies (page 25), finely chopped

2½ tablespoons apricot jam

2½ teaspoons freshly squeezed lemon juice

1 garlic clove, grated

1 small shallot, finely minced

CREPE X

2 tablespoons whole black mustard seeds

½ cup (63 g) all-purpose flour

3 tablespoons (25 g) tapioca flour (see page 6)

½ teaspoon light brown sugar

½ cup (120 g) water

1 tablespoon (15 g) fish sauce

1 heaping tablespoon finely minced fresh mint leaves

1 heaping tablespoon finely minced cilantro

1 heaping tablespoon finely minced scallion

2 tablespoons (26 g) unsalted butter, melted

MAKE THE ROASTED TOMATO CHUTNEY

1. Set a baking rack at the highest level of the oven and preheat the broiler.

2. Arrange the cherry tomatoes on a sheet pan with the *cut side up* and place them on the baking rack. Roast for 6 to 9 minutes, until charred, softened, and a little dehydrated, watching carefully to avoid too much burning.

3. Meanwhile, in a small saucepan, bring the chile pickling juice to a boil and cook until it is *reduced by half.* Add the cherry tomatoes, using scissors to roughly cut them into small chunks, along with the Pickled Chilies, jam, and lemon juice. Cook for 2 minutes or so, until the mixture is thickened. Mix in the garlic and shallot and let cool completely before using. The chutney can be kept in an airtight container in the fridge for up to 2 weeks.

MAKE THE CREPES

4. In a small skillet, toast the mustard seeds over medium heat, swirling the skillet frequently until the seeds are *just starting* to pop (don't let them burn, please). Quickly transfer the seeds to a large bowl and let them cool for a couple of minutes. Add the all-purpose flour, tapioca flour, brown sugar, water, fish sauce, mint, cilantro, and scallion and whisk until completely lump-free. Let the batter rest for 20 minutes.

5. Start with a *cold, nonstick* skillet about 7 to 8 inches (18 to 20 cm) wide. Brush the skillet lightly with melted butter, then add about one-third of the batter and swirl the skillet to spread it out evenly. Turn the heat to medium to medium-high. *When the top surface of the crepe is no longer liquid, brush it with melted butter,* then flip the crepe back and forth with a spatula a couple of times until the crepe is *lightly browned* on both sides. Repeat to make the remaining 2 crepes.

6. Brush the hot crepes with a bit more butter before serving. Serve with the chutney.

SMOKY DADDY

Ever since watching an episode of The Mind of a Chef *by Gabrielle Hamilton of Prune in New York City, my mind has been infected with the idea of scorching eggplant directly over the burner into blackened, smoky, juicy, tender lumps of flesh. That episode has thus far disabled my ability to imagine cooking eggplants any other way, with frequent side effects including The Soloist (page 146) and a newfound obsession with the Levantine dish called baba ganoush. Did you know that* baba *means "father" in Arabic? The word* ganoush *is said to be a person's name—someone who invented the dish, perhaps? But in conjunction with* baba *it could mean "pampered daddy." To be honest, I never really cared about this dish before; sad as it is, in my previous experience, there was not much else that interesting about this* baba. *A conforming suburban dad, at best.*

Enter Smoky Daddy.

This infinitely more sultry version of baba ganoush draws inspiration from other mentors besides Gabrielle Hamilton, such as a Chinese appetizer from Hunan Province of steamed eggplants mashed with fried chilies. The bits and pieces of broken and seemingly unrelated recipes together make a creamy, fiery, cooling yet burning concoction of contrasting yet balanced flavors. The brown and almost syrup-like liquid smoke emitted from the blackened eggplants is mixed with extra-virgin olive oil to wet the craggy surface, from where it will smolder in the back of your mouth like the breath of a gentle burning hearth. I don't know about your dad, but this one is cool for sure.

MAKES 2 SNACK-SIZE SERVINGS

SPECIAL EQUIPMENT: *grill rack; mortar and pestle (optional)*

1 pound (450 to 500 g) eggplants (I use the slender Asian ones)

2 small shallots, peeled and grated

2 garlic cloves, peeled and grated

3 tablespoons Greek yogurt, the thicker the better

2 tablespoons tahini

2 teaspoons juice from Pickled Chilies (page 25) or juice from other pickled chilies

1½ teaspoons freshly squeezed lemon juice

1 teaspoon fish sauce

½ teaspoon toasted sesame oil

¼ teaspoon ground cumin

¼ teaspoon ground fennel

⅛ teaspoon freshly ground black pepper

Fine sea salt to taste

TOPPING

2 tablespoons Fried Chile Verde Sauce (page 15)

1 tablespoon charred eggplant juice (from above)

2 tablespoons extra-virgin olive oil, for drizzling

Finely chopped fresh mint leaves and cilantro

Helldust (page 28), for sprinkling

Orange Chile Sambal (page 23; optional)

My Ultimate Chile Oil (page 24; optional)

1. Wash the eggplants and place them on a grilling rack set on top of a burner. Turn the heat to high and roast the eggplants, turning and repositioning them as needed, *until every square inch of the skin is completely blackened and charred and the flesh is soft.* If some parts of the skins are not charred thoroughly, it will make peeling them a lot harder. Transfer the eggplants to a large bowl, cover with plastic wrap, and set aside. (The eggplants will emit some dark brown juices as they sit, which will be used later on.)

2. In another large bowl, combine the shallots, garlic, yogurt, tahini, chile pickling juice, lemon juice, fish sauce, and sesame oil and whisk until smooth. Lightly toast the cumin, fennel, and black pepper in a small skillet over medium heat until fragrant, then add to the bowl as well.

3. The eggplants should be cooled by now. Cut off the stem tips, then peel away the charred skin (leave the liquid left by the eggplants in the bowl). I like to peel the eggplants right by a running tap to rinse off the charred skins that stick to my hands as I remove them. If there are some tiny black specks left on the eggplants, don't worry about it. Finely chop the eggplants and add them to the bowl with the shallot mixture. With a large fork, whisk vigorously until the mixture is creamy, without large lumps. Taste and season with a bit of sea salt if needed.

4. Transfer the Smoky Daddy onto a serving plate. Add the Fried Chile Verde Sauce on top and give it a little swirl. Mix 1 tablespoon of the smoky juice emitted from the eggplants with the 2 tablespoons extra-virgin olive oil, then drizzle that evenly over the top. Sprinkle with fresh chopped mint and cilantro and Helldust for extra heat. You could also use Orange Chile Sambal and/or My Ultimate Chile Oil as the topping, which will be equally good.

SHIT I EAT
WHEN I'M BY MYSELF

I don't cook for myself.

*Or at least, not the way it looks on my blog or in the rest
of this book outside this section. I don't know how it reflects
on me as someone who's selling recipes, but in my view,
cooking and eating are two very different, entirely separate
areas of investigation. Cooking, to me, is about curiosity,
the insatiable need to know beyond necessity, the compulsion
in the process of unwrapping a question, rephrasing it
again, moving on to the next, the hunt.*

Eating is about comfort.

*I rarely find enthusiasm in repeating the same recipes,
answering the same questions. But I can eat the same things
over and over again. These things don't involve a lot
of thinking and rationalizing; they aren't even bothered
by common decency or responsibilities. I eat them free of
my own judgment.*

HUANG FEI HONG SPICY COLD PEANUT NOODLES

Think Pringles . . . Doritos . . . the most iconic American savory snacks that everyone grew up with. This thing called Huang Fei Hong—fried peanuts seasoned with chilies and Sichuan peppercorns—is the cultural equivalent in China. It's everywhere, eaten by everyone, spicy, numbing, salty, and unstoppable, the perfect beer food. But very few people realize the true potential of this humble snack that they pop aimlessly into their mouths without a second thought, and that is, when pureed into a thick and velvety sauce, it can be used for the best, most life–changing spicy cold peanut noodle dish you've ever tasted. If you tend to go senseless in the presence of cold peanut noodles, don't make this.

MAKES ENOUGH SAUCE FOR 4 MAIN-DISH OR 6 APPETIZER SERVINGS

HUANG FEI HONG PEANUT SAUCE

5 ice cubes (about 1-square-inch/2.5-square-cm cubes), plus more as needed

½ pound (210 g) bag of Huang Fei Hong spicy peanuts

¼ cup plus 2 tablespoons (90 mL) soy sauce, plus more as needed

½ cup (120 mL) water

2½ tablespoons honey

2 tablespoons toasted sesame oil

1½ teaspoons rice vinegar

TO FINISH *(for 1 main-dish serving)*

A couple bricks instant ramen noodles

1 large handful mixed chopped aromatics and herbs (scallions, cilantro, and so on)

Toasted sesame oil to taste

Freshly grated black pepper to taste

My Ultimate Chile Oil (page 24), for drizzling

Turbinado sugar, for sprinkling (optional)

MAKE THE HUANG FEI HONG SAUCE

1. Place the ice cubes (these prevent the mixture from overheating and breaking), and the rest of the peanut sauce ingredients in a blender. Blend on high speed for 2 minutes, until the mixture is extremely smooth and silky, like mayonnaise. If it's too thick, blend in more ice cubes. Transfer to an airtight container and keep in the fridge until needed.

TO FINISH

2. Cook the ramen noodles until just done. Drain well and shock in an ice water bath until completely cold. Drain well again, and mix together with the chopped herbs and a generous splash of toasted sesame oil to coat. Then add an obnoxious amount of Huang Fei Hong sauce to thickly coat every strand and toss again. Season with more soy sauce if needed and give it a few grinds of black pepper. Drizzle with My Ultimate Chile Oil. I like to sprinkle some coarse turbinado sugar to get that occasional sugary crunch, but Jason doesn't like it. So you be the judge.

KARE RISOTTO

I ate Japanese curry growing up. Every Taiwanese kid did. We love this stuff. As thin-skinned as all children are during elementary school, I loved this stuff so much that I was willing to endure the savagery of the "diarrhea rice" joke from other stupid worthless kids at lunch. That's how much I love it. And now, three decades of mental fortification later, I have no problem telling you that this stuff is awesome. So awesome that I don't even have to do it properly to appreciate it. Five minutes is all the patience I have for my kare.

MAKES 1 SERVING

1 cup (240 mL) chicken stock

3 tablespoons whole milk, plus more as needed

1 ounce (30 g) Japanese curry bricks, I prefer medium spicy to spicy (see Note)

0.3 ounce (8 g) unsweetened dark chocolate or 2 teaspoons cocoa powder

1 tablespoon Caramelized Onion Powder Paste (page 22)

1 garlic clove, grated

½ teaspoon grated ginger

2 teaspoons curry powder

½ teaspoon Dijon mustard

½ teaspoon honey

⅛ teaspoon ground cumin

A few grinds of black pepper

1¼ cups (180 g) cooked Asian short-grain rice (leftover is fine)

1 egg yolk

Kraft Parmesan cheese, for serving

Combine everything *except* the rice, egg yolk, and Parmesan in a medium saucepan. Bring to a simmer over medium heat, stirring constantly, until smooth and even. Add the rice and mix evenly. If your rice is cold to begin with, heat until warmed through. Adjust the consistency with more milk if it's too thick. Serve with a raw egg yolk in the middle and lots of Parmesan cheese.

NOTE ON JAPANESE CURRY BRICKS: *Japanese curry bricks are usually packaged like Kit Kats, in connected but individual "bricks." Each brand's sizing may vary, so you may have to cut the bricks or do some basic math based on the total weight provided on the packaging (for example, if the whole package weighs 90 grams, you'll need one-third of the package). Japanese curry usually comes in sweet, medium spicy, and spicy levels and can be easily found in Japanese supermarkets or online.*

FAST AND FURIOUS CARBONARA

The secret to making carbonara is to not make it for anybody but yourself. Carbonara is like that one unpredictable relative in every family who is **hidden away at any social gatherings.** *It is very likely to crack under pressure and shit all over your perfect little dinner party. But in a safe cocoon of privacy, carbonara is allowed to be free, outspoken, sometimes even fun. It doesn't really matter if the egg curdles a bit or not. In fact, it doesn't even have to be Italian! Just you and your (maybe) slightly curdled, spicy, savory, aromatically pungent slurps alone in an empty room, minding your own business. Still good, more than good, absolutely delicious as a matter of fact, and that's all that matters when it comes to solitary dining.*

MAKES 1 SERVING

2 bricks instant ramen noodles

2 large eggs, thoroughly whisked

1 garlic clove, grated

3 tablespoons My Ultimate Chile Oil (page 24)

1½ tablespoons Dry Fried Shallots (page 17) or Fried Garlic Powder (page 27)

1 tablespoon soy sauce

1 tablespoon juice from Pickled Chilies (page 25)

1½ teaspoons Sichuan broad bean chile paste (doubanjiang; see page 8 and Note)

½ teaspoon light brown sugar

¼ teaspoon ground white pepper

Chopped herbs of your choice, such as cilantro, scallions, and so on

Bring a pot of water to a boil and cook the instant ramen noodles until done. Transfer the noodles to a sieve and pour all the water out of the pot, then return the noodles to the pot. Use a fork to vigorously mix the eggs into the hot noodles, whisking fast and constantly for 1 minute, until the eggs are slightly thickened. Add the chile oil, fried shallots or garlic powder, soy sauce, chile pickling juice, Sichuan broad bean chile paste, brown sugar, white pepper, and chopped herbs and mix until evenly combined. Slurp immediately.

NOTE ON SICHUAN BROAD BEAN CHILE PASTE (DOUBANJIANG): *You can theoretically substitute gochujang or dark miso paste, but it won't be nearly the same or as good. So please don't.*

FREEZER DUMPLING RAVIOLI

Once upon a time in a high school somewhere in Vancouver, there lived a school cafeteria that sucked. The word cafeteria itself was a gross exaggeration; human-operated vending machine *would have been more appropriate. Because, aside from soda and gum, the cafeteria sold one thing and one thing only—reheated canned ravioli in tomato sauce. To this day I can't quite decide whether it's because it was the only hot dish available or because it was actually delicious, but it holds a small, nonetheless lasting spot in my heart. If this recipe appears somewhat crude to your liking, consider it an upgrade from my public school offering.*

A quick note on Asian freezer dumplings: their convenience and availability are as vital to maintaining social stability and domestic peace as delivery pizzas are in the United States. They are almost always cooked in boiling water, but this one-pot method lets the dumplings absorb the flavors from the sauce as it reduces, and in reverse, helps the sauce thicken as well. That one teaspoon of sugar is the key to turning a grown-up, respectable tomato sauce into the childish version that we all secretly crave. Don't let go of it.

MAKES 1 SERVING

SPECIAL EQUIPMENT: *immersion blender (optional)*

One 14-ounce (400 mL) can peeled plum tomatoes

1 tablespoon extra-virgin olive oil, plus more for serving

1 garlic clove, thinly shaved

Leaves from 2 fresh thyme sprigs

Pinch of chile flakes

2½ teaspoons fish sauce

1 teaspoon light brown sugar

12 pork freezer dumplings of your choice, unthawed

1 tablespoon heavy cream

Grated Parmesan cheese, for serving

1. Canned plum tomatoes are usually submerged in some kind of tomato water/juice. If your tomato juice from the can is nice and thick, great, but if it's very watery, pour out a couple of tablespoons. I like to use an immersion blender to make a smooth puree of the tomatoes, but you can crush them with your hands as well.

2. In a small pot over medium-high heat, combine the olive oil, garlic, thyme, and chile flakes and simmer, stirring, until the edges of the garlic just start to barely brown. Add the pureed tomatoes, fish sauce, and brown sugar and cook for 5 minutes, until reduced slightly. Add the dumplings, turn the heat to medium, and cook, maintaining a gentle simmer and stirring frequently to keep the dumplings from sticking to the pan, until the sauce has reduced to a thick tomato sauce consistency.

3. Stir in the cream, then serve with lots of Parmesan and dashes of extra-virgin olive oil.

CAT FOOD

Everyone knows I am a canned sardine whore. I consider people who don't appreciate canned sardines to be of a less evolved genome, born involuntarily, with a set of erroneous taste buds. Not their fault—a thought that helps me not to go dark on them. Another thought is that perhaps they just haven't had a good can of sardines. But the fact that I'm using the Waitrose brand at $1.80/can tells me that my standards aren't exactly strict. So if you tell me that you can't enjoy a 2 × 4-inch tin can packed with fatty, luscious, incredibly deep-flavored miniature fishes, and are unable to savor every last drop of that precious liquid gold, I just can't help but label you as "the others." My husband used to be "the others," but I turned him, so there's still hope for everybody else to get in on this gastronomic delight. Starting with cat food.

MAKES 1 SERVING

One 4.2-ounce (120-g) medium-high-quality can sardines in olive oil

1 small handful mixed fresh mint leaves, basil leaves, and chopped scallions (green parts only)

½ teaspoon Makrut Lime Leaf Oil (page 13)

¼ teaspoon fish sauce, plus more to adjust

¼ teaspoon juice from Pickled Chilies (page 25) or other pickled chilies

¼ teaspoon ground white pepper

1 teaspoon grated ginger

Chile flakes

1 bowl of steamed rice (I prefer sushi rice, but jasmine rice works fine as well)

1. Drizzle a bit of the olive oil from the canned sardines over the fresh herbs to coat them (this keeps them from oxidizing prematurely) and chop them as finely or as coarsely as you prefer. Transfer to a small bowl and add the rest of the oil from the can, along with the lime leaf oil, fish sauce (the amount depends on how salty your fish is), chile pickling juice, and white pepper. Mix well and set aside.

2. Place the sardines on top of a bowl of steamed rice, then spoon the herb mixture on top and let it run marvelously through every grain of rice. Top with grated ginger and chile flakes. Meow~

SPAMOCADO TOAST

At a certain point in your life, you'll find yourself wavering on one particularly low night when you feel as though the meaning of life is dribbling away from your grasp. Try mixing mashed Spam drenched in My Ultimate Chile Oil with a spritz of soy sauce, a few drops of vinegar, a drizzle of toasted sesame oil, and a good amount of diced scallions served over soft, gently steamy sushi rice, then feel the jolt of resurgence throbbing through your veins once again. It is the encrypted message from the universe showing you why it is still good to be alive, the very thing that we are put on this earth to feel, the unmistakable sign that tells you to keep living on.

But on any other day, add a healthy avocado to it and make it a toast. Because, after all, we are still responsible human beings.

MAKES 1 SERVING

Roughly ¼ cup (100 g) low-sodium Spam

2 tablespoons My Ultimate Chile Oil (page 24)

3 teaspoons toasted sesame oil

½ teaspoon soy sauce

⅛ teaspoon ground white pepper

1/16 teaspoon (a pinch) light brown sugar

1 medium avocado, peeled and pitted

¼ teaspoon fine sea salt

1 large slice country bread, plus olive oil for coating

Finely diced scallions, green parts only

1. With a sturdy fork, mash the Spam in a bowl until broken into small pieces. Add My Ultimate Chile Oil, 1 teaspoon of the sesame oil, the soy sauce, white pepper, and brown sugar and toss to combine evenly. In another bowl, mash the avocado with a fork and mix with the remaining 2 teaspoons sesame oil and the sea salt.

2. In a large flat skillet over medium-high heat, coat the country bread with a drizzle of olive oil, then toast until crispy on the edges on both sides. Spread the avocado mixture over the bread, then top with the Spam mixture. Sprinkle the scallions on top and serve.

CHONGQING MELTED CHEESE

Inspired by the bloodbath that is today's pop-culture Sichuan cuisine, in which everything is baptized in a flaming red pool of chile oil, I thought, why not cheese, too? This is its bare-bones version, which is a sinful delight on its own, but feel free to kick it up if you have any other cheeses of your fancy, or top with leftover shredded braised meats (for example, the mala smoked meat on page 245), roast chicken, or whatnot. It can't go wrong. It can't.

MAKES 1 SERVING

1½ tablespoons My Ultimate Chile Oil (page 24)

¾ cup (68 g) shredded Pepper Jack cheese

¾ cup (68 g) shredded mild Cheddar cheese

1 large egg

Freshly ground black pepper

Finely chopped herbs and aromatics, such as mint, parsley, and scallions

Crusty bread, for serving

1. Add the chile oil to a small, heavy skillet (7 to 8 inches/18 to 20 cm; best to use a skillet in a material that retains heat well, like cast iron) and swirl to spread it around. Scatter the cheeses on top and make a small well in the middle, then crack the egg into the well. Place over medium-low heat *with the lid on* and cook until the cheeses are melted and the egg is just cooked, with the yolk still runny. You can peek a couple of times during the process; it's fine.

2. Crack some fresh black pepper on top and sprinkle with whatever fresh greens and herbs you have on hand, such as scallions, mint, or parsley. Serve immediately with crusty bread.

5

THE CHIMNEY

Unexpected things started to happen. Unfathomable things. Strangers—utterly unrelated people who weren't my mom and didn't owe me money—talked back.

I know there are a lot of people out there, mostly younger and smarter people, who approach blogging and this whole social media thing as a window to a new frontier. But when I started my blog, it didn't feel like a window, not even a chimney (at least that's where Santa comes in), but more like a slamming door (wet with paint) in my face.

Don't let my modesty fool you; I excel at negativity.

But I'm not telling you this to be a downer. Thing is, judging by my time spent with Richard and what's happening generally in the world at large, honesty is not a favored commodity in this day and age. So it's probably wiser, or more frankly, business-friendly, for me to display a more polished side of my story, even spin it a little bit, pretending not to be the angry ("passionate"), confused ("searching"), malcontented ("hungry"), and bitter ("critical") woman who didn't know what she was doing at the awkward junction of thirty-two years of age ("a dreamer at a crossroads").

But none of that would be the truth. I was fucking lost.

I hope I won't offend "my people" by saying this; I cross my fingers that the blogger community will understand the peculiar self-doubt and dilemma that I was going through when I started blogging. But at the very beginning, I didn't hold much regard for this business. At the time, with a sodden mixture of emotions, it felt like submitting to defeat—gutless, a pathetic excuse for my voluntary unemployment, the white towel. Forget about being an architect (what I had studied to be). Forget about being the Nancy Silverton of dog food in New York (when I decided I didn't want to be an architect). Forget about being *more*—this was what I was going to spend the last flow of my trickling enthusiasm on: whisking, blogging, and letting myself dribble anonymously into reality-induced early menopause.

In April 2012, as an obituary for the official death of my career aspirations, I published my first blog post on Wordpress, a platform not particularly well received in the eyes of Richard. Of course, the idea of a democratic space where anyone can gather and express, publish, or even fight for whatever the hell is their point of view is a deeply, deeply unsettling thought that puts Richard on edge. *It was just what I wanted.* I didn't care if my access to Wordpress in China was patchy at best, or at times, maddeningly difficult even with a VPN; I did it almost out of spite.

It was my last act. Then I jumped.

But strangely, the sound of my skull cracking against the asphalt of reality did not follow.

Very much to my surprise, I found myself falling down a surreal, eccentric rabbit hole, as frightening as it was fascinating. Unexpected things started to happen. Unfathomable things. Strangers—utterly unrelated people who weren't my mom and didn't owe me money—talked back. And not just people who wanted to talk about cooking, but more astonishingly, those who wanted to offer their unpackaged kindness, support, and tolerance for this obnoxious pre–middle age ranter. Fellow bloggers who probably work ten times harder than I do wanted to help me grow my audience. A terminally ill woman took precious time out of her life to write and say, "Please keep going." A total stranger from the United States offered to send me medications that were unavailable in China for my severely ill fur-children. Some of the most talented, generous, supportive, and compassionate people I know came to me through blogging—strangers whose capacity for kindness and tolerance not only put my own to shame, but made me question the basis of my cynical truth. I mean, aren't we all innately selfish beings? Don't we all measure our success against others' shortcomings? Isn't glee an unspoken response to neighboring miseries? Are these not the basic flavors of our unsavory nature? In this day and age, when clicking "like" on Facebook is considered a sufficient act of compassion, I sat in awe.

I thought I was lost on the edge of a cliff. But instead I found friendships.

I would have never started blogging if it weren't for Richard, during the most emotionally destructive period of my life, to say the least. But looking back, would I rather none of it had happened? I ask myself this sometimes. And the answer is no. Because I wouldn't have known the people whom I have had the fortune to meet.

I'm not trying to make anybody throw up in their mouth with saccharine talk. Trust me, hyper-positivity gives me acne. But I want to take the time here to say thanks to each and every one of the people who have been a part of this journey. Thank you, stranger friends.

In 2016, with the generous help of many others, an e-mail came into my inbox asking if I wanted to write a cookbook.

Hm, I guess that really was a chimney after all.

for SWEETS

*They say that sugar can kill you. Which makes it real
tempting for moments when you're sitting under dim light,
contemplating whether there's anything in this world worth
living for anymore. Death by sugar . . . there are worse ways
to go, right? But what they don't tell you is that when
you stuff a handful of buttery cookies in your mouth in a clear
act of despair, thinking it's going to help you check out,
it often, fortunately, backfires.*

*I find that, in most cases, a really great piece of something
sweet makes it feel damn good to be alive.*

*So whether you yourself are the subject in need, or you're
picking up some really troubling signs from loved ones,
neighbors, or anyone else who you think could use a fucking
break, consider this chapter a potential line between
life and death.*

SPEED-FOLDING LAMINATED DOUGH

So far in life, I haven't had my heart broken maliciously, really. I broke up with a couple of guys before I met my first real boyfriend when I was twenty-one, who then became my husband, and we've been happily married ever since. I'm not flaunting anything—I'm just saying that dating assholes was never quite my thing.

But that was before I met Mr. I'm-Too-Good-for-You. **Pastries.**

Fuck *pastries.*

In my experience, all pastries are assholes. But if I must warn you about anyone in particular, there's no doubt in my mind that it's this guy: **laminated dough.** *Oh, you've met him for sure, most likely dressed as a potential croissant, pain au chocolat, or morning bun, with all his sweet, sweet promises. Tall, gorgeously tanned, handsome, and complicated with all his vulnerable layers.* **Textbook asshole.**

Girl, if you're looking to bake something nice in your kitchen and you see this guy posing around the corner, **run.** *Call your high school sweetheart Pillsbury and never look back. Because laminated dough will require sometimes up to two days of intensive labor—which involves endless folding and refolding, and all the long hours of chilling in between— but still, when the time finally comes and you wait excitedly by the oven door, he may very well turn out to be a complete failure and disappointment.*

He hurt me. He really did.

So here I'm proposing an alternative. Someone who isn't temperature-sensitive, time-sensitive, or commitment-sensitive, yet still looks devilishly handsome in all circumstances.

Friends, meet speed-folding laminated dough.

You read correctly. In order to get those beautiful laminations, you don't need to constantly keep everything super cold, nor do you have to fold it a gazillion times. You can actually—listen—simply roll the dough out into a much longer sheet, spread the butter on top (at room temperature), and do only two foldings after that, and there you have it—Magic Mike. The theory is, as long as the texture and softness of the dough and the butter are within close proximity—a technique inspired by Asian puff pastries like Su-style mooncakes—the layers should form without the chilling process in between.

I first tested this theory armed with skepticism and a handful of Xanax, just in case it turned out to be another throbbing disappointment. But it didn't. It worked. Marvelously. Just like that.

Here is the recipe for speed-laminated dough, followed by my favorite way to use it.

MAKES 1 BRICK OF LAMINATED DOUGH

DOUGH

1 recipe mochi bread dough (see page 44)

1 cup plus 2 tablespoons (250 g) unsalted butter, slightly softened

3 tablespoons (24 g) all-purpose flour

¼ teaspoon table salt

1 egg, beaten

1.　Avoid making this recipe in a hot room, say, above 73°F/23°C. It's not impossible but it's unnecessarily messy. If you're making this during a hot summer, do it in an air-conditioned room. Prepare one recipe of mochi bread dough. After the dough is kneaded, cover the bowl with plastic wrap and let it rest for 15 minutes on the counter. Meanwhile, in a medium bowl, mix the slightly softened (*not room temperature*) butter, flour, and salt until absolutely lump-free (*the consistency of the butter mixture should be just spreadable but not melty*). Set aside.

2.　Now, before you start rolling, please try your hardest to follow the dimensions given as closely as possible. *Do not eyeball it. Measure it with a ruler.* These dimensions are designed to maximize the layering and lamination to their utmost potential. Stretch the dough too far and you may lose the layers. Underdo it and you may not have enough layers. So: Scrape the dough onto a well-floured surface and shape it into a rectangular block, then roll it into a super-long, 10 × 30-inch (25.5 × 76-cm) rectangular sheet. You may feel at times that the dough is resisting your effort by bouncing back. Relax and take

your time. This recipe is not particularly time-sensitive, and the more straight-edged and controlled the shape of your dough is, the easier the next step will be. Now, when you have the rectangle, scoop dollops of the mixed butter and scatter them evenly across the dough, then spread it out into an even layer with a spatula, *leaving about 1 inch (2.5 cm) of margin* along the edges of the sheet. Brush the butterless margin with beaten egg, then make gentle dents on the dough that mark the sheet crosswise into 6 equal segments of 10 × 5 inches (25.5 × 13 cm). Now fold the sheet according to the marks you made, with each fold gently pressing down the dough to eliminate air bubbles and pinching the edges where you applied the egg wash to close the seam (this traps the butter inside).

3.　When you finish folding, you will have a rectangular block that's about 10 × 5 inches (25.5 × 13 cm). Pinch the two seam ends tightly together, then cut off the uneven bits with a pastry cutter to get a straight edge.

4.　Rotate the block 90 degrees. This is the second and final folding. Take a wooden skewer and make a few holes across the block. These holes will release air bubbles trapped inside, which will make it hard to roll the dough out evenly. Now roll the block out again into a long, 5 × 30-inch (13 × 76-cm) rectangular sheet. Again, the dough will resist you a bit, but relax and take your time. If you feel that there are trapped air bubbles being pushed around, just

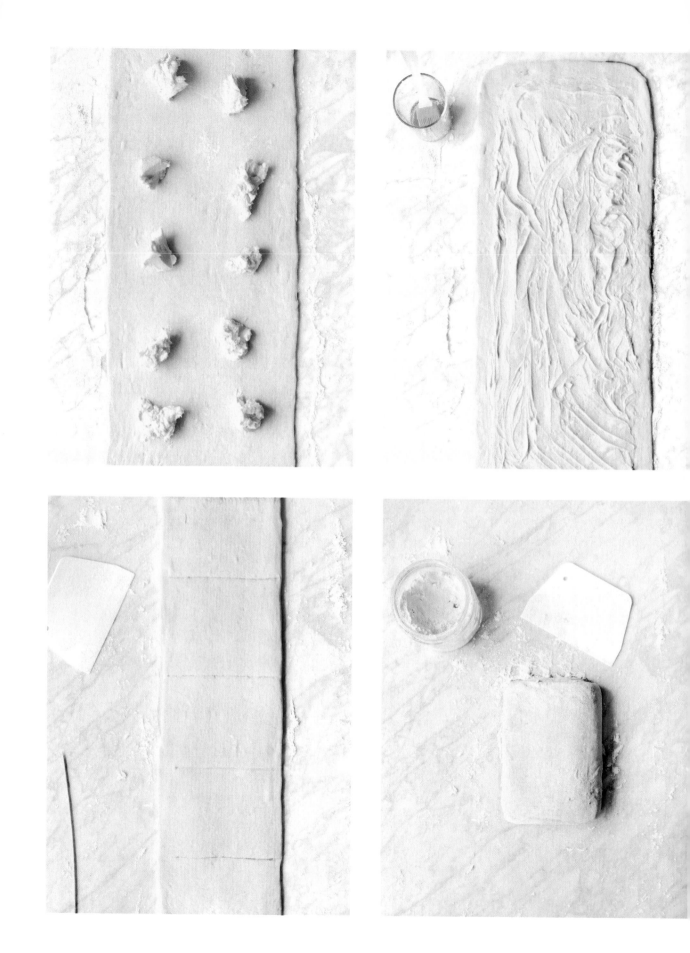

poke a hole to release them. And if there is a bit of butter being squeezed out, don't panic, it's okay—just dust a bit of flour to cover it.

5. When you have the rectangular sheet, this time brush the *entire* top surface with egg wash (this helps the folds stick together and makes the final rolling easier). Make dents that mark the sheet crosswise into 6 equal segments of 5 × 5 inches (13 × 13 cm), then fold the sheet according to the marks you made, just like before.

6. Now you should have a block roughly 5 to 6 inches (13 to 15 cm) square. Place the block

on a floured baking sheet, cover with plastic wrap, and press it down with another baking sheet with something heavy on top (you want the weight to be wide and even, like a book, so it doesn't slide off to the side). Place the whole setup in the fridge and let it rest for at least 1 hour, 2 hours at most. This technique is different from that for a traditional laminated dough; in this recipe, the butter will lose its pliability if it's too cold and becomes lumpy when it's rolled out.

7. *How to use the laminated dough . . .*

CRUFFINS WITH SALTED YOLK CUSTARD

You know about the cruffin, right? The genetically modified love child of a croissant and a muffin? It's the work of people who are no longer happy with the already exceedingly buttery piece of pastry that is the croissant, but are also too utterly ashamed to throw it into a fryer to turn it into a cronut, who ultimately want something that fits just between the cracks of their conscience but is stuffed with a boatload of custard nonetheless. Yeah, that would be a cruffin. So let's enjoy it while it still exists, before it mutates again into a hamburssant *or whatever.*

I'm suggesting making this with salted duck yolk—infused custard, adapted from an infamous dim sum poetically named "liquid sand bao," which would make this a liquid sand baossant.

MAKES 16 CRUFFINS

SPECIAL EQUIPMENT: *sixteen 3¼-inch- (8.2-cm-) wide, 2½-inch- (6.3-cm-) deep muffin molds; pastry piping bag*

SALTED YOLK CUSTARD

1 cup (240 mL) whole milk

¼ cup (50 g) sugar

3 cooked salted duck egg yolks (see Note on page 326)

2 large fresh egg yolks

3 tablespoons all-purpose flour

3 tablespoons unsalted butter

CRUFFINS

1 tablespoon unsalted butter, for the molds

¼ cup (50 g) granulated sugar, for dusting

1 block Speed-Folding Laminated Dough (page 320)

Flour, for dusting

½ cup (100 g) light brown sugar, for tumbling

MAKE THE SALTED YOLK CUSTARD

1. In a blender, blend the milk, sugar, salted duck egg yolks, fresh egg yolks, and flour until smooth and lump-free. Transfer to a medium saucepan and cook over medium-low heat, whisking constantly, until the mixture has fully thickened and starts to bubble gently. Turn off the heat and whisk in the butter until fully incorporated. Let cool slightly, then transfer to a pastry piping bag. (The custard can be made up to 3 days ahead of time and kept cold in the fridge.)

MAKE THE CRUFFINS

2. Butter sixteen 3¼-inch- (8.2-cm-) wide, 2½-inch- (6.3-cm-) deep baking molds and dust them evenly with sugar.

3. Place the block of laminated dough on a lightly floured surface and roll it out into a 10 × 16-inch (25.5 × 40.5-cm) sheet. Cut it crosswise into 16 strips that are 1 inch (2.5 cm) wide. Roll up each strip tightly like a little snail and place it inside a cruffin mold; the mold will be about 45 percent full. (If your molds are smaller than what's called for, make the strip shorter to fit accordingly.)

4. Cover the molds with plastic wrap and let the dough rise until it has more than doubled its original size, to about 210 percent, meaning it will peek over the top of the mold. Depending on the warmth of the room, this will take 1½ to 2½ hours. (Alternatively, after shaping and plastic wrapping, you can place the molds in the fridge to rise overnight, about 8 hours—but if the dough hasn't more than doubled, you have to let it finish rising on the counter before baking. Or, after shaping and plastic wrapping, you can place the molds into the freezer, then allow 4 to 6 hours for the dough to thaw and double before baking.)

5. Preheat the oven to 350°F/180°C.

6. Remove the plastic wrap and set the molds on rimmed baking sheets. Bake the cruffins for 15 minutes, until puffed and golden brown. Right out of the oven, remove the cruffins from the molds and tumble them in brown sugar to coat. Let cool on a cooling rack for 15 minutes.

FILL THE CRUFFINS

7. When the cruffins are cooled and ready, make a small opening on the top of each cruffin, then pipe the custard directly into the cruffin until it fills the cavity. You'll have up to a 4-hour window in which to enjoy them at their best.

NOTE ON SALTED DUCK EGGS: *Salted duck eggs are a common item in Chinese supermarkets. They are usually sold in egg cartons and come in both cooked and uncooked options. In this recipe we use the cooked ones. If you can't buy them locally, they can easily be found online.*

OTHER WAYS TO USE SPEED-FOLDING LAMINATED DOUGH: *After rolling out the dough in step 3, cut it into 3 long strips and braid them together as if you're braiding hair. Let the dough rise in a long pullman loaf pan, covered, until fully doubled. Bake in a 355°F/180°C oven for 45 to 50 minutes for a buttery Danish loaf.*

MOCHI BREAD DOUGHNUTS WITH SALTED HONEY AND CARDAMOM

Here's another way to use the mochi bread dough. I know, I know, doughnuts, *hardly creative, almost a foregone conclusion, but I love them too much to give a shit about any of that, especially when they're simultaneously soft and chewy like these. The prominently salted honey–butter syrup and the earthy yet sharp fragrance from the cardamom bring them up a notch.*

MAKES ABOUT 15 DOUGHNUTS

SPECIAL EQUIPMENT: *4-inch (10-cm) doughnut cutter*

1 recipe mochi bread dough (see page 44; see Note on page 329)

Flour, for dusting

¼ cup (60 mL) honey

1 tablespoon unsalted butter

½ teaspoon sea salt

1 teaspoon ground green cardamom (see Note on page 329)

½ teaspoon ground cinnamon

Canola oil, for frying

SHAPE THE DOUGHNUTS

1. After you've kneaded the mochi bread dough, cover it and let it rise at room temperature until doubled, about 1 to 2 hours. Dust the working surface with flour, then roll the dough into a large sheet about ⅜ inch (1 cm) thick. Use a 4-inch (10-cm) doughnut cutter to cut out doughnuts. You can do it with or without doughnut holes.

2. Cut out a 5-inch (13-cm) square of parchment paper for each doughnut. Transfer the doughnuts onto the squares, set them aside on large sheet pans, and cover loosely with plastic wrap. Let them rise again until doubled (this will mostly show in thickness instead of width), 1½ to 2 hours.

MAKE THE GLAZE AND TOPPING

3. Meanwhile, combine the honey, butter, and sea salt in a small saucepan and cook over low heat, stirring constantly, until the mixture has come to a simmer and the butter is melted. Set aside to let cool to room temperature and thicken.

4. Mix the cardamom and cinnamon in a small bowl and set aside.

FRY THE DOUGHNUTS

5. When the doughnuts are proofed, add 1½ inches (4 cm) of canola oil to a deep frying pan. Heat over medium-high heat until the

oil reaches 325°F/160°C. Lift one parchment paper with a doughnut on it and gently lower it into the frying oil (including the parchment). Use a fork or chopstick to press the parchment paper down so the hot oil can flood the bottom of the doughnut, which will release it from the parchment. When the parchment is free, remove it with tongs. Fry until one side of the doughnut is golden brown, about 1 minute, then flip and fry until the other side is golden brown, about 1 minute more. *If it takes way faster or slower than 1 minute for each side of the doughnut to brown, the oil is either too hot or too cold. Adjust accordingly.* Drain well and set aside on a cooling rack. Repeat to make the rest of the doughnuts.

TO SERVE

6. Drizzle the salted honey over the warm doughnuts and dust with the cardamom mixture (a little goes a long way). Enjoy immediately.

NOTE ON MOCHI BREAD DOUGH: *If you prefer a softer doughnut, you can substitute all-purpose flour for half of the bread flour in the recipe.*

NOTE ON GREEN CARDAMOM: *You probably won't be able to find ground green cardamom for purchase. Grind whole green cardamom pods in a spice grinder until finely ground (you'll need about 10 cardamom pods' worth for the grinder to work).*

NUTELLA FOCACCIA DI RECCO

This is not a pizza. And despite its name, this is not a typical focaccia bread, either. What this is is a specimen of human ingenuity originating in a little commune called Recco in a little place called Italy. It probably existed in its peaceful little universe for a long time without disturbance until it was brought to worldwide stardom by none other than the Nancy Silverton in her restaurant Chi Spacca in Los Angeles. She not only made it a star, but she perfected it: a flat saucer of unleavened dough that is stretched to its physical limit, then stuffed with dunes of stracchino cheese and baked into a brilliantly browned and crispy disk from heaven.

I realized that I cannot outdo it. And so I brought in Nutella.

Try to imagine a terrain of roaming hills consisting of paper-thin and film-like dough, largely brittle and crispy, partly chewy and stretchy, ballooned with blisters and underground chambers flowing with molten Nutella, whipped cream cheese, and a touch of honey. I'm fully aware that this sounds like a lot, which is why I'm giving you a full pardon to forgo your meal and eat just this. No one will object.

MAKES ONE 12-INCH (30-CM) PIE

SPECIAL EQUIPMENT: *stand mixer with a dough hook; pizza stone (optional); shallow, heavy 13½-inch (34-cm) pizza pan; pastry cutter (optional)*

DOUGH

1¾ cups (215 g) bread flour, plus more for dusting

½ cup (120 g) water

1½ teaspoons (9 g) fine sea salt

¼ teaspoon (1 g) light brown sugar

1 teaspoon (6 g) extra-virgin olive oil, plus more for the pan

FILLING

½ heaping cup (4 ounces/115 g) cream cheese, at room temperature

1½ tablespoons whole milk

½ heaping cup (140 g) Nutella

2 tablespoons honey

Extra-virgin olive oil, for drizzling

MAKE THE DOUGH

1. In the bowl of a stand mixer with a dough hook attachment, combine the bread flour, water, sea salt, brown sugar, and the 1 teaspoon (6 g) olive oil. Mix on low speed until a cohesive dough comes together, then turn to high speed and knead for 10 minutes, until the dough is extremely elastic and smooth. The dough should pull away cleanly from the bowl during mixing but stick back when the machine stops. It should feel very soft and tacky but not stick obsessively to your hands.

2. Cover the bowl with plastic wrap and let rest for *at least* 2 hours. You need the dough to be extremely relaxed in order to stretch properly. You can also prepare the dough the day before, wrap it in plastic wrap, and keep it in the fridge,

but let it sit at room temperature for at least 1 hour before using.

3. Forty-five minutes before baking, preheat the oven to 500°F/260°C, with a pizza stone (if available) set on the middle rack. Lightly brush a shallow, heavy 13½-inch (34-cm) pizza pan with olive oil and set aside.

MAKE THE FILLING

4. While the oven is preheating, whisk the cream cheese and milk until creamy and set aside.

SHAPE THE FOCACCIA

5. Transfer the dough to a floured surface and divide it into 2 equal portions. Dusting one dough portion with more flour as needed, roll it out into a thin sheet almost as big as the pizza pan. Drape the sheet onto the pizza pan and gently stretch the sheet over the edges until it's so thin that it's slightly translucent. Drop the Nutella in 6 or 7 large dollops across the dough, then do the same thing with the cream cheese mixture. Drizzle the honey all over it. Roll out

the other portion of dough and drape it on top, again stretching it gently over the edges until it's thin and almost translucent. Gently use the heels of your hands to contour the dough around the fillings, resulting in a surface with multiple domes. Pinch the edges of the dough to enclose the two sheets, then use a pastry cutter or knife to press down on the edges and cut off any excess dough from the rim. Now, cut a 3-inch (8-cm) opening directly over *each* lump of filling, to let the filling spill over a little during baking.

TO BAKE

6. Gently brush the surface with a bit of olive oil (it doesn't have to be perfect), then place the pizza pan on top of the pizza stone (or directly on the oven rack) and bake for 11 to 13 minutes, until the entire pie is puffed, blistered, and golden brown. If the bottom of your focaccia isn't crispy enough at this point, heat it over high heat on the burner for 20 seconds to crisp it up a bit. Generously drizzle more extra-virgin olive oil on top and serve immediately.

MOCHI

I want to dedicate a few recipes in this chapter to something that I hold with absolute high regard in my heart: mochi, the softly chewy, slippery, smooth, and bouncy dough made with sticky rice that is a cherished culinary focus in pretty much all parts of Asia. It has dozens of different names and forms, but for good measure, here I'm going to call it mochi across the board.

I adore mochi. I adore it like dancers adore rhythm and painters adore colors, as a constant necessity that feeds inspiration. Which is precisely why it saddens me to see it underappreciated in the broader international food scene, as many from the West fail to understand what's its big fucking deal.

You see, mochi is a textural thing. It does carry a mild yet distinct sweetness from the sticky rice, but to fully understand its appeal, one has to be willing to recognize texture as a stand-alone culinary element, equal in importance to flavor. Just as one can gradually acquire a taste for whiskey, coffee, or more pungent cheeses, the slippery and chewy texture of mochi is an acquired appreciation that, once registered, is a lifelong source of satisfaction and endless possibilities.

I've incorporated a hint of this texture already in recipes like the mochi bread dough and sticky rice tortillas, but now we're headed into a full frontal dive. Here are three of my favorite ways to incorporate mochi into sweets.

MOCHI WITH PEANUT BROWN SUGAR AND ICE CREAM

In very traditional Taiwanese street food, white and puffy mochi are fished right out of a roiling water bath and tumbled in either black sesame sugar or peanut sugar, then served with shaved ice. The warm and chewy comfort of the mochi weaves with the aroma of the blended sugar in your mouth, tangling in a sensational conflict with the sub-zero streams of melted ice, often conjuring a long queue of salivating patrons around the block in night markets. Here I've replaced the shaved ice with ice cream, both because I suspect that nobody will have an ice shaver at home and also, more important, because ice cream is never wrong. Never.

MAKES 5 SERVINGS

MOCHI DOUGH

1½ cups (180 g) sticky rice flour (see page 6)

2 teaspoons light brown sugar

½ cup (120 g) simmering water (210°F/100°C)

1½ tablespoons (20 g) canola oil

PEANUT BROWN SUGAR

⅓ cup (42 g) salted roasted peanuts

⅓ cup (70 g) dark brown sugar

ICE CREAM

Choose your flavor: green tea, coconut, taro, chocolate, coffee, hazelnut, pistachio

MAKE THE MOCHI

1. Combine the sticky rice flour and brown sugar in a medium bowl. Bring a small pot of water to a simmer (if your water isn't hot enough, the dough will not come together properly), then pour ½ cup of it evenly over the flour mixture. The water should cook the flour on contact, turning it partially translucent. With a large fork, stir everything together into a clumpy mixture, then let it sit until cool enough to handle. Add the oil and knead the mixture with your hands for 5 minutes, until smooth. The dough should be very smooth, slightly shiny, soft, and not overly sticky. If it feels too dry and is cracking here and there, knead in a bit more water.

2. Divide the dough into 5 equal portions. Roll each into a large ball, then gently pat it down into a thick disk. Cover with plastic wrap until needed. You can also make the disks ahead of time and keep them in the freezer.

MAKE THE PEANUT BROWN SUGAR

3. Pulse/run the peanuts in the food processor until they have the texture of fine wet sand, but be careful not to overgrind them into peanut butter. Transfer them to a large bowl and add the brown sugar. Use your fingers to crumble any clumped peanuts and mix them evenly with the sugar.

COOK THE MOCHI

4. Bring a pot of water to a boil, then add the mochi disks (either fresh or frozen) without

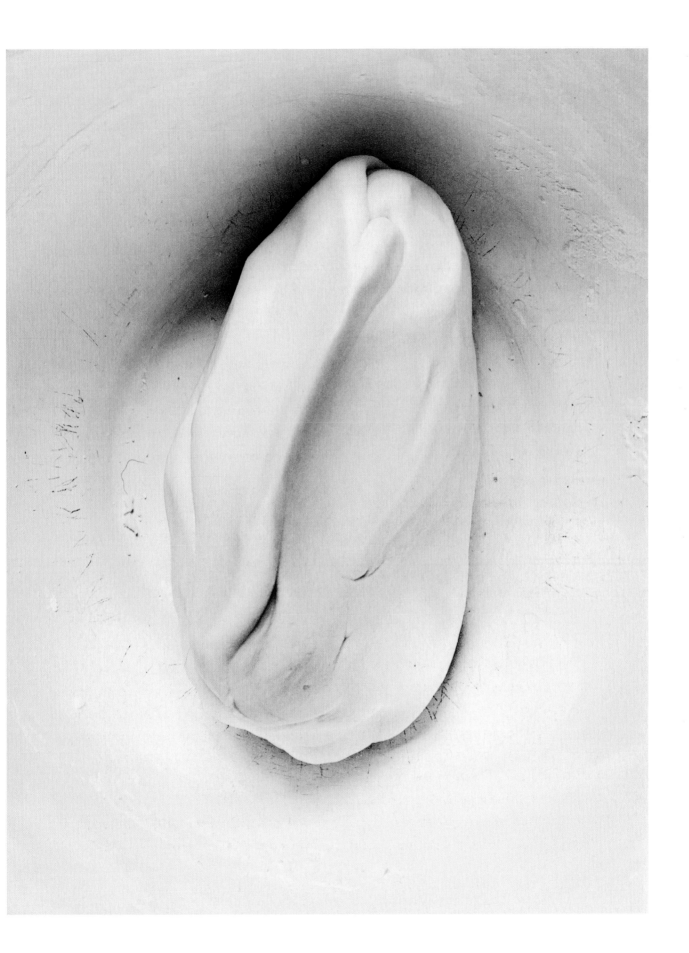

crowding the pot. Turn the heat down to maintain the water at a *gentle boil,* making sure that the dough is not sticking to the bottom of the pot, then *put the lid on* and cook for 5 minutes. Come back to flip the mochi, *put the lid back on,* and cook 3 to 4 minutes for fresh mochi or 5 to 6 minutes for frozen mochi. When done, the mochi will float to the top and be swollen, soft, and cooked through.

TO SERVE

5. Remove the mochi with a slotted spoon and rinse them for a few seconds under cold water. You want to shock and tighten the mochi but still keep them warm. Drain well and tumble them in the peanut sugar just to coat, then serve with a large scoop of ice cream of your choice and extra peanut brown sugar on top.

MOCHI-STUFFED DATES IN SPICED TEA SYRUP

In Shanghainese cuisine, something like this would be called "Hearts Too Soft," which is mochi-stuffed Chinese red dates braised in a simple syrup. I've ordered it just about as many times as I've seen it on a menu, **any menu,** *inside or outside of China, which, regrettably, has never proved to be a memorable decision. Perhaps taking its name too literally, the mochi centers are often too mushy, a self-defeating mistake as confusing as warm beer. Then, as much as I would like to overlook such a problem, the thick skins of the Chinese red dates are an abrasive reminder between my teeth, while the overall bland flavor leaves me wishing,* **Maybe the next one will be different.**

Despite these disappointments, my faith is unwavering because I believe this dish has true potential. What's not to like about the hollowed body of a sweet, fruity date gently hugging a soft pillow of chewy sticky rice, glistening in a syrup that cares about what people say about it on Instagram? If it's made this way, nothing.

MAKES 6 SERVINGS

MOCHI DOUGH

¾ cup (90 g) sticky rice flour (see page 6)

¼ cup (60 g) simmering water (210°F/100°C)

2 teaspoons (9 g) canola oil

DATES AND SYRUP

12 to 15 large, thin-skinned dates (I like Mejdool dates)

1½ cups (360 mL) water

2 tablespoons honey

2 small strips orange peel, each about ½ × 3 inches (1.5 × 8 cm)

1 small cinnamon stick

3 whole cloves

1 hefty pinch of black tea leaves

1 small pinch of ground allspice

Flaky sea salt, for sprinkling

MAKE THE MOCHI DOUGH

1. Place the sticky rice flour in a medium bowl. Bring a small pot of water to a simmer *(if your water isn't hot enough, the dough will not come together properly)*, then pour ¼ cup (60 g) of it evenly over the flour. The water should cook the flour on contact, turning it partially translucent. With a large fork, stir everything together into a clumpy mess, then let it sit until cool enough to handle. Add the oil and knead it with your hands for 5 minutes, until smooth. The dough should be very smooth, slightly shiny, soft, and not overly sticky. If it feels too dry and is cracking here and there, knead in a bit more water.

STUFF AND COOK THE DATES

2. With a small knife, cut the dates open on the side and remove the pits. Dust the dough with more sticky rice flour to prevent sticking, then stuff a nub of sticky rice dough (the proportion should be about 1:1 to the date) tightly into each date cavity. Pinch to close it up slightly; the dough should ooze out on the side a bit. When you've stuffed the dates, divide the rest of the dough into 1½-teaspoon portions and roll them into small sticky rice balls.

3. In a saucepan *that will allow all the dates to be submerged in a single layer,* combine the water, honey, orange peels, cinnamon, cloves, tea leaves, and allspice and bring to a gentle boil over medium heat. Add the dates and cook for 5 minutes, until the mochi is cooked through and the dates are softened. Remove the dates and set them aside on a plate. You may notice that the skins of the dates are peeling off somewhat; I like to peel away any loosened skins because it creates a prettier final presentation and a finer texture. But that's up to you. Now reduce the remaining liquid over medium heat until there is about ¼ cup left.

4. Meanwhile, bring another pot of water to a boil and cook the sticky rice balls for 5 minutes, until they are cooked through and float to the top. Use a slotted spoon to transfer them to the reduced tea syrup. Coat them lightly in the syrup, then spoon the syrup and the sticky rice balls over the stuffed dates. It's best to serve the dates just slightly warm or at room temperature. Sprinkle with a bit of flaky sea salt before serving and eat within the hour, before the mochi becomes tough.

BASIC VANILLA MOCHI ICE CREAM

Our first prison break after moving to Beijing was to Istanbul, where we first experienced Turkish ice cream, aka dondurma.

When I say "experienced" I don't mean just eating, because getting a dondurma in Istanbul around the touristy area is in itself a complete experience. A fucking humiliating one. If you've been there, you know of what I speak. Every vendor—and I mean every single one of them, because you can't escape it—holds out their ice cream, which is sitting atop a cone at the end of a long paddle, and just when you reach out your shaky but hopeful hand, they twist and turn and spin the ice cream right out of your grasp like a satanic child teasing monkeys at the zoo, and then they repeat this until you're driven to a dark place at the brink of a violent engagement. Then and only then do they let you have it.

Any self-respecting human being would walk away empty-handed but with their head held high. But we endured the humiliation every single day, simply because I couldn't let a day go by without a fix of dondurma. I loved and hated myself while I chuckled at the sight of the ice cream cone in my hand.

So why did I choose to be subjected to such public and dignity-stripping embarrassment when I could just go to a regular ice cream shop and get a cone without losing my shit?

The same reason these vendors can spin the ice cream upside down without it slipping or falling. Dondurma is special because it's made with salep flour, a flour made from orchid tubers, which gives the ice cream an extraordinarily sturdy, sticky, and stretchy body that one has to almost chew through. But in my part of the world, salep flour is hard if not impossible to come by, whereas something similarly enthusiastic, stretchy, and chewy—sticky rice flour—is not.

You know where I'm going with this, right? To a place where enslaved dondurma lovers around the world can break away from their humiliation and rejoice under the benevolence of a generous and merciful god who doesn't make fun of them before letting them eat ice cream.

Mochi, the chewy Asian dessert made of sticky rice flour, becomes mochi ice cream.

Of course if you freeze solid mochi, it ain't gonna be pleasant. We're aiming for a batter hovering at just the right spot between mochi texture and liquid form, which when churned transforms into a remarkably stretchable mass that mimics dondurma. Mochurma? Dondurchi? *Or whatever. Either way, I get to keep my cool and eat it, too.*

MAKES 6 SERVINGS

SPECIAL EQUIPMENT: *immersion blender (optional); ice cream maker or 12 × 12-inch (30 × 30-cm) container*

1½ cups (360 mL) whole milk

1 cup (240 mL) heavy cream

⅓ cup (56 g) granulated sugar

2 tablespoons honey

⅓ vanilla bean, split down the middle

¼ teaspoon sea salt

¾ cup (90 g) sticky rice flour (see page 6)

1. In a medium saucepan, whisk the milk, cream, sugar, honey, vanilla bean, and sea salt and bring to a simmer over medium-low heat. With a wooden spoon, press on the vanilla bean to release all the seeds. Cook for 5 minutes at an enthusiastic simmer, then remove and discard the empty vanilla pod. Transfer the mixture to a blender and add the sticky rice flour (or use an immersion blender), and while it's still very hot, pulse and blend until the mixture has thickened considerably and the heat has fully cooked the sticky rice flour, scraping down the sides once. You will know it's cooked when the mixture no longer has a floury mouthfeel. (We don't use direct heat at this stage because the mixture is thick and high in sugar and will burn easily.)

2. Now, you have two options to turn the batter into mochi ice cream. Which one you choose will determine who you are and how you'll be remembered by history. The first method is to churn it in an ice cream maker *by hand* (the ice cream is too sturdy to be churned by machine), which will require an arm workout but will yield better texture. Because the churning process stretches and restretches the mochi ice cream, introducing more air into the structure, it allows you to enjoy it at its prime, fresh out of the bucket, super chewy and not rock hard. The second method is to pour the batter into a shallow container to a thickness of about 1 inch (2.5 cm), then freeze it until hardened and cut it into squares. This is obviously much easier, but it yields a denser texture and doesn't give you the whole "fresh ice cream" experience, which is how dondurma is usually served.

METHOD 1

1. Prefreeze the bucket that comes with your ice cream machine in the freezer for 24 hours. After you make the batter, cover it with plastic wrap, and chill in the fridge for at least 6 hours, until completely cold. Pour the batter into the prefrozen ice cream bucket, then use a sturdy plastic spatula (not rubber) or large metal spoon to scrape the sides and fold the batter in on itself. Don't be afraid to get a little batter on your hand, because the *closer* you hold the spatula or spoon, the *less hard* you have to work at it. The batter will become more and more stretchy and chewy as you go, and eventually you'll be able to pull long strands without breaking them. At this point, put the bucket in the freezer for 10 minutes, then stretch the ice cream again for a couple of minutes, then freeze

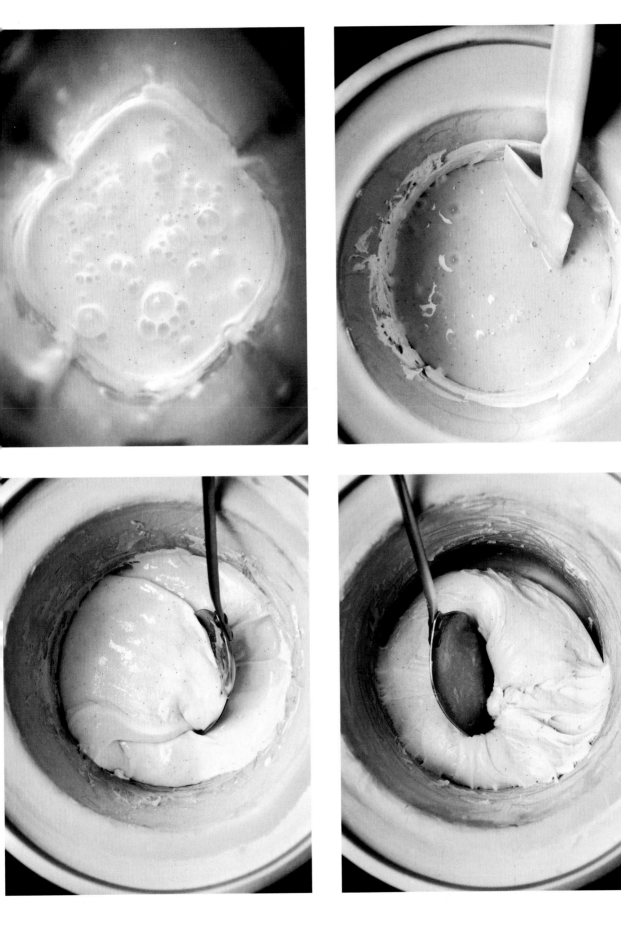

again for 10 minutes, until it becomes a sturdy, compact ball of chewy goodness. The entire process takes around 30 minutes.

2.   The best time to enjoy this mochi ice cream is now, eating it right out of the bucket with a spoon. I freeze any remaining ice cream in an airtight container and let it soften at room temperature for 5 minutes the next time I want to eat it. If you are serving this as dessert for guests, after you finish churning it, you can keep it in the bucket in the freezer for a maximum of 1 hour for optimal texture. Give it another folding before serving.

METHOD 2

Line a shallow 12 × 12-inch (30 × 30-cm) container with parchment paper, then spread the batter about 1 inch (2.5 cm) thick. Freeze until hardened enough to be cut, 3 to 4 hours. Remove the parchment paper, then cut the slab into squares and freeze until hard again. Keep the squares in a freezer bag.

NOTE: *Don't try to turn this mixture into ice pops, even though it feels perfectly logical to do so. They will not come out of the mold.*

RECYCLED NUTS AND CARAMEL APPLE CAKE

If you make a good amount of nut milk, whether it's apricot kernel for me, almond for you, or whatever, what is one to do with the leftover, stripped, ground-up nuts? This challenge used to trouble me, and as I've always done with all challenges in life, I would throw them in the trash can. But as my food waste mounted, so did my guilt, until finally one day I decided to combine this challenge with my guilt, just to better organize my negative emotions.

So I turned the leftover nuts into a cake. Then, for good measure, I threw in another lingering guilt of mine, what to do with extra sour cream. So instead of one challenge and two guilts scattered around, I now have just one single guilt, in the form of a nice and tidy cake with buttery, moist crumbs and a creamy tang. I call this life-management mathematics, and I'm pretty good at it.

MAKES ONE 6-INCH (15-CM) CAKE

SPECIAL EQUIPMENT: *stand mixer with a whisk attachment; 6-inch (15-cm) diameter nonstick round or ball cake pan*

1 tablespoon (13 g) unsalted butter plus 1 stick (8 tablespoons/113 g) unsalted butter, cut into cubes

2 Granny Smith apples (see Note on page 349), peeled, cored, and cut into ¾-inch (2-cm) dice

2 tablespoons sugar

1 tablespoon freshly squeezed lemon juice

¾ teaspoon sea salt

1 portion (about 1¼ packed cups/165 g) ground apricot kernels from making Chinese Southern Almond (Apricot Kernel) Milk (page 29) or leftover ground nuts from any other nut milk

½ cup (100 g) light brown sugar

Zest of ½ lemon

3 large eggs

½ cup (63 g) all-purpose flour

1 teaspoon baking powder

Powdered sugar, for dusting

Sour cream, for serving

1. In a medium skillet over medium heat, melt the 1 tablespoon of butter and add the apples. Cook for 5 minutes, until the apples start to soften. Add the sugar, lemon juice, and ¼ teaspoon of the salt and cook until all the liquid has evaporated and the sugar has caramelized around the apples. Transfer the apples to a bowl and put them in the fridge to cool down.

2. Preheat the oven to 350°F/180°C.

3. In a stand mixer with a whisk attachment, cream the ground kernels or nuts, the remaining

1 stick butter, the brown sugar, and lemon zest on high speed for 7 to 8 minutes, until pale and fluffy. Add the eggs, one at a time, and beat until the mixture is fluffy again. Add the flour, baking powder, and the remaining ½ teaspoon salt and mix on *low speed* until evenly mixed.

4. Transfer to a nonstick 6-inch (15-cm) standard round or ball cake pan and bake for 55 minutes, until an inserted wooden skewer comes out clean. Let cool on a cooling rack for 15 minutes. Invert the cake to release it onto the cooling rack and let cool for 1 hour. Serve with a dusting of powdered sugar and a dollop of sour cream. The cake can be kept covered at room temperature for up to 3 days.

NOTE ON APPLES: *I would highly recommend using a tart apple variety like Granny Smith for this recipe. If your apples are on the sweeter side, add 1 extra teaspoon lemon juice when you add the sugar to the skillet.*

WONTON WRAPPER CIGARS SOAKED IN ORANGE HONEY

The Middle Eastern version of this dessert is usually made with phyllo dough. The tactic of using reprocessed wonton wrappers to replace phyllo dough was employed out of desperation, but it's sort of stuck for some reason. Phyllo dough can be hard to source in most parts of Asia, whereas wonton wrappers are anything but. When rerolled super thin and pan-fried, wonton wrappers create a layer that is crispier than phyllo dough, and stays that way. They're almost shard-like, that is, if shards don't kill you, but rather get rejuvenated in tart syrup and nestle in a state where fracturability and moistness coexist. I'm quite fond of that rare state of physical matter, even though it may last only a few fleeting hours in this cruel and unforgiving cosmos. So please eat them while it lasts.

MAKES 6 OR 7 SERVINGS

NOTE: *You can also use baklava filling for this recipe.*

SPECIAL EQUIPMENT: *stand mixer with a pasta machine attachment or rolling pin*

CIGARS

12 to 14 Shanghai-style wonton wrappers (see Note on page 353)

½ cup (68 g) dried apricot kernels (see Note on page 353) or blanched almonds

⅓ cup (45 g) peeled salted roasted pistachios

¼ teaspoon ground cinnamon

⅛ teaspoon ground nutmeg

6 dried apricots

1 egg white, lightly beaten

2 tablespoons unsalted butter

1 tablespoon canola oil

ORANGE HONEY

½ cup (120 mL) freshly squeezed orange juice

4 strips orange peel, each about ½ × 3 inches (1.5 × 8 cm)

3 tablespoons light brown sugar

2 tablespoons honey

MAKE THE CIGARS

1. If you have a pasta machine attachment on your stand mixer, pass each wonton wrapper a *couple of times* through the *thinnest* setting (8 on my KitchenAid), then gently pull on the wrapper to stretch it even more thinly without tearing it. Or you can roll it by hand to get it as thin as humanly possible, then pull it to stretch it as thinly as you can. The wrappers should be so thin that you can see your fingers through them. Stack them up and trim off the uneven edges to make a large square. Cover with plastic wrap and set aside.

2. In a food processor, pulse the apricot kernels or almonds, pistachios, cinnamon, and nutmeg until finely ground. Transfer to a small bowl and set aside. Pulse the apricots in the food processor until finely ground. Set aside in a separate bowl. (You don't want to process the

nuts and apricots together because they will clump up.)

3. Lay a single wonton wrapper on a working surface and brush beaten egg white around all four edges. Scatter a thin layer of ground nuts on top, leaving a thin margin around the edges, then add a few small nubs of ground apricots here and there, about 2 tablespoons of filling in total. *Do not overstuff the cigars, because you want them to be light and crispy, not dense and hard.* Start rolling the cigar up from one side until the wrapper runs out, then pinch the two seams on the left and right sides together to close. *Again, do not roll too tightly.* The cigars should feel loose and light. Trim off the excess dough at the seams and repeat to make the rest of the cigars.

4. In a large, flat skillet, heat the butter and canola oil over medium heat. When the butter is melted, add the cigars, gently flipping them around as they brown, and cook until golden brown and crispy on all sides. Let sit on a cooling rack while you make the orange honey.

MAKE THE ORANGE HONEY

5. Strain the orange juice through a fine sieve into a small saucepan, pressing on the pulp to extract as much juice as you can. Discard the pulp. Add the orange peels and brown sugar, bring to a gentle boil over medium-high heat, and simmer until reduced by 30 to 40 percent. Whisk in the honey.

6. Place the cigars in a container where they c an fit snugly in a single layer. Pour the orange honey over the cigars and let soak, flipping once or twice, for 1 hour before serving. Eat within 4 to 5 hours or they will get too soggy.

NOTE ON WONTON WRAPPERS: *Shanghai-style wonton wrappers are white, whereas Guangdong- or Hong Kong–style wonton wrappers are yellow with added kansui (the ingredient put in ramen noodles to make them bouncy and yellow). They should be quite easy to tell apart in the supermarket even if not specifically labeled.*

NOTE ON DRIED APRICOT KERNELS: *Dried apricot kernels are also known as Chinese southern almonds (see page 29). They carry that distinct fragrance of almond extract, whereas American almonds don't. If you're not a fan of that flavor profile, you can substitute blanched almonds or walnuts.*

MILK TEA SWAMP CAKE WITH SAGO PEARLS

I have a sick addiction to boba milk tea—yeah, the strange Taiwanese beverage with black, chewy tapioca balls that doesn't seem to make any sense at all and yet is definitively the country's most successful cultural export around the world. I admit that it's a baffling thing—chewy black balls floating around in milk tea? But as Taiwanese, we are hardwired from birth to adore this stuff. And if you find yourself unable to stop sucking on it without even knowing why, then you are officially one of us.

This cake is not quite a boba milk tea cake. However, it certainly draws inspiration from the idea that anything can benefit from a few slippery, chewy balls adding textural fun in the mouth, even a cake that I like to call swamp cake.

Swamp cake is also baffling, in that it's a cake batter that is flooded with liquid before going into the oven and still comes out as an edible thing. More than edible, actually. The cake comes out with a fluffy upper layer that's moistened and is soaked on the bottom with an undercurrent of intense, Hong Kong–style milk tea. It's typically served with ice cream (and if you're doing that, may I suggest coffee-flavored?), but here I'm opting for a playful swarm of sago tapioca pearls. Strange? Yes. But if you find yourself unable to stop spooning it up, then you are officially one of me.

MAKES 4 SERVINGS

SPECIAL EQUIPMENT: *spice grinder; stand mixer with a whisk attachment or handheld mixer*

MILK TEA

⅔ cup (160 mL) evaporated milk

½ cup (120 mL) water

2 tablespoons finely ground black tea leaves (use a spice grinder, or see Note on page 357)

3 tablespoons light brown sugar

TAPIOCA PEARLS

¼ cup (38 g) small or medium sago tapioca pearls (see Note on page 357)

3 tablespoons light brown sugar

CAKE BATTER

5½ tablespoons (70 g) unsalted butter, softened

⅔ cup (125 g) light brown sugar

1 large egg

½ teaspoon pure vanilla extract

1¼ cups (156 g) all-purpose flour

¼ cup (37 g) cornstarch

2 teaspoons baking powder

¼ teaspoon fine sea salt

1 teaspoon instant coffee

½ cup (120 g) whole milk

FOR SERVING

Powdered sugar

1. In a small saucepan, whisk the evaporated milk, water, ground tea leaves, and brown sugar. Bring to a simmer, then turn off the heat and let steep and cool *completely* to room temperature.

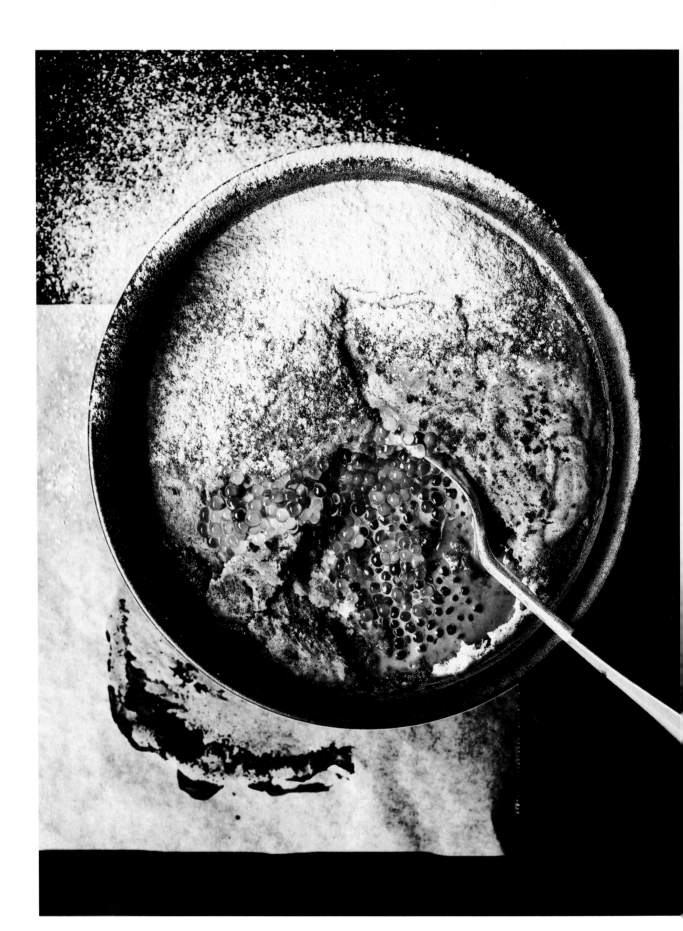

Strain through a fine sieve, squeezing on the grounds to extract as much liquid as you can, then discard the grounds.

2. Meanwhile, bring a small saucepan of water to a boil and add the tapioca pearls. Keep the water at a gentle boil and cook until about 50 percent of the outer layer of the pearls has turned translucent, with a dot in the middle that is still opaque (small pearls will take about 15 minutes and larger pearls will take 20 to 30). Strain the pearls through a fine sieve and rinse under cold water until *completely cooled*. Transfer to a medium bowl, add the brown sugar, and mix to combine. Set aside.

3. Preheat the oven to 340°F/170°C.

4. In a stand mixer with a whisk attachment, cream the butter and brown sugar on high speed until light and fluffy, about 3 minutes. Scrape the sides and bottom of the bowl, then add the egg and vanilla and cream again on high speed until pale and velvety, about 5 minutes. Whisk the flour, cornstarch, baking powder, and salt in a large bowl, then add to the mixer and mix just to combine. Whisk the coffee in the milk until dissolved, then add into the mixer. Mix on low speed just until the batter is evenly combined.

5. Divide the batter evenly between two large ovenproof bowls or cups for double servings or four small ovenproof bowls or cups for single servings. Gather the batter in a mound in the middle of the bowls, then equally divide and pour the milk tea around the batter. *Do not completely submerge the batter with liquid, or it will get absorbed into the cake while baking.* Instead, we want it to seep down to the bottom on the sides. The bowls and cups should be filled to 60 percent max.

6. Bake for 23 to 28 minutes, until the center of the batter appears completely cooked and the milk tea puddle has completely sunk to the bottom. On the surface it will look like a normal cake.

7. Dust the cakes with powdered sugar and serve immediately with the tapioca pearls.

NOTE ON TEA: *Grinding black tea leaves gives this dessert an intense tea flavor. But if you don't have a spice grinder, you can use 3 tablespoons of whole tea leaves.*

NOTE ON SAGO TAPIOCA PEARLS: *I use medium sago pearls here, but you can use large or small sago pearls if you prefer. The cooking time will vary.*

6

THE PUPS

"If all you can do is crawl, start crawling." —RUMI

In March 2016, in the middle of writing this book, we left Richard. Obviously I had no lack of intention to do so, but the abruptness was triggered, mainly, for one reason only: Dumpling passed away.

Dumpling was my toy Maltese, my son who had been with me since I was a nineteen-year-old child myself. My love for him was unmeditated, incautious, and raw. However, during his fifteen years of life, he was best remembered for his relentless unlikability. Dumpling regrettably modeled his life after what he considered to be the most inspirational character ever created: the Grinch. Not only did he meticulously mimic his mentor's methodical and complete social isolation beyond his immediate family, he also practiced his patterns of self-absorbency, political incorrectness, unpredictable mood swings, and unprovoked violence. Say hello, and he would hurt you.

Then in late 2013, as a final climactic tribute to the Grinch, he too, grew his heart three sizes bigger. Little did he know that, outside of Whoville, that would be called congestive heart failure. For two years, Jason, Dumpling, his broken heart, and I huddled around as a single living organism. We ate, we slept, we hoped, and we crashed in repeated unison. I barely left the apartment, let alone Richard, in two years of physical and emotional confinement. But in the end, only two hearts were left beating.

Those two years were saturated with unrelenting depression and anxiety. But perhaps I would have been more equipped to handle the situation if we hadn't lost Dumpling's younger sister, Bado, just two months before his diagnosis.

Bado was a French bulldog who had joined the family during our blissful years in New York. Before her untimely departure right before her ninth birthday, she took her role as a French bulldog seriously. She left not a ball unplayed, a mess unmade, a cookie unstolen, a heart unconquered. She soiled highly absorbent furniture plus or minus a hundred times—while her eyes exuded a remorse that skillfully helped her evade scolding. She once walked right through a midnight dump so she could come back to our bed to finish a masterpiece of painting, with brown footprints contouring two human silhouettes. She stole and ate in one sitting twenty-four pieces of spicy Sichuan peanut brittle—including the plastic wrappers—and spent the subsequent eighteen days filtering the wrappers through her majestic waste-processing system.

It had seemed that the only way to stop Bado from being a French bulldog was over her dead body. And so in October 2013, violently and without our consent, a brain tumor delivered just that.

If all you can do is crawl, start crawling.

In the wreckage that was left after the loss of Bado and then Dumpling, there was only one place I wanted to crawl out of. So just like that, five months later, we left Richard. I was simply no longer able to accommodate living there. Was I fleeing or renouncing? Was it cowardice or ultimately determination? I have since asked myself these questions, but I still can't define it, and perhaps it's not necessary to do so.

If I haven't encouraged you to stress-eat yet, good. Because, as generally advised, I actually want to end this cookbook on a happier note.

In March 2016, we settled back in Hong Kong together with Shrimpy, a mutt-boy of suspected Pekingese descent whose custody we wrested out of Richard. You know how some cats are claimed to be dog-like? Well, Shrimpy is a cat-dog. He's never made any mess, never peed on a wrong thing, never cared about a toy, never thrown a tantrum. You could say he mostly keeps to himself. Unless of course if there is a transaction to be made with a treat, at which time he allows a few questions: Do you love Mommy? Are you happy? Do you even care?

He answers the questions with unenthusiastic compliance before disappearing, again, for the next six hours.

His psychologist said that, in most cases, a sibling would help.

So one year later, enter Sesame and SRB (sticky rice ball), two Rottweiler-mix sisters whom we adopted in Hong Kong. Why the weird names? Both are actually named in Mandarin (like all our dogs): Zhima ("sesame") and Tangyuan ("sticky rice ball"). Together they make up the name for a popular Asian dessert. But, like many Asians, they also have English names and are known as Ashley and Mary-Kate Olsen. I think that explains itself.

As I'm sitting here in front of my computer writing the end of my book, I watch Sesame chewing dirt that she dug up from the balcony on our no longer pristine white carpet, and SRB sticking her head in between my back and the chair with the rest of her body drooping on the floor as usual, and I feel an inexplicably stupid joy. Things come. Things go. Things come again. Not always in the way I like, and almost never as expected. I'm not trying to sound all philosophical and positive, because I'm sure good stuff just keeps coming unstoppably for plenty of other lucky motherfuckers. I'm just saying, I guess for me in this life, sometimes there's no window without walls, no happy ending without heartbreaks. And finally, in my thirty-nine years of curbing positivity, I think . . . that ain't half bad.

for PUPS

So, actually, did I mention I had a company while I was living in New York that made and delivered home-cooked dog foods? Yeah, it was called Big Bone. Originally it was meant to be "Big Boned," but I forgot to add the letter d when I filled out the LLC application. This not only completely erased the intended pun, it also made registering and marketing our website slightly tricky later on. Turned out, bigbone.com was a lot more popular among lonely adults than hungry canines.

Who knew.

To anyone who ever tried to Google my dog food service ten years ago but was instead flashed by unsolicited male parts, I deeply and sincerely apologize.

OMBRE BIRTHDAY MEATCAKE

I baked my first-ever meatcake for my Dumpling's fifteenth birthday on an August day, almost two years into our uphill battle against his congestive heart failure. Unspoken, but we knew what was to come, and maybe he did, too, and that broke my heart. I think a lot about the love I feel for my dogs. How it isn't hard-coded in blood; how it isn't supported by future hopes and prospects; how it is in no way an extension of my existence after death; how it isn't a byproduct of animal procreative instincts; how the only thing I am guaranteed is a finite happiness and one absolute heartbreak; how helplessly stupid it is; how special it is; and how truly unconditional.

They say dogs are not children. I agree.

When something I love and need that much is no longer going to exist, it compresses my heart into broken coals. With his lungs flooded with fluid, every breath so exhausting that his eyes drooped, and a ticking muscle in his chest so tired it was begging to stop, Dumpling was without much appetite in those days. So I baked a special meatcake for him— one not that much different from this recipe—and when it came out of the oven, I saw a gleam of liveliness in his subtly moving ears, like a sudden flare on a guttering candle. Please don't go out. Please don't go out . . .

With every calculated morsel—what was meticulously included in the meatcake, and what was meticulously not—I pleaded to transmit to him what could not be spoken: that he was loved. If nothing else, then please just know this: that he was loved.

On a full stomach, he passed away in October.

MAKES ONE 6-INCH (15-CM) CAKE

SPECIAL EQUIPMENT: *two 6-inch- (15-cm-) diameter cake pans; parchment paper*

1 pound (450 g) skinless boneless chicken thighs, cut into medium chunks

3.5 ounces (100 g) chicken livers

1 packed cup (200 g) blanched and squeezed broccoli, frozen is fine

¾ packed cup (150 g) blanched and squeezed spinach, frozen is fine

1 large celery stick, roughly chopped

1 large egg

½ cup (60 g) rolled oats

¼ cup (30 g) ground flaxseed

2 tablespoons toasted sesame oil

1 teaspoon ground cumin

½ teaspoon ground allspice

3 medium russet potatoes

3 medium sweet potatoes

MAKE THE MEATCAKE

1. Preheat the oven to 350°F/180°C. Line the cake pans with parchment paper.

2. In a food processor, pulse the chicken thighs until finely ground. Transfer to a large bowl. Pulse the chicken livers until coarsely chopped, then transfer to the bowl. Process the broccoli, spinach, and celery and transfer to the bowl as

well. Add the egg, oats, flaxseed, sesame oil, cumin, and allspice and mix everything evenly with your hands.

3. Divide the mixture between the prepared cake pans. Bake for 20 to 25 minutes, until a wooden skewer inserted into the center comes out clean. Remove the meatcakes from the pans and set them aside to cool on a cooling rack.

PREPARE THE "ICING"

4. While the meatcakes are baking, bring a large pan of water to a boil. Peel and cut the russet potatoes and sweet potatoes into 1½-inch (4-cm) chunks and cook them *separately* for about 10 minutes each, until soft and cooked through. Strain well and let cool slightly. Run the cooked russet potatoes through the food processor until you have a sticky, gummy paste (gummier than you'd want for mashed potatoes), then transfer to a large bowl. No need to clean the processor. Run the sweet potatoes in the processor until you have a thick paste. Transfer to a separate bowl. These are the two "icing" colors.

"ICE" THE MEATCAKE

5. Use a long serrated knife to cut each meatcake horizontally into two slabs, so you have four slabs total. Place one slab on a serving plate and smear a layer of sweet potato puree on top, then top with another slab of meatcake. For the next two layers of icing, reduce the ratio of sweet potato puree while mixing in russet potato puree to make the color lighter as you go up the layers. (These inner layers of icing won't

have a significant effect on the overall look, so they don't have to be exact.) Place the final slab of meatcake on top and ice the top with pure russet potato puree.

6. With an icing knife or butter knife, smear the bottom side of the cake with sweet potato puree, then mix the sweet potato puree gradually with more russet potato puree to get a color gradation as you move toward the top. Ice the top of the cake with russet potato puree. Use the straight edge of the knife to smooth out the coloring. And there you go—an ombre celebration meatcake for your pups.

VARIATION: *You can substitute peas, zucchini, or any other green vegetables that you have on hand for the broccoli and spinach.*

PIGS IN A JAR

Why can you never find pork in dog foods? It's cheaper than fish and lamb, more easily sourced than duck, and tastier than chicken, and yet there's never a pork option in the major brands of dry dog food out there.

Well, here's something your dog has probably been waiting for his or her entire life: a protein-rich, nutritious pork mixture cooked inside glass jars, with fiber-rich vegetables and skin-friendly flaxseed, appetizingly seasoned with five-spice powder and toasted sesame oil to give it a sweet and wholesome aroma.

I like to color-coordinate the ingredients in my dog food recipes—none of that all-in-one, unpalatable brownness. The tomatoes, carrots, and ground sweet paprika give this recipe a pleasantly orange hue. And even better, the jars can be stored in the freezer, making it easy to cook for your pups in bulk and convenient to bring a jar to a picnic or as a little edible gift.

This dog food can be fed straight or in conjunction with dry food.

MAKES ABOUT 11 CUPS OF DOG FOOD

SPECIAL EQUIPMENT: *assorted 2- to 4-cup glass jars with lids*

2 pounds (900 g) ground pork

2 large eggs

1½ cups (150 g) rolled oats

¾ cup (180 mL) low-sodium chicken stock

½ cup (60 g) ground flaxseed

3 tablespoons toasted sesame oil

2 tablespoons ground sweet paprika

2 teaspoons five-spice powder

½ pound (220 g) pig's liver (or if unavailable, chicken liver), cut into large chunks

1 medium skin-on carrot, cut into large chunks

1 large skin-on russet potato, cut into large chunks

1 skin-on apple, cut into large chunks

One 14-ounce can (400 g) white beans, drained

One 14-ounce can (400 g) peeled tomatoes

1. Preheat the oven to 350°F/180°C.

2. In a large bowl, combine the ground pork, eggs, oats, chicken stock, flaxseed, sesame oil, paprika, and five-spice powder. In a food processor, pulse the liver until finely chopped (not pureed), then add it to the bowl. Repeat with the carrot, potato, apple, beans, and tomatoes, pulsing each separately, then adding everything to the bowl. You want each ingredient to be in small bits, not pureed, which improves the final texture and flavor for your pups.

3. With your hands, mix everything together evenly, then transfer the mixture into the glass jars, leaving about 1 inch (2.5 cm) of room at the top to prevent spillover during cooking. Place the jars, *without lids,* on a rimmed baking sheet, then bake for about 45 minutes, until the mixture at

the center of the jars is cooked through. I check this by cutting through the center with a dinner knife.

4. Let cool completely, then put the lids on the jars. Label the jars and put them in the freezer.

5. Alternatively, you can make the jars sterile. Put the lids on right after filling the jars, then submerge the jars completely in a large pot of boiling water. Keep the water at a gentle boil and cook for 45 minutes. Remove the jars and let cool completely at room temperature, which will result in a vacuum seal. Since the content of the jars is nonacidic (meaning bacteria could still grow even after canning), I would still recommend storing the jars in the freezer to keep them at maximum freshness.

6. The night before you need a jar, place it on the counter to defrost. If you're in a hurry, remove the lid and defrost in the microwave.

VARIATIONS:

Ground beef, zucchini, celery, and peas

Turkey, pumpkin, sweet potato, dried cranberries, and cinnamon

BOMBAY JERKY

A treat is by definition a reward. If after helping my mom do the dishes as a child, I got a whole wheat cracker in return, I'm not sure I'd be the highly functional and positive member of society that I **obviously** *am now. So if you don't want your dog to grow up to be a psychopath, please, let them* **taste** *something,* **savor** *something—when it comes to treats if nothing else.*

This exceptional jerky is minimally seasoned with fish sauce and toasted sesame oil, which act as an adhesive for the intense ground spices like turmeric, cumin, coriander, and cinnamon. It's vividly aromatic while retaining a firm, bouncy chew, inducing canine salivation without artificial seasonings and coloring. Turmeric is a great anti-inflammatory spice, but if you don't like the way it tinges your fingers with a yellow hue (or if your dog has white, easily stained fur or hair), you can omit it.

MAKES ABOUT 1 DOZEN THIN STRIPS

1 pound (450 g) lean beef, pork, chicken, duck, or other meat, cut into long, thin strips

1½ teaspoons toasted sesame oil

1½ teaspoons fish sauce

1 teaspoon ground cumin

1 teaspoon toasted sesame seeds (see page 100)

½ teaspoon ground turmeric

½ teaspoon ground coriander

¼ teaspoon ground cinnamon

1. Preheat the oven to 200°F/95°C (if you have a fan-on option, do it). Line a rimmed baking sheet with parchment paper and set a baking rack on top.

2. Arrange the strips of meat on the baking rack without them touching. Bake for 1½ to 2 hours, until the meat feels leathery with a firm bounce (it shouldn't be completely dry, like wood). *Flip the strips when they're about halfway cooked, and open the oven door periodically to let the steam escape.*

3. Place the sesame oil and fish sauce in a large bowl and toss the strips evenly in the mixture. Lay the strips on the baking sheet. Mix together the cumin, sesame seeds, turmeric, coriander, and cinnamon and sprinkle evenly over the jerky. Toss again until evenly coated with the spices.

4. Bake for another 15 minutes, until the jerky is dry to the touch but with a little give (if you apply the spices too soon they'll lose their aroma).

5. Keep the jerky in an airy environment, such as inside a brown paper bag, for up to 1 week at room temperature or up to 3 weeks inside the fridge. Cut the jerky into pieces that work for the size of your dog.

CHEESE COOKIES

If you've ever eaten a commercial dog biscuit, you'll understand the occasional sorrow and lonesomeness tinged with a trace of resentment you see in your dog's eyes. It's not the cat. It's you. So spend a few minutes of your life baking some delicious yet nutritious cookies for your dogs—buttery, mildly sweet, and boosted with flaxseed and caramelized Cheddar cheese. The effort involved is nothing compared to the devotion your dog has so generously offered you. Dogs will take a bullet for humans, man. It's possible that no one on earth loves you as much. I think that's worth a homemade cookie.

MAKES APPROXIMATELY 45 COOKIES, DEPENDING ON SIZE

SPECIAL EQUIPMENT: *cookie cutters*

6 tablespoons (78 g) unsalted butter, diced

2 tablespoons (40 g) molasses

2 large eggs, plus 1 large egg white, for brushing

1¼ cups (156 g) all-purpose flour or whole wheat flour

1 packed cup (100 g) shredded Cheddar cheese

½ cup (60 g) ground flaxseed

½ cup (50 g) rolled oats

¼ cup (40 g) cornstarch

½ teaspoon baking powder

1. Preheat the oven to 350°F/180°C. Line a baking sheet with parchment paper.

2. In a food processor, combine the butter, molasses, and the 2 eggs and blend until smooth. It's okay if the butter is in bits. Add the flour, Cheddar, flaxseed, oats, cornstarch, and baking powder and pulse until the mixture comes together in an even dough.

3. Transfer the dough to a floured surface and roll it out into a ¼-inch- (0.5-cm-) thick sheet. Cut it into shapes with your favorite cookie cutters. Arrange the cookies on the prepared baking sheet and brush the tops with egg white.

4. Bake for 11 to 12 minutes, until the surface is lightly browned. Gather the dough scraps and roll out and bake more cookies until the dough is used up.

5. Let the cookies cool on a rack, then store in an airtight bag at room temperature for up to 5 days or in the fridge for up to 2 weeks.

ACKNOWLEDGMENT

I would not have been able to write this book if not for the unrelenting—if not irrational—faith that my husband, Jason, has in my pathetic ability to carry anything through. Frankly, even my parents wisely avoid such expectations of me. There is really one person, and one person only, who has stood strong and supportive all these years in the face of my explosive, unthankful, childish bitching and moaning, and that is Jason.

So, thank you. I'm so glad we met.

UNIVERSAL CONVERSION CHART

OVEN TEMPERATURE EQUIVALENTS

250°F = 120°C   350°F = 180°C   450°F = 230°C

275°F = 135°C   375°F = 190°C   475°F = 240°C

300°F = 150°C   400°F = 200°C   500°F = 260°C

325°F = 160°C   425°F = 220°C

MEASUREMENT EQUIVALENTS

Measurements should always be level unless directed otherwise.

⅛ teaspoon = 0.5 mL

¼ teaspoon = 1 mL

½ teaspoon = 2 mL

1 teaspoon = 5 mL

1 tablespoon = 3 teaspoons = ½ fluid ounce = 15 mL

2 tablespoons = ⅛ cup = 1 fluid ounce = 30 mL

4 tablespoons = ¼ cup = 2 fluid ounces = 60 mL

5⅓ tablespoons = ⅓ cup = 3 fluid ounces = 80 mL

8 tablespoons = ½ cup = 4 fluid ounces = 120 mL

10⅔ tablespoons = ⅔ cup = 5 fluid ounces = 160 mL

12 tablespoons = ¾ cup = 6 fluid ounces = 180 mL

16 tablespoons = 1 cup = 8 fluid ounces = 240 mL

INDEX

HarperCollins books may be purchased for educational, business, or sales promotional use. For information, please email the Special Markets Department at SPsales@harpercollins.com.

FIRST EDITION

DESIGNED BY RENATA DE OLIVEIRA

ALL PHOTOGRAPHS BY MANDY LEE
except page viii by Lintao Zhang/Getty Images

Library of Congress Cataloging-in-Publication Data has been applied for.

ISBN 978-0-06-280237-8

19 20 21 22 23   LSC   10 9 8 7 6 5 4 3 2 1